Question&Answer
TORT LAW

Liverpool

Community

College

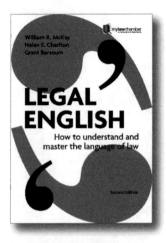

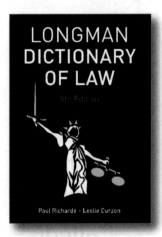
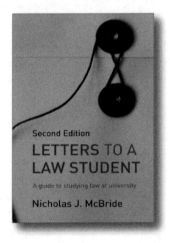

Question&Answer
TORT LAW

Neal Geach
University of Hertfordshire

Longman
is an imprint of

Harlow, England • London • New York • Boston • San Francisco • Toronto • Sydney • Singapore • Hong Kong
Tokyo • Seoul • Taipei • New Delhi • Cape Town • Madrid • Mexico City • Amsterdam • Munich • Paris • Milan

Pearson Education Limited
Edinburgh Gate
Harlow
Essex CM20 2JE
England

and Associated Companies throughout the world

Visit us on the World Wide Web at:
www.pearson.com/uk

First published 2012

© Pearson Education Limited 2012

ISBN: 978-1-4082-4115-8

British Library Cataloguing-in-Publication Data
A catalogue record for this book is available from the British Library

Library of Congress Cataloging-in-Publication Data
A catalog record for this book is available from the Library of Congress

10 9 8 7 6 5 4 3 2 1
15 14 13 12 11

Typeset in 9/12pt Helvetica Neue by 3
Printed in Great Britain by Henry Ling Ltd., at the Dorset Press, Dorchester, Dorset

Contents

Supporting resources

Visit the **Law Express Question&Answer** series companion website at
www.pearsoned.co.uk/lawexpressqa to find valuable learning material
including:

- Additional **essay and problem questions** arranged by topic for each chapter
  give you more opportunity to practise and hone your exam skills.
- **Diagram plans** for all additional questions assist you in structuring and writing
  your answers.
- **You be the marker** questions allow you to see through the eyes of the
  examiner by marking essay and problem questions on every topic covered in
  the book.
- Download and print all **Attack the question** diagrams and **Diagram plans**
  from the book.

Also: The companion website provides the following features:

- Search tool to help locate specific items of content.
- Online help and support to assist with website usage and troubleshooting.

For more information please contact your local Pearson sales representative or
visit www.pearsoned.co.uk/lawexpressqa

Acknowledgements

I would like to thank Zoë Botterill for giving me the opportunity to write this book, as well as all of the academics and students who have reviewed this work. Primarily though I would like to acknowledge the constant support and encouragement that I have received from far too many people to list here individually, but hopefully you know who you are. Thank you all very much.

Publisher's acknowledgements

Our thanks go to all reviewers who contributed to the development of this text, including students who participated in research and focus groups which helped to shape the series format.

What you need to do for every question in Tort Law

Books in the *Question and Answer* series focus on the *why* of a good answer alongside the *what,* thereby helping you to build your question answering skills and technique.

This guide should not be used as a substitute for learning the material thoroughly, your lecture notes or your textbook. It *will* help you to make the most out of what you have already learned when answering an exam or coursework question. Remember that the answers given here are not the *only* correct way of answering the question but serve to show you some good examples of how you *could* approach the question set.

Make sure that you refer regularly to your course syllabus, check which issues are covered (as well as to what extent they are covered) and whether they are usually examined with other topics. Remember that what is required in a good answer could change significantly with only a slight change in the wording of a question. Therefore, do not try to memorise the answers given here; instead use the answers and the other features to understand what goes into a good answer and why.

It is also important not to worry about trying to learn all of the case citations. These are listed in the answers for information purposes only. You are unlikely to be expected to include these in an exam. Tort is predominantly a case-based subject and so you would be using a lot of your time if you listed the citations every time. However, you should obviously just confirm this with your tutors. Citations for journal articles are slightly different. While, again, it is very unlikely that you will be expected to write the full details of articles, you should give some indication as to where it is from, such as the journal abbreviation and year.

All torts have an inherent structure because of the elements which make up each tort. Use these elements to form the basis of your structure, particularly for problem questions. Deal with the first element and then move on to the next. The key is to spot how much weight you need to give each element, as questions are likely to focus on particular elements of the tort.

Tort also has a large amount of theory underpinning it and is influenced by certain principles. Make sure you learn these and try to incorporate these into your answer. This is particularly beneficial when the question is an essay assessing the merits of a tort or the elements for the tort required by the courts.

Guided tour

What you need to do for every question in Tort Law

What to do for every question – Find out the key things you should do and look for in any question and answer on the subject in order to give every one of your answers a great chance from the start.

How this topic might come up in exams – Learn how to tackle any question on this topic by using the handy tips and advice relevant to both essay and problem questions. In-text symbols clearly identify each question type as it occurs.

 Essay question

 Problem question

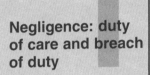

Negligence: duty of care and breach of duty

How this topic may come up in exams

While negligence is examinable as a whole (see Chapter 3), the various individual components can be, and often are, examined separately as essays. Duty of care is particularly ripe for essay questions because of its complexity and differing components; the specialist duty situation, psychiatric injury and economic loss will usually form their own examinable areas. You will probably find that individual questions on duty of care are more common than questions on breach. However, in respect of breach questions you need to ensure that you know what the factors are which the courts considered, and are able to evaluate how and why they are used as well as when they will be adapted.

Attack the question – Attack attack attack! Use these diagrams as a step by step guide to help you confidently identify the main points covered in any question asked.

2 NEGLIGENCE: CAUSATION, REMOTENESS AND DEFENCES

■ Attack the question

Causation	Remoteness	Defences
• Is the situation one of distinct, alternative causes or cumulative causes?	• What was the original test under *Re polemis*?	• Has the claimant voluntarily assumed the risk of injury?
• Has the breach of duty caused or materially contributed to the injury?	• Is the injury one which is of a type, kind or class which was reasonably foreseeable as required by the modern approach under the *Wagon Mound No.1*?	• Is the injury one for which liability can be excluded or limited?
• Is the injury one which is actionable?		• Is the claim substantially based on an illegal act by the claimant?
• Is there any medical uncertainty which permits the normal rules to be relaxed?		• Has the claimant contributed to his injury through his own negligence?
• Did the breach materially increase the risk of injury?		
• Are there		

Answer plans and Diagram plans – Clear and concise answer plans and diagram plans support the planning and structuring of your answers whatever your preferred learning style.

Diagram plan

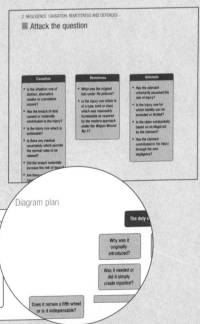

The duty c

Why was it originally introduced?

Was it needed or did it simply create injustice?

Does it remain a fifth wheel or is it indispensable?

Answer plan
→ Provide the historical context and background to the role of the duty concept, discussing whether its creation was necessary.
→ Evaluate the modern role of the duty concept, including how it is established.
→ Assess the extent to which injustice arises or whether the concept can actually help to achieve justice.
→ Conclude whether it is essential or could negligence function without it.

Answer with accompanying guidance – Make the most out of every question by using the guidance to recognise what makes a good answer and why. Answers are the length you could realistically hope to produce in an exam to show you how to gain marks quickly when under pressure.

[3]This is your most important paragraph: you need to show that while there are some factors which pertain to the defendant which are considered, these are still viewed objectively. This allows the latter part of your answer to explore these factors for their justifications and explains why your answer has gone in this direction.

factor is the nature of the situation. Where there is an emergency, it is reasonable to act less cautiously than where there is more time to consider what one is doing.

However, notwithstanding these impersonal factors, it is not entirely accurate to say that the standard of care is completely without reference to the defendant.[3] As *Street* (Murphy, 2007a)[4] states, to finalise the definition of the reasonable man the phrase 'in the circumstances' from *Paris* needs to be considered; and these words require the particular defendant to be taken into account. Although, as *Street* also highlights, the courts still eliminate considerations related to the defendant's idiosyncrasies and instead consider their attributes which are characteristic of a class of which they are a member. Objectively considering characteristics attributable to the defendant's class is necessary for justice as clearly a child cannot be expected to reach the same standard as expected of an adult. Yet, focusing on the class rather than the actual individual prevents the key principle of negligence, namely that a required standard of behaviour must be reached, is not distorted.[5] Clearly, a subjective approach would negate tort's purpose as in regulating social conduct

[4]You ought to give an indication of what you have read and state this as your authority for the proposition. However, in the exam do not worry about trying to get the full citation down, simply give sufficient indication as to what you have read.

[5]It is around this point that you can, and should, include

[6]Even if you recognise straightaway that this is not a 'but-for' scenario, you should follow a logical progression through what the law requires. Therefore, set out how this normally applies first rather than jumping to the relaxed rules.

[7]As there have been two operations, identify which one is in issue here, particularly as the first operation appeared successful.

613, provided there is a negligent contribution which is more than negligible, it will suffice as a causative factor. While the hospital may claim that the evidence here does not even show that the lack of hydration made any contribution to the heart attack, this may not matter. The **Wardlaw** principle was developed in **McGhee v National Coal Board** [1973] 1 W.L.R. 1 so that causation can be satisfied where the evidence shows the negligence made a material increase in the risk of the harm suffered. This is the situation here as we told that the risk of the heart attack was 'heightened'[16] by Mick's increased weakened state which resulted from the rehydration failure. It was doubted, following **Wilsher**, that this relaxation of the causation rules would apply to medical negligence cases and instead were limited to industrial cases. However, following **Bailey** the

Case names clearly highlighted – Easy to spot bold text makes those all important case names stand out from the rest of the answer, ensuring they are much easier to remember in revision and in the exam.

Make your answer stand out – Really impress your examiners by including these additional points and further reading to illustrate your deeper knowledge of the subject, fully maximising your marks.

✓ Make your answer stand out

- Explain the rationale and merit for imposing strict liability on producers of defective products.
- Consider the distinction made between manufacturing defects and design defects and discuss the different approach to each by the courts, explaining what sort of the phone is.
- Explore the problems which exist with each action and make a deeper comparison of the merits of Kamui bringing an action under each.
- Read C. Hodges (2001) 'Compensating patients: case comment on *A v National Blood Authority* [2001] 2 All E.R. 289', 117 L.Q.R. 528 in order to obtain some academic criticism of the judicial interpretation taken to the meaning of 'defect' under s.3.
- Discuss the difference between standard product defects and non-standard product defects.

Don't be tempted to – Avoid common mistakes and losing easy marks by understanding where students most often trip up in exams.

! Don't be tempted to …

- Ignore either of the possible claims in favour of solely talking about the other in depth. As the question does not set any limits, you need to discuss both. Even if you do not do so because you feel that claim is futile, it may look like you did not realise there is a chance of the claim. At the very least raise it to dismiss the possibility of success.
- Get into a discussion of loss of a chance and *Gregg v Scott* [2005] 2 A.C. 176 with regards any chance of the kidney damage occurring.
- Merge your discussion as to both injuries, as arguably the outcome will be different and so you may find you compromise the clarity of your argument.
- Set out all of the defences within s.4 unless you can make the case for them being relevant; otherwise you will use up valuable time without gaining any real benefit.

Bibliography – Use this list of further reading to really explore areas in more depth, enabling you to excel in exams.

Bibliography

Arden, M. (2010) 'Human rights and civil wrongs: tort law under the spotlight', Public Law, Jan.: 140–59

Beever, Allan (2009) 'Transferred malice in tort law?', Legal Studies 29 (3): 400–20
Buckland, W.W. (1935) 'The duty to take care', 51 L.Q.R. 637
Buckley, R.A. (1984) 'Liability in tort for breach of statutory duty', 100 L.Q.R. 204

Guided tour of the companion website

Book resources are available to download. Print your own **Attack the question** and **Diagram plans**

Additional **Essay and Problem questions** with **Diagram plans** arranged by topic for each chapter give you more opportunity to practice and hone your exam skills. Print and email your answers.

You be the marker gives you a chance to evaluate sample exam answers for different question types for each topic and understand how and why an examiner awards marks. Use the accompanying guidance to get the most out of every question and recognise what makes a good answer

All of this and more can be found when you visit **www.pearsoned.co.uk/lawexpressqa**

Table of cases and statutes

■Cases

■ Non-English Cases

■Statutes

◼International Conventions

Negligence: duty of care and breach of duty

How this topic may come up in exams

While negligence is examinable as a whole (see Chapter 3), the various individual components can be, and often are, examined separately as essays. Duty of care is particularly ripe for essay questions because of its complexity and differing components; the specialist duty situations, psychiatric injury and economic loss will usually form their own examinable areas. You will probably find that individual questions on duty of care are more common than questions on breach. However, in respect of breach questions you need to ensure that you know what the factors are which the courts considered, and are able to evaluate how and why they are used as well as when they will be adapted.

Attack the question

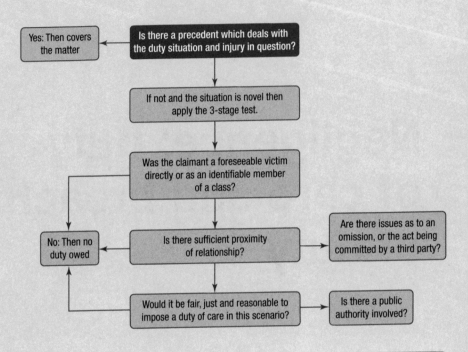

Breach factors extraneous to the defendant

- What was the likelihood of harm?
- What was the likely magnitude of harm?
- Was there social utility in the defendant's conduct?
- What was the cost of avoiding the harm?
- Was the act in accordance with a trade or community practice?
- Was it an emergency?
- How much was the situation part of the demands of everyday life?

Breach factors pertaining to the defendant

- What was their age?
- Do they possess any disability?
- Were they able to foresee the acts of third parties?
- Did they possess special knowledge of the claimant?
- What was their level of intelligence or knowledge?
- Were they a skilled professional?

A printable version of this diagram is available from www.pearsoned.co.uk/lawexpressqa

Question 1

'While historically it may have been possible to argue that the concept of the duty of care was an unnecessary element in negligence, prone to cause injustice, today it acts as an essential device for the purposes of determining whether liability will be imposed or not.'

In light of this statement critically evaluate the modern role of the duty concept in negligence.

Answer plan

→ Provide the historical context and background to the role of the duty concept, discussing whether its creation was necessary.

→ Evaluate the modern role of the duty concept, including how it is established.

→ Assess the extent to which injustice arises or whether the concept can actually help to achieve justice.

→ Conclude whether it is essential or could negligence function without it.

Diagram plan

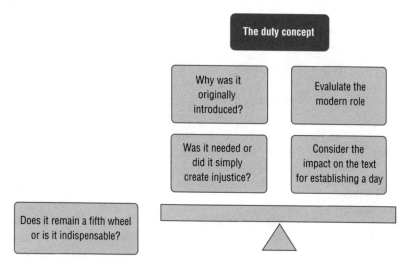

A printable version of this diagram is available from www.pearsoned.co.uk/lawexpressqa

Answer

The issue to be determined is whether the duty concept is needed in negligence or whether it merely creates injustice and thus its role should be performed by the other aspects of negligence. This is important as establishing a duty is the first hurdle which a claimant must overcome; a failure to do so means that notwithstanding their injury, they will have no redress. It will be argued that the duty concept plays a useful function in seeking to achieve justice for those injured, while preventing punitive liability for those who are negligent.

While of the utmost importance today, the duty concept has not always been seen this way. Buckland (1935) saw the duty concept as merely a fifth wheel: he argued that the more rational explanation for cases is that, as in Roman law, there is a duty to everyone which is then limited on the basis of remoteness, intervening acts and contributory negligence. This view is shared by Winfield whose research argued that historically no case was in fact ever lost through the absence of a duty because in the cases from which the independent tort of negligence grew, and the cases arising during its early development, the concept of duty was never raised. He felt the issues of establishing a duty could just as easily be dealt with when establishing the presence of negligence or breach and limited in the ways suggested by Buckland. Interestingly, Lord Bingham in **D v East Berkshire Community Health NHS Trust** [2005] 2 A.C. 373 also stated that he would 'welcome' such a shift.[1]

By not insisting on its existence in order to bring an action, claimants may now lose claims on a basis which they would not have lost on historically. As such, in Buckland's view by holding that a duty does not exist in certain situations, injustice is created. A good example of this can be seen in relation to negligently inflicted psychiatric injury where, even if all of the other elements of negligence are present, the concept has long been used as the basis for denying liability. However, if liability can be justifiably limited by other factors and the duty's presence would not have mattered, then it is perhaps questionable how much injustice is caused. Arguably, using, say, remoteness to limit liability rather than duty was not any fairer.[2]

Today, the modern role of the duty concept is, as Lord Goff noted in **Smith v Littlewoods Organisation** [1987] A.C. 241, to specifically

[1] The point here is for you to say that, notwithstanding the time lapse and the changes to the law since these views were first aired, there is prominent, recent support. You can then use this as the basis for arguing that the concept is not indispensable, if you wish.

[2] While you have advanced Buckland's view, even with Lord Bingham's apparent support, you still need to subject it to some critical evaluation – is there a link between the concept and injustice or would it exist anyway?

identify when liability will not be imposed. As such, it is a control mechanism seeking to prevent indeterminate and crushing liability on a defendant for what could amount to only a momentary lapse in care. Such a role has arguably been played by the concept since its existence as an important requirement in negligence. However, the need for this role became more important following **Anns v Merton L.B.C.** [1978] A.C. 728. The test proposed here for establishing a duty was seen as expanding negligence into areas where the law had been reluctant for it to explore, particularly economic loss. The duty concept, thus, is the device whereby the law controls the expansion of negligence into new situations. Generally, a claim will have to fit within an existing precedent which has recognised a duty in that situation. This rejects arguments of corrective justice whereby a person should have redress for any injury suffered through a want of care. Although, it could be argued that by performing this role it reflects the fact that the law should also be just towards defendants.

However, negligence is not completely rigid and it may expand into new situations, but the role of the duty concept is to firmly dictate when this will occur so as to keep the law within acceptable bounds.[3] This role is reflected in the test for establishing a new duty. In **Caparo v Dickman** [1990] 2 A.C. 605 it was determined that the following factors would need to be present on the facts. Firstly, it must be reasonably foreseeable that the particular claimant would suffer the particular type of loss which did in fact occur. The issue of the foreseeable claimant leads to the second factor which is proximity. There must be a sufficient closeness between the parties in view of the type of loss which justifies imposing a duty. This, in turn, leads to the third element which is that it is 'fair, just and reasonable' to impose the duty. The presence of the first two factors means it generally will be, but this element is also where public policy comes in, which even today leads to injustice to still be caused as with psychiatric injury, although the judges rather than talking specifically about policy can use the policy to find that there was insufficient proximity or foreseeability.

The converse can also said to be true though. The third element and the presence of policy can lead to justice for the defendants and thus it reinforces the modern role of the concept. A good example of this would be **Caparo** where the auditor's negligence was argued to have caused the claimant to buy firstly, a significant shareholding,

[3]This part of your answer is quite important. Naturally, if you are discussing duty of care, you need to discuss how it arises. You need to link, though, how it arises to the wider discussion about what the role is and how well the test for establishment performs the role given to the concept.

5

[4]As the reasoning is from a specific judge, name him/her as this shows a greater level of knowledge and understanding of the case, and that you have read, learnt and understood the judge's views.

[5]Whereas normally you would not need the journal's full name, where it is one from another jurisdiction it is worth stating it in full, because the marker may not be familiar with the abbreviated initials, unlike, say, L.Q.R.

[6]This is where you could still expand on a comparative evaluation if you have not chosen to include a paragraph in the main body on other jurisdictions. The benefit of doing this is that the quote suggests the concept is indispensable. Show how other jurisdictions get by without it. This will then tie in to your discussion of the history of English law from Buckland and Winfield.

and then the entire third-party company. The claim was rejected by Lord Bridge[4] because to hold otherwise would result in an indeterminate amount of liability, owed to an indeterminate class of people for an indeterminate length of time. If a duty was owed to potential shareholders, or even shareholders in relation to publicly released information, there was nothing to stop banks and merchants supplying credit to the company in reliance of the accounts having a claim. Therefore, for these reasons it was determined that it would not be fair, just and reasonable to impose what would have been a potentially crushing duty of care on the auditors.

In conclusion, notwithstanding the arguments that the duty concept serves no function, or simply duplicates a role which could be performed by another aspect of negligence, as Winfield (1934) noted,[5] it is so deeply entrenched in the law now that only legislation can eradicate it. This is even more the case today, and therefore the debate now really is purely academic in nature even though different jurisdictions also provide a model as to how the law could operate without it.[6] However, clearly the modern approach does utilise the concept as a way of balancing when to justify liability on the one hand while restraining the potential liability from being too crushing on the other. Although as the cases show, this may not always be satisfactorily achieved, depending on how strictly one adheres to corrective justice.

 Make your answer stand out

- Read in full the following articles: W. W. Buckland (1935) 'The duty to take care', 51 L.Q.R.: 637; and P. H. Winfield (1934) 'Duty in tortious negligence', Columbia Law Review, 34(1): 41–66.

- Consider in more depth if it really is indispensable, particularly if it does cause injustice.

- Draw a comparison with other jurisdictions, such as France, highlighting how they manage without resort to the idea of a duty of care.

- Consider briefly the debate as to whether there is a single, general duty of care or a series of different duties – see Howarth (2006) 'Many duties of care: or a duty of care? Notes from the underground', 26 O.J.L.S. 449.

Don't be tempted to ...

- Get bogged down describing the historical development of the duty concept.
- Go off on a tangent and consider in great detail on all the specialist duty situations and their merits; just draw on specific examples.

Question 2

'There are sound reasons why omissions require different treatment from positive conduct.'
Per Lord Hoffman in *Stovin* v *Wise* [1996] A.C. 923 at 943

Evaluate when a duty of care will be imposed for an omission and assess whether the reasons for restricting such an imposition are indeed 'sound'.

Diagram plan

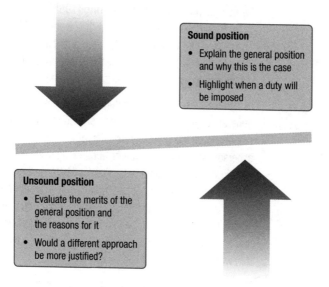

Sound position
- Explain the general position and why this is the case
- Highlight when a duty will be imposed

Unsound position
- Evaluate the merits of the general position and the reasons for it
- Would a different approach be more justified?

A printable version of this diagram is available from www.pearsoned.co.uk/lawexpressqa

Answer plan

→ Explain the general position regarding omissions and evaluate the reasons for this, assessing their merits.

→ Discuss the alternative view of Lord Mackay in *Smith* v *Littlewoods Organisation Ltd* [1987] 1 A.C. 241.

→ Analyse the limited scenarios when a duty will exist and whether these offer, in light of the policy reasons, a justifiable departure from the general position.

→ Conclude by determining whether the general position is 'sound' or whether adopting the approach of Lord Mackay is better.

Answer

The general position in English law is that a duty of care will not be imposed for what is a pure omission to act and thus it is treated differently to positive conduct. Otherwise, as Lord Keith observed in **Yeun Kun Yeu** *v* **A.G. of Hong Kong** [1988] A.C. 175, one would be liable for not warning another that they were walking off a cliff edge. The reasons for this will be evaluated and it is argued that these are indeed 'sound', partly owing to the scope that they in fact give for exceptions to the rule which are also analysed.

In **Stovin** Lord Hoffmann categorised the 'sound' reasons for the general position in political, moral and economic terms. The political reason is that it is a greater invasion of a person's freedom to compel a person to rescue or protect another than simply requiring them to take care for positive acts. From a libertarian perspective this is indeed hard to argue against. The alternative would be for the state to impose how we should act. It could be argued that the state would be justified in compelling people to be proactive in certain situations; this is arguably the case with some of the limited exceptions to the rule which will be discussed below.[1]

[1] You have a bit of a balance to strike. There is an argument for saying that if you mention the point here, you should explain it more, but you need to bear in mind what part of your answer you are dealing with – the reasons for the general rule. If you go off into the exceptions you will lose the structure of your argument, so the safest thing to do is to raise the point and show that you will be discussing it in depth at some point. You could give an example of such a situation here though.

The moral reason was referred to as 'the why pick on me argument'. The rationale was that the duty could be imposed on an indeterminate class of people therefore, the argument being why one individual should be held liable for the omission, and not another. It is hard to justify, in the absence of other factors, why that person is picked. It is easy however, to justify why a duty should be owed for positive conduct. This explains the repeated insistence that mere foreseeability of harm is insufficient (See Lord Hope in **Mitchell v Glasgow C.C.** [2009] UKHL 11). In **Stovin** Lord Hoffman highlighted that a duty will be imposed where a person has undertaken to do something or induced that person to rely on them doing something. This illustrates the prominence of proximity when justifying the imposition of a duty in such cases, which is why one exists, for example, between employers and employees; the class of potential claimant is clearly identifiable and limited in scope. This proximity makes the duty fair and just, while foreseeability of harm is generally quite obvious in such situations.

The economic reason is based on the concept of efficient allocation of resources. Economic theory dictates that the market is distorted if the cost of performing an activity is passed on to others; as the activity becomes cheaper to perform, the activity should, therefore, bear its own costs. As such, it is justifiable, as a benefit is being gained from the activity, to make people factor in the potential liability costs of their activities into its price. Compensation payments for negligent performance mean that the activity will be performed more efficiently, or safely, so as to limit the cost of the activity. However, Lord Hoffmann noted that there was no equivalent justification for imposing a cost on someone who is not performing an activity so that another can benefit. As the justification rests on the fact that there is a benefit gained from performing the activity, it is clear why this position is correct in relation to omissions.[2]

[2]This is obviously the comment as to the merit of the reasoning and why it is 'sound' not to have a duty for omissions. Naturally, if you disagree with the reasoning, explain that here.

The orthodox position as stated by Lord Goff in **Smith v Littlewoods Organisation Ltd** was directly challenged in **Mitchell** where it was argued this was not the majority opinion. This was therefore a call to endorse the contrasting opinion of Lord Mackay who appeared to depart from orthodoxy by recognising a notional duty of care.[3] Indeed he expressly rejected counsel's argument that there could not be a duty on policy grounds. As Markesinis argues in the L.Q.R. (1989),[4] while Lord Mackay referred to foreseeability, he also stressed that it fell to be decided on the facts of each individual case and thus his opinion can be equated with the idea of likelihood of harm when determining the standard of care to be exercised. The case being decided on this basis was that there was no breach on the particular facts as opposed to any general principle. It could be that Lord Mackay felt, again in contrast to Lord Goff, that the situation was

[3]The point that you should be seeking to make here is to show that Lord Hoffman was wrong, as the earlier case of *Smith* appears to have accepted a duty in relation to omissions.

[4]You would not need to give the full citation and title but you should give the marker some reference point as this enables them to check it if they wish and adds to the validity of the reference.

[5]After raising the issue and the argument for it, you should then make a decision as to which view is better and why.

within the scope of the limited exceptions. However, without Lord Mackay explaining why the policy reasons for the non-imposition of a duty are overcome, their Lordships were correct in **Mitchell** to follow Lord Goff's view that the general position is one of no duty.[5]

Notwithstanding this endorsement of the general position, as indicated, the law will justify a departure from the general position in certain limited situations. While Lord Nicholls in **Stovin** felt that the established situations for imposing a duty are not closed, however, it is clear that for a new category to be recognised it must be fit within the circumstances outlined by Lord Goff in **Smith**. The first was described by his Lordship as 'special circumstances' which warrant the duty's imposition. This heading includes where there is an assumption of responsibility, arising through contract or a fiduciary position,[6] between the maker of the omission and the claimant such as in **Stansbie v Troman**[7] [1948] 2 K.B 48. Where the harm is caused through the acts of a third party, a duty may also be imposed if there is a special relationship between the maker of the omission and that third party, as was the case in **Dorset Yacht Club v Home Office** [1970] A.C. 1004. Therefore, there is a clear element of proximity which indicates why the individual is being chosen to owe the duty, overcoming any moral objection. Proximity also explains why it is fair for that individual to be required to act in a certain way which overcomes the political reason.

[6]This firmly sets out when this situation would arise.

[7]This is just to give a firmer example of the situation and so the facts are not necessary; your marker should know the facts of the examples that you give in this section of your answer, so you do not have to use time explaining them. If you are doing fine for time, you could give some brief words, such as 'where a contracted decorator left the house unlocked'.

Lord Goff then added two general circumstances when a duty may be imposed. The first is when someone causes, or allows to be created, a source of danger and it is reasonably foreseeable that a third party will interfere sparking off the danger. The second is where an occupier has knowledge that a third party has created a fire, or the risk of one, on the premises and fails to prevent the fire's spread to the neighbouring land. As Lord Hoffmann explained in **Stovin**, a mutuality of benefit between the occupiers exists in these circumstances which justifies the reasons.

In conclusion, the law does have sound reasons for treating omissions differently as otherwise unjustifiable burdens and personal intrusions are placed on individuals. When these reasons can be questioned owing to certain factors being present, the law has responded by creating justifiable, limited exceptions which maintain fairness and achieve justice.

✓ **Make your answer stand out**

■ Read B. S. Markesinis (1989) 'Negligence, nuisance and affirmative duties of action', 105 L.Q.R. 104 and refer to this in support of your arguments.

■ Provide a comparative evaluation from the jurisdictions which are covered in the above article.

■ Make sure you do offer an opinion as to the soundness of the reasons for the law's position. Do not just describe what that position is.

■ Explore in more depth whether the approach which Lord Mackay appeared to adopt has more merit than the general position.

❗ **Don't be tempted to …**

■ Produce a list of situations when a duty for an omission does exist; make sure the answer flows from one to another.

■ Provide every specific example of a situation when a duty will arise. In the interests of the clarity of your structure and time, discuss the overall categories and then draw on specific examples.

■ Get tied down in specific situations, such as employer/employee relationships.

📝 Question 3

'The standard of foresight of the reasonable man is, in one sense, an impersonal test. It eliminates the personal equation and is independent of the idiosyncrasies of the particular person whose conduct is in question.' *Per* Lord MacMillan in *Glasgow Corporation v Muir* [1943] A.C. 448, at 457

Evaluate the statement's validity in light of the factors pertaining to the defendant which the courts consider in assessing breach of duty.

Answer plan

→ Establish the role played by breach within negligence.

→ Explain what the standard of care of is.

→ Outline the factors considered which are impersonal to the defendant.

→ Contrast those with an evaluation of the factors which do relate to the defendant.

→ Conclude by assessing the overall validity of the statement.

Diagram plan

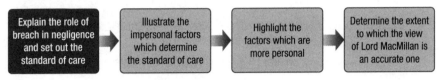

A printable version of this diagram is available from www.pearsoned.co.uk/lawexpressqa

Answer

When determining whether a person has reached an acceptable standard in their conduct, various factors are considered. The issue is the extent to which personal characteristics should be included. This is important as liability will vary according to how their conduct is assessed, while certain characteristics may prevent someone reaching a standard reachable by others. It is argued that while certain factors pertaining to the defendant are considered, Lord MacMillan's statement is correct owing to the objective nature of assessing those factors.

Breach is a crucial element of negligence as determining the standard expected to be shown impacts on whether the duty of care is discharged and thus potential liability. Breach is a mixture of law and fact. Firstly, the standard required by law needs establishing; then it becomes a question of fact whether the standard was reached or not. The legal standard to reach, as seen in **Paris v Stepney B.C.** [1951] A.C. 367, is reasonable care in the circumstances of the case. The scope of looking at the circumstances of the case allows the court to assess a range of factors in determining how the reasonable man would have acted.

Clearly, the emphasis on the reasonable man demonstrates that the factors are assessed objectively and therefore, are impersonal. There are several but the main ones[1] are the likelihood and magnitude of harm, plus the preventability of that harm. The greater the likelihood of the harm occurring, the more care should be taken, particularly where the harm can easily be prevented. A prime example is the case of **Paris** where supplying goggles would have prevented the harm occurring; it was more likely in view of the work and would be greater owing to his already limited eyesight.[2] A further external

[1] Use this to show that you know that there are more but also to indicate that you are consciously looking at a limited few. Looking only at the main factors will also allow you time to explore the factors which relate to the defendant in more depth.

[2] It is beneficial to show some of your knowledge of case law but remember that the question asks for a consideration of the factors more attributable to the defendant, so do not dwell too long on these points.

[3]This is your most important paragraph: you need to show that while there are some factors which pertain to the defendant which are considered, these are still viewed objectively. This allows the latter part of your answer to explore these factors for their justifications and explains why your answer has gone in this direction.

[4]You ought to give an indication of what you have read and state this as your authority for the proposition. However, in the exam do not worry about trying to get the full citation down, simply give sufficient indication as to what you have read.

[5]It is around this point that you can, and should, include some evaluation as to why these factors are needed and why a full subjective account of the defendant's characteristics is not undertaken. This will prevent your answer coming across as just a list of factors.

[6]Explain why this is the case by relating your discussion to the primary principles and theories of tort. This will show your deeper understanding of the subject as a whole.

[7]As such factors are not considered, use them as a contrast to how young age is considered within this paragraph rather than as a separate paragraph.

factor is the nature of the situation. Where there is an emergency, it is reasonable to act less cautiously than where there is more time to consider what one is doing.

However, notwithstanding these impersonal factors, it is not entirely accurate to say that the standard of care is completely without reference to the defendant.[3] As *Street* (Murphy, 2007a)[4] states, to finalise the definition of the reasonable man the phrase 'in the circumstances' from **Paris** needs to be considered; and these words require the particular defendant to be taken into account. Although, as *Street* also highlights, the courts still eliminate considerations related to the defendant's idiosyncrasies and instead consider their attributes which are characteristic of a class of which they are a member. Objectively considering characteristics attributable to the defendant's class is necessary for justice as clearly a child cannot be expected to reach the same standard as expected of an adult. Yet, focusing on the class rather than the actual individual prevents the key principle of negligence, namely that a required standard of behaviour must be reached, is not distorted.[5] Clearly, a subjective approach would negate tort's purpose in regulating social conduct by stressing how one should act.[6]

As indicated, one characteristic assessed is whether the tortfeasor is a child. If so, the question asks what degree of care and foresight is reasonable to expect of a child of that age (**Mullin v Richards** [1998] W.L.R 1304). This is necessary to allow children to indulge in natural horseplay and enjoy their youth without unduly stifling them with thoughts of potential injury while playing games like tag, as in **Orchard v Lee** [2009] E.W.C.A. Civ. 295. By contrast, any disability or infirmity of the defendant[7] will not be considered as it will be deemed that by doing the act in question with knowledge of their disability they have been negligent (**Roberts v Ramsbottom** [1980] 1 W.L.R. 823).

Whether the defendant has, or ought to have, special knowledge of the claimant is another assessed factor attributable to the defendant (**Paris**). If the defendant knows of a condition which makes the claimant more susceptible to injury, or injury of a greater extent, then clearly it is right to expect a greater degree of care. As such this can be seen as overlapping with the external factors consider earlier as it means they should be more aware of the likelihood magnitude of harm.

Arguably, the most significant factors relating to defendants are their skill and knowledge. Negligence is not excused simply because someone is of lower intellect (**Vaughan v Menlove** 132 E.R. 490) nor does failing to use one's higher intellect necessarily attract liability (**Wooldridge v Sumner** [1963] 2 Q.B. 43). The reasonable man simply has normal intelligence; however, where the defendant has a status which is relevant to the conduct in question, this is considered. For example, where a reasonable chief engineer would have known of the risk of discharging the oil in the **Wagon Mound (No. 2)** [1967] A.C. 88, liability resulted. Such circumstances warrant altering the reasonable man's knowledge to that of someone of the defendant's status so as to fully and fairly assess their conduct.

This leads into consideration of the defendant's skills and whether someone possessing certain skills who injures another when exercising that skill should be judged by reference to the reasonable man who does not have that skill or to someone who does. The law takes a tough stance answering this question. For example, learner drivers are judged to the standard of reasonable, qualified drivers (**Nettleship v Weston** [1971] 2 Q.B. 691). This scenario is based on policy as otherwise there would be problems in determining insurance and assessing liability based on experience. However, unlike scenarios such as **Chaudhry v Prabhakar** [1989] 1 W.L.R. 29, it cannot be said that the learner holds themselves out as having more skill, hence their learner plates.[8] Similarly, professionals are judged to the standard of the reasonable person of their profession, regardless of their experience (**Bolam v Friern H.M.C.** [1957] 1 W.L.R. 582). Patient confidence dictates doctors cannot plead inexperience for poor operations, thus also enhancing tort's deterrence and economic efficiency principles. However, under **Bolam** professionals do have leeway if they can show that a respected body of opinion from that profession would have acted in the same way even if others would not have so acted. Provided the opinion supporting the conduct withstands scrutiny (**Bolitho v City and Hackney H.A.** [1998] A.C. 232), this is permissible to reflect legitimate variations in professional opinions as to such conduct which makes it harder to say what is unreasonable.

In conclusion, it is clear the statement is largely correct as breach is firmly determined on an objective basis. That reasonableness is determined objectively in view of the circumstances means some

[8]This section is needed in order to illustrate why there is a tough stance taken. Use this to try and either justify or argue against the approach the law takes with regard to these factors.

considerations of factors pertaining to the defendant are needed. However, these are still viewed objectively by looking at how a reasonable person of that class would have acted, thus reinforcing the statement.

✓ Make your answer stand out

- Ensure that you offer some evaluation and academic commentary on each factor. It is quite easy to have your answer to this question simply slide into a descriptive narrative. This will only get so many marks.
- Ensure that you do reach a decision as to whether breach of duty is assessed from a purely objective basis and is completely impersonal to the defendant; do not just sit on the fence.

! Don't be tempted to ...

- Just list the different factors, make sure you evaluate each one. As noted above, it is easy to do this but you will lose out on marks.
- Turn your answer into a list of cases and facts if giving an example for each factor.
- Cover all aspects of negligence; the question is very specifically concerned with breach of duty.
- Go through all the factors which are considered. You will struggle to get through them all in any significant depth and will end up with a series of brief points. Focus on the main ones and use your time and space to add depth to them.

Negligence: causation, remoteness and defences

2

How this topic may come up in exams

As with the previous chapter, these elements of negligence are closely interlinked and will all feature in the same problem question, as shown in the next chapter. However, each element can be examined as an essay in its own right particularly causation which has many different complex subsections and so is popular for essay questions with examiners. You will also need to have a firm understanding of the judicial reasoning in cases on causation and be able to evaluate whether those opinions have merit. Therefore, make sure you also have read sufficient academic opinion to support your argument.

■ Attack the question

Causation

- Is the situation one of distinct, alternative causes or cumulative causes?
- Has the breach of duty caused or materially contributed to the injury?
- Is the injury one which is actionable?
- Is there any medical uncertainty which permits the normal rules to be relaxed?
- Did the breach materially increase the risk of injury?
- Are there consecutive causes of the injury?
- Can any of these be classed as an intervening act?

Remotness

- What was the original test under *Re polemis*?
- Is the injury one which is of a type, kind or class which was reasonably foreseeable as required by the modern approach under the *Wagon Mound No.1?*

Defences

- Has the claimant voluntarily assumed the risk of injury?
- Is the injury one for which liability can be excluded or limited?
- Is the claim substantially based on an illegal act by the claimant?
- Has the claimant contributed to his injury through his own negligence?

A printable version of this diagram is available from www.pearsoned.co.uk/lawexpressqa

Question 1

'Certainly in *Wilsher's* case the House of Lords applied strictly the "but-for" test and rejected the Court of Appeal's interpretation of *McGhee's* case but it was not a case of causes cumulatively causing injury but a case where there were different distinct causes.' *Per* Waller LJ in *Bailey* v *Ministry of Defence* [2009] 1 W.L.R. 1052 at 1069

Evaluate how the 'but-for' test is adapted depending on whether the case involves a cumulative cause scenario rather than a distinct, alternate cause scenario and consider whether the law is satisfactory.

Answer plan

→ Outline the standard 'but-for' test.

→ Demonstrate its application in scenarios such as *Wilsher*.

→ Highlight what further problems there can be with applying the 'but-for' test.

→ Chart the development of modifying the test through the material-contribution test to the material increase in risk test.

→ Conclude assessing the current state of the law.

Diagram plan

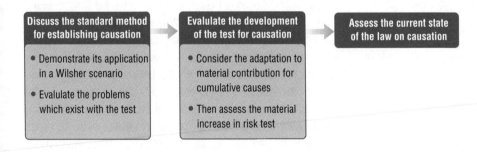

Discuss the standard method for establishing causation	Evaluate the development of the test for causation	Assess the current state of the law on causation
• Demonstrate its application in a Wilsher scenario • Evalulate the problems which exist with the test	• Consider the adaptation to material contribution for cumulative causes • Then assess the material increase in risk test	

A printable version of this diagram is available from www.pearsoned.co.uk/lawexpressqa

Answer

The issue to address is the test used for determining causation in negligence and how it is modified depending on the circumstances. Strict adherence to the traditional approach has led to many

CE: CAUSATION, REMOTENESS AND DEFENCES

claimants going uncompensated, whereas in certain circumstances claimants benefit from a relaxation of the rules. It will be argued that this discrepancy in the law can be justified and so the law is satisfactory.

The standard approach for determining causation was devised in **Cork v Kirby Maclean** [1952] 2 All E.R. 402, and is to apply a simple test to the facts. One asks whether, 'but for' the negligent act, the claimant would have suffered their injury. This requires looking at whether, on the balance of probabilities, the negligent act was the most likely cause of the claimant's injury. Where there was an over 50 per cent chance that the negligent act was the cause, it is treated as the 100 per cent cause. Where it is shown that the injury was likely to have occurred even without the negligence, the defendant cannot be deemed the factual cause of the injury. **Hotson v East Berkshire AHA** [1987] A.C. 750 illustrates this with the judge holding that as there was only a 25 per cent chance that without the negligence the condition would have been avoided, the injury was already in place prior to the negligence.[1] In **Bonnington Castings Ltd v Wardlaw** [1956] A.C. 613 Lord Reid noted the authorities supported the proposition that the question is whether on the balance of probabilities the defendant caused or materially contributed to the injury. Although **Wardlaw** concerned cumulative causes, the issue of material contribution to the injury applies where the cause is one of several distinct factors as seen in **Wilsher v Essex AHA** [1988] A.C. 1074. Here a prematurely born baby was given excessive oxygen by the hospital and later suffered blindness, but there were four other completely separate risks which the baby was exposed to which could have caused the blindness. Lord Bridge framed the question throughout as one of showing that the excess oxygen administered to the baby was the cause or material contribution of the blindness. However, the problem was the presence of the other factors meant that it could not be shown that 'but for' the contribution of the negligent cause, the injury would not have occurred. The application of the 'but for' test for the material contribution of injury in such a case was affirmed in **Bailey v Ministry of Defence**.

As **Wilsher** shows, the test has been rigorously applied in medical negligence cases; however, in cases of negligent exposure to industrial illnesses[2] the courts have been willing to relax the 'but for' test to overcome causal uncertainties. In **Wardlaw**, while the

[1] It is the decision of the case and its reasoning here which you need to illustrate your point, so there is no need to give a fuller factual account.

[2] The fact that these cases are set in a different context is important as to why the same policy factors as *Wilsher* have not been applied. Therefore, you need to flag up this difference in setting.

fact that a material contribution would suffice as opposed to actually causing the injury, the issue was complicated by the fact that the case concerned a cumulative cause scenario. Wardlaw contracted pneumoconiosis from inhaling silicon dust while at work. There were two sources of inhalation, an innocent cause from using a pneumatic hammer which could not be avoided; and a negligent cause by his employer who had failed to maintain the extraction plant. Wardlaw succeeded as while it could not be said that 'but for' the negligence the injury would not have occurred – indeed the evidence showed it was insufficient to have caused it – the evidence showed that his employer's contribution to his contracting the illness was more than negligible.[3] In **Fairchild v Glenhaven Funeral Services Ltd** [2002] U.K.H.L. 22 Lord Rodger expressly stated[4] that the 'but for' test is departed from in such situations.

[3]Do not forget this qualification to the decision as this forms part of the justification to the decision.

[4]By referring to Lord Rodger in *Fairchild*, you have high level authority for the statement which you are making.

The approach was developed further by **McGhee v National Coal Board** [1973] 1 W.L.R. 1. McGhee, through his job, was non-negligently exposed to brick-dust and then negligently not provided with washing facilities, which prolonged the exposure while he travelled home. Subsequently, he developed dermatitis which medical evidence showed was from the exposure. However, the evidence only showed that the prolonged exposure increased the risk of dermatitis but not that this negligent exposure had caused it. Lord Reid felt that there was no distinction between a material contribution and a material increase in risk, although this was rejected in **Fairchild**. Lord Wilberforce justified liability on the basis that where a person creates a risk by breaching a duty, and injury ensues from within the area of risk, he should bear the loss unless he can show there was another cause. This was a matter of justice as the employer should be taken to foresee the possible injury and thus bear the consequences.[5] At first glance this might seem unfair on the defendant who becomes liable for injury which it is unclear that he caused. However, it certainly achieves justice for the claimant and would seem to be grounded in tort principles such as ideas of corrective justice and loss distribution. A wrong has been done with a foreseeable outcome, the employer is in a better position to bear such a loss through insurance and could prevent liability through better working practices, another aim of tort.

[5]This is still part of Lord Wilberforce's reasoning which you need to set out before considering whether *McGhee* was an acceptable departure from the traditional position.

Therefore, a shift in approach has been undertaken by the courts in relation to causation and the application of the 'but for' test, with

[6]Although a judicial quote has just been stated as to how/when the principle operates, you ought to demonstrate that you understand it by explaining it and developing the point.

[7]It is important to explore why the distinction existed and the nature of that distinction, i.e. you comment on whether it is right or wrong that *Bailey* has exposed the medical profession to potentially more litigation.

[8]You should write something like this to tie your point to the question.

[9]Refer to your previous comment to justify your point without repeating in full what you have already said.

[10]If you are arguing that there is a distinction, you need to highlight why this is the case and then argue whether there is a good reason for it or not.

departure permitted where, as Lord Rodger states in **Fairchild**, 'it is inherently impossible for the claimant to prove exactly how his injury was caused'. The principle, started in **Wardlaw** and developed in **McGhee**, can be applied where the claimant has proved all they can, with the causal link of the injury needing scientific investigation which cannot be concluded because science itself is uncertain as to the cause.[6] **Wilsher** appeared to make a distinction between industrial cases and medical cases. While justified on the grounds of protecting NHS funds, this has now rightly been removed by **Bailey** which stated there is no policy reason for not applying **McGhee** in cumulative-cause medical cases which does provide some consistency.[7]

However, a distinction does remain, even after **Bailey**, as the quote shows,[8] between cases where the cause is cumulative but flowing from essentially the same substance or where there are distinct, alternative causes as in **Wilsher**. In the former, to alleviate the evidential uncertainty the 'but for' test is departed from, and possibilities are considered rather than probabilities. As noted above,[9] this is justifiable under tort principles but it raises questions as to why the same tort principles are not applied to a **Wilsher**-style case. However, the key distinguishing factor is that in **Wilsher** there were several independent causes.[10] No commonality existed and so it is hard to say that the hospital's negligence even contributed to the injury; the uncertainty is too great. Imposing liability would be too unfair and thus ensures justice between the parties in question; no wrong needs correcting.

 Make your answer stand out

- Offer a view as to whether material contribution is different to material increase in risk; if you think that they are, are they equally justifiable?
- Consider whether, if damages are awarded for material contributions and increased risks, those damages should be awarded on a proportionate basis.
- Evaluate the merits of the single agent theory as the basis for continuing to distinguish *Wilsher* from *McGhee*. Look at the opinion of Lord Hoffman in *Fairchild* who did not think it was satisfactory although he did change his mind in *Barker* v *Corus UK Ltd* [2006] 2 A.C. 572.
- Consider the potential overlap with issues for loss of a chance.
- Include academic opinion to support your view as to the merits of the judicial comments which you use in your answer.

! **Don't be tempted to …**

■ Frame your answer too narrowly by focusing on mesothelioma if you rely more on *Fairchild* and *Barker* for your discussion.

■ Forget the merits of the policy factors which underpin why each case was decided. These are needed to more fully assess whether the decisions reached in the cases as to test of causation to apply are justifiable for those situations.

Question 2

'The common law imposes duties and seeks to provide appropriate remedies in the event of a breach of duty. If negligent diagnosis or treatment diminishes a patient's prospects of recovery, a law which does not recognise this as a wrong calling for redress would be seriously deficient today.' *Per* Lord Nicholls in *Gregg* v *Scott* [2005] 2 A.C. 176 at 185E

Critically evaluate whether the law on causation is 'deficient' and loss of a chance should be an actionable head of damage.

Answer plan

→ Outline the factual background of *Gregg*.

→ Set out the majority's view, evaluating the compatibility of each judge's reasoning.

→ Discuss whether the decision leaves the law 'deficient'.

→ Evaluate whether the opinion of Lord Nicholls satisfactorily counters the majority's concerns.

→ Conclude which view is more justifiable.

Diagram plan

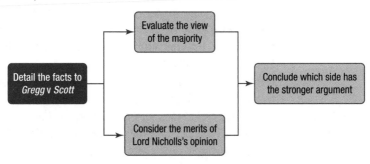

A printable version of this diagram is available from www.pearsoned.co.uk/lawexpressqa

Answer

Whether loss of a chance is an injury which warrants being an actionable head of damage in negligence is an important issue, as recognising such harm would give effect to a fundamental principle of tort, namely corrective justice. However, it would potentially increase litigation against the NHS and lead to defensive medical practices.[1] It will be argued that theoretically the stronger argument is that it should be adopted while equally any practical complaints can be overcome.[2]

[2]This is just my opinion and not necessarily what you should write. As with other areas, this question lends itself to having your own opinion which you should express and then seek to substantiate in your answer.

In **Gregg** the defendant misdiagnosed a lump under the claimant's arm as harmless when in fact it was cancerous. The misdiagnosis was revealed nine months later when Gregg visited another GP after the lump had grown.[3] Resultantly, the cancer spread reducing Gregg's chances of recovery from 42 per cent to 25 per cent, therefore no injury had occurred which was caused by Scott. On the balance of probabilities, there was no chance of recovery to lose. Gregg unsuccessfully appealed on two grounds, the second being that loss of a chance should be an actionable injury itself.

[3]Save yourself time by being brief with the factual background to the case. This is needed just to provide the context to the debate on the issue in the House of Lords.

Lord Hoffman dismissed this ground[4] for lacking a principled basis. He regarded the law as deeming everything has a determinate cause even if that cause is not known. A lack of knowledge and evidential difficulty do not make the cause indeterminate. He considered economic loss cases could be explained owing to an act of an independent third party which was not the case here; it was simply whether the defendant caused the injury.

[4]You need to state what position each of their Lordships was coming from as this was a majority decision.

[5]This indicates that you have read the case in full and know the full range of arguments advanced before their Lordships.

Responding to counsel's argument that a wrong required remedying,[5] he argued any remedy required widening the limited exception for departing from the normal rules of causation from **Fairchild v Glenhaven Funeral Services Ltd** [2003] 1 A.C. 32 and departing from **Wilshir v Essex AHA** [1988] A.C. 1074 and **Hotson v East Berkshire AHA** [1987] A.C. 750; yet the arguments had not changed since those cases. Gregg argued that the **Fairchild** principle could be narrowly extended by confining it to cases in which the claimant had already suffered an injury. Lord Hoffman felt this was artificial and akin to limitations which had 'disfigured' the law on psychiatric injury. Such a restriction had no underlying principle to it nor did the alternative restriction of limiting the principle to cases

[6]This sentence allows your answer to flow naturally into how Lord Nicholls saw the matter.

[7]Make sure you show that you are aware that he was not in the majority, to give the context of why he took the opposite view.

[8]Starting with this part of his opinion straightaway gives weight to the comparative evaluation which you should be seeking to provide in your answer, as it in direct contrast to the argument which you have advanced.

[9]As you are seeking to rebut the arguments of the majority and show why it should be actionable, you must show how Lord Nicholls countered the arguments of the majority and tie it back to the points you advanced earlier.

where medical knowledge as to the cause was lacking. While Lord Hoffman was adamant that the claim should not succeed, no reason was advanced against the latter restriction and it was the complete opposite of how Lord Nicholls saw that issue.[6]

Lord Nicholls, allowing the appeal,[7] felt the matter was, in principle, 'clear and compelling';[8] actionable loss should cover the loss of a favourable outcome rather than just the lost outcome itself. He argued this would 'match medical reality' and recognise what, in practice, the patient had before the negligent act and thus what has been lost. He further argued that the extent of the duty owed by doctors is to exercise care and skill when diagnosing and treating patients. This is hollowed by stating that just because a favourable outcome was originally less than 50 per cent it can be negligently reduced; there would be no need to exercise the requisite care on a patient in such a position.

Underlying this reasoning was the recognition that tort's principal objective is to provide redress where a duty has been breached. The principle of corrective justice centres on injuries being corrected by the payment of compensation; it is hard to see even on grounds of distributive justice why the former should be departed from. Lord Nicholls argued that leaving a claimant without redress in this situation would leave the law deficient and, notwithstanding Lord Hoffman's view, 'open to reproach' in light of the differing approach taken to loss of financial opportunities.

He furthered countered Lord Hoffman's argument by considering that it is not always true that the patient's actual condition at the time of the negligence will determine the answer to the hypothetical question which must be asked as to what would have happened 'but for' the negligent act. As such, **Gregg** was not covered by authority as Lord Hoffman suggested. In **Gregg**, the answer to the latter question was laced with uncertainty and could only be answered by recourse to statistics expressed in percentage terms. Reflecting this, there were no theoretical grounds for holding that compensation could not be awarded for the diminution of recovery. By restricting the development to where the claimant already has the illness complained of, he felt it also left the **Fairchild** principle unaffected.[9]

It does appear that tort is placing financial interests above the chance of achieving personal well-being, which is strange considering that claims for pure economic loss are tightly restricted. The justification could lie in the practical difficulties in adopting this change. Lord Nicholls addressed some of these implications although not in as much depth as the theoretical arguments. He simply stated that the fear of floodgates was not a convincing enough reason for departing from the principal objective of tort. In terms of increased costs to the NHS, he felt, while a formidable argument, it was 'unacceptable' and by keeping the development to the tightly defined circumstances which he did and insisting on a significant reduction in the chance of recovery this would combat the issue. Finally, regarding claims that defensive medical practices would result, he noted that doctors are already aware that they face being sued if they are negligent and thus this argument was unimpressive.

It could be said that his failure to go into more depth weakened his opinion and he certainly does not counter the argument of Lady Hale that nearly all claims based on loss of an outcome could be changed to a loss of a chance of that outcome. This would result, if both were retained, in the defendant always being liable, as the claimant would always have the fallback position of a proportionate claim. This could be unfair but it misses the fact that they have been at fault and therefore, based on corrective justice principles, it is not necessarily an unfair situation. A stronger argument was that for some claimants this could be a negative development. If both types of claims could not be retained and the latter was adopted, then claimants who currently get 100 per cent compensation would suddenly get less. This is detrimental to claimants but arguably fairer for defendants and would further best recognise the medical reality of the situation.

[10]Throughout your answer you will have been looking at the merits of both sides of the argument; however, in your conclusion it is essential, in order to fully answer the question, to come down on one side.

In conclusion, in principle a lost favourable outcome should be actionable.[10] **Gregg** differed to **Hotson**, the eventual outcome 'but for' the negligent act was not determined at the time of that act. Even Lady Hale's concerns could be argued as having some positive consequences, with any issues as to quantifying damages being resolved in practice. Potential implementation difficulties should not prevent the law's development in a fair manner consistent with fundamental principles. The potential impact on the NHS needs to be monitored, with Parliament stepping in if it proves detrimental.

✓ **Make your answer stand out**

- Look at the basic objective of tort in order to determine which view in *Gregg* was right.
- Explain the extent of the principle in *Fairchild*.
- Draw on the arguments of academics such as Helen Reece (1996) in her article 'Losses of chances in the law', 59 Modern Law Review: 188.
- Consider whether loss of a chance needed to be actionable if the majority had been persuaded by the quantification argument within the first ground of appeal.

! **Don't be tempted to …**

- Put too much factual background surrounding the illness and misdiagnosis and get too technical in terms of medical terminology.
- Cover all the points raised by their Lordships in *Gregg* as you will simply run out of time for your answer.
- Dwell on the first ground of appeal, the quantification argument, as the question centres on the second ground. Therefore, in light of the point above you do not need to worry about Lord Hope so much in this question.

Question 3

'… the *Polemis* rule works in a very strange way. After the event a fool is wise. But it is not the hindsight of a fool; it is the foresight of the reasonable man which alone can determine responsibility.' *Per* Viscount Simonds in *Overseas Tankship (UK) Ltd* v *Morts Dock & Engineering Co. Ltd (The Wagon Mound (No. 1))* [1961] A.C. 388 at 424

In light of this statement evaluate the judicial approach to the issue of remoteness of damage.

Answer plan

- Outline the requirements and operation of the test in *Re Polemis*.
- Discuss what problems arose through the test's use.
- Highlight the approach adopted in the *Wagon Mound (No. 1)*.
- Evaluate the requirement for change and whether it has solved the highlighted problems.
- Have there been adverse consequences because of the change?

Diagram plan

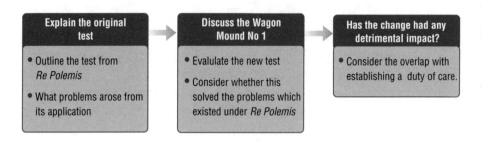

A printable version of this diagram is available from www.pearsoned.co.uk/lawexpressqa

Answer

For any claim to be successful in tort, the injury suffered must not be too remote from the act of the defendant. Therefore, the issue is how the courts should best go about determining whether negligent acts will be deemed to be the legal cause of injury. This has implications for claimants, as even if the defendant factually caused the injury they may still not receive compensation. The current approach will be evaluated to explain why it is better than the original approach from **Re Polemis**.

[1]Before you can discuss whether the approach to remoteness is appropriate, you need to explain what this aspect of negligence is about and what it attempts to do.

Remoteness is the law's attempt to limit liability on policy grounds even where the defendant has factually caused the injury.[1] This restriction is justified[2] as liability is based on the risk that the negligent creates. If the injury is outside of this risk, it is unfair to impose liability. The issue therefore, is how the law determines whether the injury was within the scope of risk for which liability should result.

[2]By then discussing whether the actual purpose of remoteness is justified, you have more scope to argue that perhaps the law should be different; would a change in approach allow the law to be more justifiable, or strengthen its overall purpose?

Originally, following **Re Polemis**, remoteness was determined by looking at whether the injury was a direct consequence of the negligent act regardless of its foreseeability. In the case a ship was destroyed when, through the negligence of the stevedores, a rope from a sling led to a wooden plank dropping into the ship's hold which in turn caused a spark because the hold contained benzine vapour.[3] The court acknowledged that this outcome was not a foreseeable consequence of the negligent act. However, they

[3]You need the key facts in order to highlight how the test operates, and then you can decide whether the approach is fair or not by using these as an illustration.

held that provided the outcome was a direct cause of the negligence, it was irrelevant whether the defendant could anticipate that outcome. Foreseeability of the consequences went towards negligence not compensation. What would amount to 'direct' was not explained and questions could be asked how someone is meant to guard against such an outcome if they do not know what they may be liable for. However, the decision itself can be said to be fair; a negligent act was performed which caused damage. As such, liability should ensue as that damage was caused by the negligence, thereby sanctioning negligent behaviour and awarding compensation for loss suffered, which are two functions of tort.[4] The decision could also be justified owing to the circumstances of the time. As Davies (1982) notes, the case was tried during a slump in the shipping industry[5] and so the decision would have had been a further blow to a struggling shipping industry if liability was not found. While not stated as a reason within the case, Davies argues it must surely have played a part; owing to the importance of shipping at the time this seems a fair assessment.

Although no criticism regarding excessive liability was made following the decision, negative comment did emerge after **Donoghue v Stevenson** [1932] A.C 562 established a general principle for imposing a duty of care in novel situations. Academic criticisms over excessive liability were also combined with judicial comments, subsequent to **Donoghue**, which were at odds with **Re Polemis** and which never wholeheartedly endorsed the principle.

This culminated in the Privy Council[6] decision of the **Wagon Mound No. 1**. Viscount Simmonds felt that the **Polemis** approach overcomplicated matters with a prime example being a defence based around intervening acts. Furthermore, he felt that the basis of **Re Polemis** whereby the issue of foreseeability related to liability rather than whether compensation was payable, was false. He noted that liability is founded upon the consequences of the act, not the act itself.

Therefore a new approach was adopted whereby the question to ask is simply: was the injury of a type which was reasonably foreseeable to occur from the negligence? His Lordship felt that it was unjust to impose liability simply because an injury is a natural consequence, especially if completely unforeseeable.[7] Although he noted the

---

[4] Give your own view on whether the test has merit. Your purpose here is to help set up the debate later in your answer as to whether a change was needed.

[5] The point of highlighting this is so you can give some context to the decision and then also argue whether, even if the principle behind the case is flawed, there is still some justification to the decision. You are looking to provide an explanation for the case.

[6] By including reference to this you could explore how binding this decision should be.

[7] As you are stating that the law was changed, you need to explain what his reasoning was. This then allows you to evaluate whether the reasoning, and by extension the change, was justifiable.

opposite was true, where injury is reasonably foreseeable, even if an indirect consequence of the act, liability is fair and just. To hold otherwise would be at odds with principles of civil liability that a man is only liable for the probable causes of his acts, while still leaving minimum standards to be observed by society.

Interestingly, he did not feel that many cases would be decided any differently, and that in fact where damage was a direct or natural consequence of the act they would be reasonably foreseeable. However, by insisting on reasonable foreseeability as the limitation of liability, it meant that liability was kept within the bounds of common conscience. It is significant that the problems with **Re Polemis** began to emerge following the change to imposing duties in **Donoghue**; indeed Viscount Simmonds states that to base remoteness on **Re Polemis** would be a departure from the sovereign principle of **Donoghue**. This ignores that **Re Polemis** was pre-**Donoghue** and decided at a time when the duty concept was narrowly applied to particular relationships. A wider test of remoteness only became an issue when the application of the duty concept was widened in **Donoghue**. However, this development means it is more logical to treat compensation the same as culpability with both based on foreseeability. The injury suffered must be within the scope of any duty owed, otherwise the act cannot be said to be negligent. If duty is restricted on this basis, it is indeed unjust to still award compensation for injury which, while a cause of the act, was not something which the defendant could have foreseen and so taken steps to prevent.

However, the equating of remoteness with reasonable foreseeability has created an overlap with the imposition of the duty of care.[8] This was seemingly accepted by Viscount Simmonds, as he states that culpability dependant on reasonable foreseeability is determined by reference to the foreseeability of what actually happened. This raises the question as to why this separate element of the tort is needed.[9] Arguably, for remoteness to have any independent purpose, notwithstanding the opinion of Viscount Simmonds, hindsight must play a part.[10] If the aim of remoteness is to determine whether the injury was one that was one within the risk to which a duty was owed, then hindsight must be used to establish what risks were created by the act of the defendant. Otherwise, the test advanced by his Lordship does not work.

[8]Even if you feel that the change was justified, you ought to explore what the consequences have been. Just because something has merit in theory you still need to look at how it works in practice.

[9]The point here is to question whether the purpose of the element which you identified earlier is being carried out following this change.

[10]This ties your answer back to address the suggestion of Viscount Simmonds in the quote.

In conclusion, while it was in fact **Donoghue** that caused the problems for **Re Polemis** and not the test itself, the argument has merit; it is clear that with the approach to duty of care firmly established, a test based on foreseeability makes more sense. While this approach does raise questions as to the overall need for such a test, it does create an extra precaution against liability, helping to ensure that liability and the resultant compensation only occurs where justified.

 ✓ Make your answer stand out

- Read the article by Martin Davies (1982), 'The road from Morocco: *Polemis* through *Donoghue* to no-fault', Modern Law Review, 45(5): 535–55 to gain more depth to your argument around *Re Polemis*.
- Make sure you use part of your answer to address the point in the quote that hindsight has no place in the test of remoteness.
- Ensure that you do consider whether the direct consequence test has merit, as this enhances the overall evaluative nature of your answer.

! Don't be tempted to ...

- Get too tied down with the facts of either *Re Polemis* or the *Wagon Mound No. 1*. The key points can be used to illustrate the application of the particular test but you will lose time if you go into too much depth.
- Start a more in-depth account of duty of care and what was said in *Donoghue* and why it was said.

Question 4

'The reason there are not many defences to a claim in negligence is that before any defence is required the claimant must have shown that the defendant behaved unreasonably in breach of duty and that this contributed to harm which was reasonably foreseeable; if all this is established, extenuation is bound to be difficult ...' T. Weir (2006), *An Introduction to Tort Law*, Clarendon Law Series, at p. 129

Evaluate what defences exist for a defendant in a claim for negligence to rely on as extenuation for their act.

Answer plan

→ Take each defence in turn and evaluate how and when it operates.

→ Consider what is required to make out the defence and assess where it is needed.

Diagram plan

Consent
- What situation does it operate in?
- Elements of the defence
- Why is it needed?
- Statutory limitations– UCTA 1877 and RTA 1988

Illegality
- What situation does it operate in?
- Elements of the defence
- Why is it needed?

Contributory negligence
- What situation does it operate in?
- Elements of the defence
- Why is it needed?

Defences to negligence

A printable version of this diagram is available from www.pearsoned.co.uk/lawexpressqa

Answer

As negligence liability is determined by fault, once fault is proven, an extenuation of liability may be difficult to justify. An assessment of these defences shows that their application is needed owing to policy considerations. However, in view of the overall purpose behind negligence liability, the fairest outcome results from a wider application of contributory negligence.

The main reason for a defendant's liability being extenuated, notwithstanding his fault, is that the claimant consented to the injury or the risk of it. As such, a defence of consent makes good sense and is just (**Smith v Baker & Sons** [1891] A.C. 325). If one voluntarily invites the risk of injury, they cannot complain if it materialises.

[1]Academically, it is worth acknowledging the debate and assessing the merits of each view, but demonstrate that you are aware of the practical implications of the defence more by highlighting that, in practice, it makes no difference to the individual relying on it.

It's unclear whether a successful pleading of the defence removes the existence of the duty or negates liability for its breach. However, in any event, the overall outcome is the same with the courts determining the final issue on the facts of the case before them.[1]

The first requirement is informed consent as to the nature of the risk of injury. In **Smith** it was said that consent can be implied from a course of conduct; however, the consent must be to the specific thing being done which brings the future risk. Therefore, full knowledge is needed as to the extent of the risk that the claimant faces which the claimant then consents to. Either factor alone is insufficient.

Secondly, the claimant must freely volunteer to assume the risk. Therefore, the defence is generally not applicable in cases involving employees, and never to rescuers. Such people are compelled to act: they cannot be said to have taken the risk of their own volition. This is justifiable on policy grounds, as otherwise employers would never be responsible for the safety of their workplaces and rescuers may be deterred from acting. It also does not apply to suicides. Attempting suicide would seem a clear, voluntary act of risking death, however, applying the defence hollows the specific duty owed by the defendant (**Reeves v Metropolitan Police Commissioner** [2000] 1 A.C. 360). This might seem strange in light of the defence denying the existence of a duty and, as Weir notes, it is at odds with the concept of personal autonomy. Yet, the non-application of the defence is justified, as the duty is to prevent that very outcome from occurring and the negligence allowed it to in fact occur.

[2]The logical place for you to discuss these is after the main discussion on consent, as they restrict the situations when that defence could be said to operate.

[3]Make sure you offer some form of explanation as to why the defence is limited by the statute when at a first glance it appears it should apply. The same applies to UCTA.

[4]As this is a standard abbreviation for the Unfair Contract Terms Act 1977, there is no need to write it in full first as it will be clear what you are referring to.

The defence is further limited by statutes.[2] In relation to road accidents, s.149 of the Road Traffic Act 1988 provides that a passenger does not consent to the risk of injury by entering a vehicle. As the driver must have insurance for this scenario, it is fair to leave the burden of liability there.[3] UCTA[4] also limits the defence's application for liability arising out of things done, or to be done, in the course of a business, and on business premises. Liability for negligently caused death or personal injury can never be excluded or limited (s.2(1)); however, other injuries can be if the relevant clause is reasonable (s.2(2)). Further, under s.2(3) agreement or awareness of a term purporting to exclude or limit liability for negligence is not to be taken as voluntarily assuming the risk. Policy underlies this; the consent cannot be said to be voluntary as it is extracted from the

[5]Although the question is on negligence, by acknowledging this you show that you appreciate its wider operation without losing the focus of the question.

[6]While your answer will go on to explore how the defence operates and on what basis, make sure you explain why it is needed. This is particularly important with this defence, which has been criticised for its lack of coherence.

[7]Use *Revill* as a reference point to offer a view about how best to explain the defence throughout your discussion of the defence, as it does seem at odds with the reasoning for the defence.

[8]Again, you can use your knowledge of the defence's application in other torts to question its operation in negligence without straying from the focus of the question.

[9]Make sure that you offer your own explanation of the operation of the defence which provides an explanation for *Revill*.

[10]This shows that you are aware of the change brought about by the Act more succinctly than giving a fuller account of the background to the defence. You can then get on more quickly to how the defence operates.

person who needs to enter the contract and as such lacks equality of bargaining power to negotiate the term.

Another defence is that of illegality, which also applies to intentional torts.[5] This is, again, based on policy, namely that those engaged in criminal acts should not be compensated for injuries resulting from participating in such acts. Therefore, even where the defendant is at fault for the injury, policy dictates that their liability warrants being extenuated. [6]

However, not all illegal acts will defeat a claim as in **Revill v Newbery** [1996] Q.B. 567 where a burglar was shot but obtained compensation.[7] In **Pitts v Hunt** [1991] 1 Q.B. 24 the defence was deemed to arise where the illegality of the act means that the court is unable to determine the standard of care owed. However, in **Pitts** the standard was determinable as it was a car accident; it was more the case that the court did not want to acknowledge the standard due to the illegality. A further difficulty with this reasoning is that it fails to explain the defence's applicability to intentional torts.[8] Therefore, the better view in **Pitts** was that of Beldam LJ who viewed the matter of compensation as being determined by whether the public conscience would be outraged by the claimant obtaining compensation. While more plausible, it also accords with the policy behind the defence and offers some explanation for **Revill** in that the defendant's response was disproportionate.

However, this was rejected in **Hewison v Meridian Shipping PTE** [2003] I.C.R. 766 in favour of an approach which looks at whether the claim is substantially based on the illegal act. This still leaves questions regarding **Revill**, as his injury only occurred because of his illegal act. Therefore, arguably, the unifying rationale to the defence is that it applies where the injury suffered is related to the illegal act and was proportionate to that act.[9]

Revill is illustrative of an increasing reluctance by courts to apply the full defences in favour of reducing the quantum of damages under the Law Reform (Contributory Negligence) Act 1945. This has been considered a far more appropriate tool for ensuring justice (**Vellino v Chief Constable of Greater Manchester** [2001] E.W.C.A. Civ. 1249). Following the Act, contributory negligence is now a partial defence.[10] Damages are reduced to reflect the amount that the claimant contributed to their injury through their negligence. If the

[11]Include the merits of the defence here, before the requirements, to link into the comment from *Vellino*.

defendant is not liable for the full extent of the injury, it is justifiable to limit damages to the extent to which they are.[11] Three factors must be proved by the defendant for the defence to apply (**Fookes v Slaytor** [1978] 1 W.L.R 1293). Firstly, the injury must result from the claimant exposing himself to a particular risk. Secondly, his negligence contributed to his injury; and finally that there was fault on the claimant's part. A reduction is made where the claimant is contributorily negligent regardless of the difficulty ascertaining the exact scope of the contribution (**Capps v Miller** [1989] 1 W.L.R. 839) so as to reflect that fact.

To conclude, even though the injury is the defendant's fault, there is a need for defences on policy grounds to ensure fairness. However, moving towards relying on contributory negligence is welcomed as it strikes a fair balance between recognising the defendant's fault while also taking account of the claimant's own role in events.

✓ Make your answer stand out

- Consider the merits of the defence and whether it is actually needed in view of the circumstances that it operates in, particularly as the quote could be said to imply there is little need for them.
- Evaluate the justification for favouring the partial defence of contributory negligence over the full defences. Is there still a role which the full defences are required to play?

! Don't be tempted to ...

- Discuss the requirements for liability in negligence.
- Just describe each defence; offer some evaluation of why each is needed if liability is based upon the defendant's fault and whether it is justified.

Negligence: combined issue questions

3

How this topic may come up in exams

In the previous two chapters we looked at how the aspects of negligence may arise individually as an essay question. In this chapter we put all of the aspects of negligence together for problem scenarios. In such a question all aspects of the tort will need to be touched on and skill is needed in identifying the weight which should be given to each aspect. As this is a way of testing your knowledge and understanding of the entire tort they are very common but, provided you work through the tort logically, they should not be feared.

Attack the question

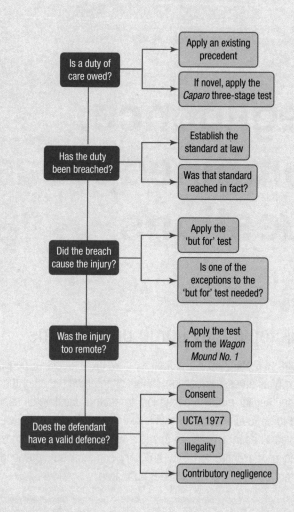

❓ Question 1

Mick had recently purchased a new sports car and, feeling excited, took it out to see how fast he could get it to go. Having got the car up to 90 mph, he saw something in the road and slammed on the brakes. Unfortunately, he lost control and hit the central reservation.

An ambulance arrived and rushed him to Keefstone Hospital where his condition was stabilised. However, following the operation, a nurse from the hospital failed to rehydrate Mick sufficiently, which left him weaker than he would have been.

Subsequently, because of a pre-existing condition which Mick had, a complication developed which required further major surgery. Owing to his increased weakened state, Mick suffered a heart attack. The evidence shows that the heart attack could have been naturally caused because of the trauma of the second surgery but this is inconclusive; in any event, his weakened state would have heightened the risk of this occurring.

Advise Mick as to whether he has a claim in negligence for his injuries.

Answer plan

→ Confirm the existence of a duty of care owed by the hospital.

→ Explain whether, and if so how, it has been breached.

→ Evaluate the difficulty Mick may face with regard to causation and the non-applicability of the 'but-for' test.

→ Discuss whether regardless of the lack of firm evidence Mick could still prove causation.

→ Consider whether the heart attack is too remote from the breach.

→ Discuss whether there is a possible defence because of Mick's own negligence in speeding initially.

Diagram plan

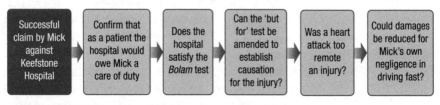

A printable version of this diagram is available from www.pearsoned.co.uk/lawexpressqa

[1] As there can be a lot of issues surrounding a negligence problem question, spell out the key issues within the scenario early to show that you have fully understood the question.

[2] The *Caparo* test only applies to novel situations and, therefore, you should not mention it when you have a scenario which is covered by precedent, as it suggests you do not fully understand its operation. While there are more long-standing authorities for the point, factually the situation is the same as *Bailey* so you can justifiably use *Bailey*, which is then easier when you refer to it again.

[3] Make sure that you explain what the duty of care in the instance case is and the extent of that duty, because this will be relevant in terms of determining breach and whether the damage is too remote.

[4] So that you can fully explore whether there has been a breach, you need to highlight, out of the facts, what the potential act is which breached the duty.

[5] Even though the question does not mention the extent of the nurse's experience, show that you are aware of the potential issue by advising Mick briefly how this will not affect his claim.

Answer

In advising Mick on his action for negligence, the rules relating to causation will need particular focus as, on the traditional rules, it seems as if the act of the hospital is not the factual cause of his injury.[1] However, it will be argued that Mick's case may warrant a relaxation of these rules and he is likely to be successful in his claim.

The first aspect of negligence which needs to be satisfied is that the hospital must have owed Mick a duty of care. As this is not a novel situation, precedent must be relied on to determine the matter, which clearly shows in this situation a duty is owed: for example, **Bailey v Ministry of Defence** [2008] E.W.C.A. Civ. 883 which is factually similar to Mick's case.[2] Therefore, the hospital can be said to have owed Mick a duty of care in relation to his operation and the subsequent treatment which would follow.[3]

Once a duty is imposed, it then needs to have been breached. This occurs when the defendant's conduct falls below a reasonable standard. Here it will need to be shown that the standard of the operation and aftercare was unreasonable owing to a failure to sufficiently rehydrate Mick following the operation.[4] Mick should be advised that there are two legal questions to ask: what is the required standard and, on the facts, does the conduct fall short of the standard? In terms of the first question, the legal standard is normally to take such care as is reasonable in the circumstances (**Paris v Stepney B.C.** [1951] A.C. 367) and determined objectively. However, when the issue is one of professional negligence, as is the case here in dealing with a surgical operation, the standard is altered to take account of the professional status of the defendant (**Bolam v Friern Management Hospital Committee** [1957] 1 W.L.R. 582), regardless of their level of experience (**Wilsher v Essex AHA** [1988] A.C. 1074).[5] Mick should be advised that the standard required becomes whether the defendant acted with the level of skill and competency expected of someone undertaking the activity in question. Therefore, the question is simply whether a reasonable nurse would have provided the level of rehydration which was given to Mick. While we are not told whether others would have provided the same level of rehydration, owing to the risks brought by the level

⁶As this part of the claim is inconclusive at this stage, and you are offering advice, emphasise that this aspect is conditional on the previous requirement. This will also illustrate your understanding by showing that you are not making firm opinions when the evidence does not necessarily confirm the view.

⁷This is the main focus of this question so you should factor in most time for this part of your answer.

⁸Even if you recognise straightaway that this is not a 'but-for' scenario, you should follow a logical progression through what the law requires. Therefore, set out how this normally applies first rather than jumping to the relaxed rules.

⁹As there have been two operations, identify which one is in issue here, particularly as the first operation appeared successful.

¹⁰Quoting the facts strengthens the suggestion that the principle applies.

¹¹By stating this you allude to knowing the issues around the overlap between duty and damage since they are both based on foreseeability following the *Wagon Mound No. 1*.

provided and following a major operation, it is unlikely to be the standard of a reasonable nurse.

If a breach is found,[6] the next issue to advise Mick on is whether this left Mick so significantly weakened as to cause or materially contribute to his heart attack[7] (**Bailey**). Normally, causation is determined on the balance of probabilities by reference to the 'but-for' test[8] (**Cork v Kirby Maclean** [1952] 2 All E.R. 402): 'but for' the negligent rehydration would the injury have been suffered? On the facts this cannot be said to be so, as the heart attack may have been caused through non-negligent means, the trauma of the second[9] operation. However, this is a cumulative cause scenario whereby, because of evidential difficulties, the 'but-for' test is not applied. Under **Bonnington Castings Ltd v Wardlaw** [1956] A.C. 613, provided there is a negligent contribution which is more than negligible, it will suffice as a causative factor. While the hospital may claim that the evidence here does not even show that the lack of hydration made any contribution to the heart attack, this may not matter. The **Wardlaw** principle was developed in **McGhee v National Coal Board** [1973] 1 W.L.R. 1 so that causation can be satisfied where the evidence shows the negligence made a material increase in the risk of the harm suffered. This is the situation here as we told that the risk of the heart attack was 'heightened'[10] by Mick's increased weakened state which resulted from the rehydration failure. It was doubted, following **Wilsher**, that this relaxation of the causation rules would apply to medical negligence cases and instead were limited to industrial cases. However, following **Bailey** the distinction is between distinct, independent causes as in **Wilsher**, or cumulative causes as in **Wardlaw**. It was held that there was no sufficient policy reason for not applying the relaxed rules for the latter scenario even where it is medical negligence. On the authority of **Bailey**, and especially in light of the similarities, it would appear that there is sufficient factual causation.

Even if the breach was the factual cause of Mick's injury, it must also be the legal cause. This means that the injury suffered must be of a type which was reasonably foreseeable (**Wagon Mound No. 1** [1961] A.C. 388) and not too remote. Arguably this is satisfied here as a heart attack is a foreseeable occurrence in such incidents and could be said to show that a duty is recognised in this situation.[11] The fact that Mick was suffering a pre-existing condition which

3 NEGLIGENCE: COMBINED ISSUE QUESTIONS

necessitated the second operation will also not matter as an 'egg-shell' skull rule applies in negligence (**Smith v Leach Brain & Co. Ltd** [1962] 2 Q.B. 405), meaning that the hospital must take Mick as they find him.

[12]Demonstrate that you appreciate this by stating it as you introduce it.

Therefore, it appears that Mick would have a valid claim for negligence; however, he should be advised that the hospital may seek to rely on the partial[12] defence of contributory negligence; if successful, this would mean any compensation is reduced to take account of his own negligence. They may argue that the only reason Mick was in hospital was through his own negligence: speeding, which caused the initial crash. However, while Mick may satisfy the first requirement of **Fookes v Slaytor** [1979] 1 All E.R 137 that the injury resulted from a risk which Mick exposed himself to, Mick's negligence needs to contribute to the injury suffered. The evidence does show that the heart attack was contributed to by his non-negligently caused weakened state following his operation and this could be traced back to him crashing his car. Therefore, this could be a contributing factor to his injury; however, Mick should be advised that as the injury occurred following the negligence and the second operation, not the operation following the crash, a contributory finding may be unlikely. Finally, the hospital must show negligence on Mick's part which, as noted, is easily satisfied as he was speeding.

[13]Remember to use consistent wording: earlier it was couched in less than absolute terms so do not make it concrete now.

To conclude, Mick was owed a duty of care by the hospital which seems[13] breached; this is likely to be deemed to have caused the injury under the principle from **McGhee**. As this injury is not legally too remote, Mick is likely to succeed in his claim; however, this would be subject to a possible reduction for his own negligence in crashing his car initially.

✓ Make your answer stand out

- Discuss how even though the negligence was the act of an individual nurse the hospital will be vicariously liable (*Cassidy* v *Ministry of Health* [1951] 2 K.B. 762).
- Discuss the potential counter to the *Bolam* principle which the hospital could make under *Bolitho* v *City & Hackney Health Authority* [1997] 3 W.L.R. 1151.
- Discuss the policy factors flowing from the decision in *Bailey* and its potential impact on the health service.

! Don't be tempted to ...

- Demonstrate that you know about the *Caparo* three-stage test and mention the aspects. You will show that you understand it better by not referring to it.
- Mention *Donoghue* v *Stevenson* [1932] A.C. 562 as it has no relevance to the question.
- Cover all of the factors considered by the courts in relation to breach.
- Discuss in length the facts of *Bailey* to show how it is similar. Your examiner will know the facts and know that the question is similar, but by all means offer a brief outline.

? Question 2

Jenna and Briana had been out at their local nightclub to celebrate Jenna passing her driving test. However, after losing track of time, when they finally left they realised that they had missed the last bus. Although they started to walk home, Brianna started to complain that her feet hurt and needed to stop. Upon doing so she noticed that a nearby car had the keys in the ignition. As a result, she shouted to Jenna that she could drive them back now she had passed her test. Jenna, who had had several alcoholic drinks, thought it was a good idea and that no one would know it was them as the area was deserted.

Both girls got in and Jenna started to drive home. To pass the time they put the radio on and a song which they had been dancing to was playing. Jenna started to sing to Brianna and stopped looking at the road and in doing so missed a red light. As they went over the junction Jenna quickly swerved to avoid an oncoming car and careered into a bus stop. Brianna suffered multiple bone fractures from the impact but was diagnosed with brittle-bone disease in the hospital and her injuries would not have been as severe in a normal person.

Advise Jenna on the matter.

Answer plan

→ Confirm that as a driver Jenna owes other road users a duty of care.

→ Establish that notwithstanding her inexperience she has breached this.

→ Identify the breach as the cause of the injuries, and using the egg-shell skull rule show how they are not too remote.

→ Consider the application of the defences to determine whether they could defeat any claim by Brianna.

Diagram plan

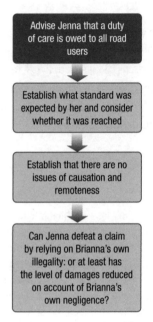

Advise Jenna that a duty of care is owed to all road users

Establish what standard was expected by her and consider whether it was reached

Establish that there are no issues of causation and remoteness

Can Jenna defeat a claim by relying on Brianna's own illegality: or at least has the level of damages reduced on account of Brianna's own negligence?

A printable version of this diagram is available from www.pearsoned.co.uk/lawexpressqa

Answer

[1]When faced with a question which just says 'Advise X', it is worth spelling out in your first line that you have correctly identified the exact thing that you should be advising the person on.

The issue to advise Jenna on is her potential liability in negligence (as the driver) for the personal injury suffered by Brianna following the crash. This will involve looking at the standard of care required by drivers and the impact on liability of the fact the injury occurred in a stolen car.[1] It will be argued that she will certainly have breached her duty of care to Brianna but may be able to defend that action on the basis of the illegality of the episode.

[2]As there is a precedent regarding the duty in this situation, there is no need to talk about *Caparo Industries plc* v *Dickman* [1990] 2 A.C. 605.

The first issue to confirm is that as the driver, Jenna, owes a duty of care to all other road users who may be reasonably foreseeably injured if care is not exercised; this extends to her passengers (**Langley *v* Dray** [1998] P.I.Q.R. P314[2]).

The main question is what standard is expected to be reached by someone who is subject to this duty. The standard expected is determined objectively by looking at what the reasonable man would do in this situation (**Blyth v Birmingham Water Works Co.** (1856) 11 Ex. 781). The reasonable man was stated by Lord MacMillan in **Blyth** to have a standard of foresight which eliminates the idiosyncrasies of the person whose conduct is in question. This is significant for Jenna as it means that the fact that she has only just passed her test will be irrelevant and she must meet the same standard as the reasonable driver regardless of her experience (**Nettleship v Weston** [1971] 2 Q.B. 691). While this may seem unfair, it is required to surmount the difficulties otherwise in ascertaining an individual standard for every driver.[3] Therefore, the standard as explained in **Langley** is to drive with such care and skill so as to avoid exposing other road users to unnecessary risk of injury. Regarding breach of duty the second question is to determine whether, on the facts, Jenna reached the required standard. Jenna should be advised that she has clearly breached the standard. Not only are we told that she drove after having several alcoholic drinks, but we also know that at the key time she was not looking at the road and instead singing to Brianna.

[3] As this standard is detrimental to Jenna's chances of defeating the claim, you should explain to her why this is the situation and, in doing so, you will show that you have more than a superficial knowledge of the law.

The next factor to establish is that this breach of Jenna's duty caused the injury to Brianna. Causation is a question of fact whereby it is asked whether, on the balance of probabilities, the injuries would have happened 'but for' Jenna's breach (**Cork v Kirby Maclean** [1952] 2 All E.R. 402). There does not appear to be any issue here as, were Jenna paying attention and looking at the road, she would not have had to swerve to avoid the other car.

While Jenna's breach was the factual cause of the injuries, it must also be determined that she was the legal cause. This means that the injury suffered was not too remote from the incident. To satisfy this requirement Brianna would need to show that the injury was a kind, type or class that was reasonably foreseeable (**Wagon Mound No. 1** [1961] A.C. 388). Broken bones from a car crash are clearly a reasonable foreseeable injury from driving in the manner that Jenna did. However, Jenna may seek to argue that as Brianna's injury was too remote in that a normal person would not have suffered such severe injuries. Therefore, Jenna should be advised as to the 'egg-shell skull' rule. This means that the defendant must take the claimant as they find them and they will be liable for the entire harm caused, even where it is greater than expected owing to a particular condition of the claimant. This might seem at odds with the principle from the **Wagon Mound No. 1**, but it has been held to still apply (**Smith v Leech Brain & Co. Ltd** [1962] 2 Q.B. 405). As the injury was a type which was foreseeable, the fact that Brianna's condition meant the injury was far more severe will not limit liability.

Jenna may avoid liability in negligence[4] by demonstrating a valid defence against Brianna. Under s.149 of the Road Traffic Act 1988, Jenna will not be able to claim that Brianna voluntarily assumed the risk of such injury by getting in a car with someone who had been drinking and was inexperienced.[5] The defence of illegality may, however, be applicable. This is a full defence absolving Jenna of all liability and requires Brianna's claim to be substantially based on the illegal act (**Hewison v Meridian Shipping PTE** [2003] I.C.R. 766). Jenna's situation is somewhat similar to that in **Ashton v Turner** [1981] Q.B. 137, whereby the claimant was injured through the negligent driving of his partner in a burglary which they were driving away from. It was held that the degree to which the claim was based on the illegal act was too high and thus there was no liability. Here the girls were in a stolen car and the negligent driving of that car led to the injury. At the time of the injury they were still in the performance of a theft of the vehicle, which arguably was incited by Brianna.

In any event, Jenna should be advised that if a court were to hold that the claim was not substantially based on the crime, she may be successful in pleading contributory negligence on the part of Brianna.[6] This is a partial defence[7] which reduces the amount of damages payable where just and equitable to reflect the level of contribution made by the claimant (Law Reform (Contributory Negligence) Act 1945, s.1). It must first be shown that Brianna was acting negligently; arguably she was, as she ought to have foreseen that by encouraging Jenna to drive, knowing she had been drinking, and getting in the car she might suffer injury. It was not the act of a reasonable person. As the injury which occurred was exactly what Brianna had exposed herself to, it would be said to have made a contribution to her injury. In terms of what reduction would be made, Jenna should be advised that under the Act damages cannot be reduced by 100 per cent even if it was Brianna's idea to take the car in those circumstances (**Pitts v Hunt** [1991] 1 Q.B. 24).

[4]Obviously, there are other actions which Jenna may face to which the following would not apply so it is worth clarifying the scope of the application of the defences.

[5]As the section will bar the defence application, there is no more that needs to be said than just this. Do not go on and explain what the defence involves, let alone apply the requirements to the scenario, as it will be a pointless exercise.

[6]Even if you think that the illegality defence would certainly apply, you should still discuss this, as there is a possibility the other defence would not be applied. Further, by doing so you show that you know not only about this issue but also how it relates to the other defences.

[7]It is because this is only a partial defence that you discuss it last. It is mentioned as a last chance for Jenna. Logically, if you were advising her you would not go to great lengths to advise her of the chance of paying less in damages if there is a chance of paying none at all. Start with the full defences and then fall back on the partial defence.

[8]While you will always have a conclusion, in a negligence problem question, as there are several issues, sum-up events by recapping what you have discussed throughout.

In conclusion,[8] Jenna should be advised that she owed Brianna a duty of care which was clearly breached. As that caused the injury, she would be liable notwithstanding that the extent of the injury was worse than that which an ordinary person would have suffered. However, owing to the illegality of the event, she will likely have a defence to any claim. At the very least the level of damages would be reduced to reflect Brianna's own negligence in the matter.

✓ Make your answer stand out

- Read *Langley* v *Dray* [1998] P.I.Q.R. P314 which provides an overview of the duty owed by motorists and this sort of scenario and draw on the points made by Lord Justice Stuart-Smith to support your assertion that Jenna owed a duty of care to Brianna.
- Mention how Jenna could also face liability for trespass to goods for taking the car (although only in passing).
- Question the validity of the 'egg-shell' skull rule.
- Explain the policy factors which justify defences to an action for negligence when liability has been made out.

! Don't be tempted to ...

- Show your wider knowledge of the tort by raising aspects which are not applicable to the scenario. For example, there is no need in relation to causation to discuss anything more than the 'but-for' test.
- Demonstrate why there is illegality at the heart of the issue.

❓ Question 3

Paddy McQueen was a long-term alcoholic and was recently told that owing to his lifestyle he only had about a 45 per cent chance of living more than three years. After an unexpected bet came off, he decided to check himself in to the Ladbroke Hills private medical centre for a liver transplant in order to prolong his life expectancy. Prior to the operation he had spoken to Dr. Done who talked him through the procedure that would be used. Reflecting the seriousness of the situation, a new and innovative procedure was to be used which, while not having wide-scale endorsement, has been supported by a leading expert in the field in a national medical journal.

However, because he believed that Paddy really ought to have the operation, Dr. Done chose not to inform Paddy that the operation carried with it a 5 per cent risk that the new liver may not be accepted by his body, which could result in death.

Following the operation, it became apparent that the new liver had not been accepted and Paddy was informed that with some medication the condition could be managed, but he would only have a 20 per cent chance of living longer than three years. Paddy has indicated that if he had been informed he may not have gone ahead with the operation.

Advise Paddy as to whether he has a successful negligence action against the medical centre.

Answer plan

→ Explain quickly how a duty of care is owed by the Centre in this situation and set out the full scope of the duty.

→ Identify the two potential breaches and deal with each, assessing whether they were breached.

→ Explain how even if the duty with regards the operation procedure was breached, it is non-actionable.

→ Apply the causation rules to the personal autonomy breach and explain how the approach is taken by the courts.

→ Address any appropriate defences that the Centre may have.

Diagram plan

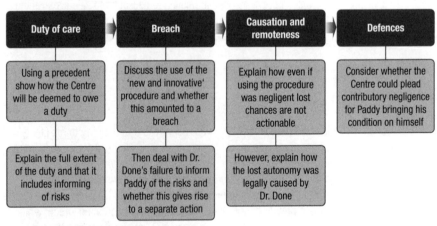

Duty of care	Breach	Causation and remoteness	Defences
Using a precedent show how the Centre will be deemed to owe a duty	Discuss the use of the 'new and innovative' procedure and whether this amounted to a breach	Explain how even if using the procedure was negligent lost chances are not actionable	Consider whether the Centre could plead contributory negligence for Paddy bringing his condition on himself
Explain the full extent of the duty and that it includes informing of risks	Then deal with Dr. Done's failure to inform Paddy of the risks and whether this gives rise to a separate action	However, explain how the lost autonomy was legally caused by Dr. Done	

A printable version of this diagram is available from www.pearsoned.co.uk/lawexpressqa

Answer

[1]It is important to highlight early that you have spotted that this is not simply a loss of chance problem scenario and that in fact it is arguably more to do with *Chester* v *Afshar* [2004] U.K.H.L. 41. To avoid your answer getting messy, clearly separate out the two issues and then explain to the reader this is what you are doing so they know and thus do not lose track of what you saying by trying to work out why you are saying it.

[2]By inserting this word, and after citing *Cassidy*, you show that you are aware of the applicability of the doctrine of vicarious liability to this situation, without getting sidetracked by a fuller explanation of it.

In advising Paddy as to whether he has a claim against the Centre in negligence, the full extent of the duty owed by the Centre will be established and then the two possible ways any action may take will be considered. It will be argued that while it would appear that he has not suffered any actionable injury, merely a lost chance of living more than three years, the presence of the issue of personal autonomy in the matter means that he should have some basis for succeeding in any action.[1]

The first point to establish is that authorities such as **Cassidy v Ministry of Health** [1951] 2 K.B. 343 clearly show that through the doctor–patient relationship the Centre will vicariously[2] owe a duty of care to Paddy when treating and operating on him. It is also important to advise Paddy that there is an additional aspect to the duty which is to warn Paddy of the risks involved even though they were small (**Chester v Afshar**). This gives effect to a person's personal autonomy and forms the basis of their consent to the treatment. This has been recognised as being an important principle since **Sidaway v Board of Governors of the Bethlehem Royal Hospital** [1985] A.C. 871.

The next issue, therefore, is whether the duty owed to Paddy was breached by the Centre. In taking the duty covering the actual performance of the operation, the standard must be that of the level of skill and competency expected of a person undertaking that activity and with the level of skill that the defendant professes to have (**Bolam v Friern Management Hospital Committee** [1957] 1 W.L.R. 582). While Paddy may argue that the new procedure is not widely endorsed, this is not necessary. Provided the Centre can show that Dr. Done acted in accordance with a respectable body of medical opinion, which can withstand logical scrutiny (**Bolitho v City and Hackney Health Authority** [1997] 3 W.L.R. 1151), this standard will be deemed to have been reached. The fact that a world leading expert has supported the procedure in an international journal would suggest that the procedure was in line with a respectable body of opinion.

Paddy would have a problem though in that, even if it is accepted the use of this new procedure was negligent, he has suffered no actionable injury. Prior to the operation he only had a 45 per cent chance of living over three years. After the operation he had a 20 per cent chance. Therefore, this makes his position near identical to that in **Gregg v Scott** where the House of Lords held that the claimants in fact lost nothing as, on the balance of probabilities, the outcome in question would not have happened, there was no chance to lose. Further, it was held that a reduction in the chance itself should not be an actionable head of injury.[3]

[3]Even if you strongly conclude that the use of the procedure was non-negligent, it is worth adding an additional paragraph on this point – to show that you have recognised that there is a similarity here to *Gregg* but that you understand the legal position and, therefore, that an action by Paddy on this basis would not work.

However, as explained, the scope of the Centre's duty was wider than merely carrying out the operation in a non-negligent manner. It extended to warning Paddy of all the risks which the operation entailed. While Lord Templeman in **Sidaway** accepted that a doctor may, in light of their training and experience, determine what needs to be said to a patient, he also stated that enough information must be given so as to enable the patient to make an informed decision whether to consent to the operation. Therefore, in light of the importance attached to an individual's personal autonomy, it appears that this aspect of the duty was clearly breached, as no information regarding the risk was provided.

[4]By highlighting this you further distance this part of your answer from the previous discussion, as it shows that passing the *Bolam* test has no bearing on this aspect of Paddy's situation.

[5]Professor Honoré was cited by both Lord Steyn and Lord Hope in the majority in *Chester* in support of their opinions; therefore, a small reference such as this allows you to demonstrate your knowledge of their opinions and the wider academic thinking on this issue.

Paddy should then be advised that the breach of the duty to inform must then be deemed to have caused the injury suffered. This is where any action becomes complicated. As stated previously, his injury simply amounts to a reduction in his chance of survival, which is non-actionable. Even proceeding on the basis that the lost ability to make an informed choice was the injury has some difficulties. This is because on conventional principles it must be shown that, on the balance of probabilities 'but for' the negligence, the injury would not have occurred. The issue here is that Paddy may well have proceeded and, therefore, the risk for which the duty was to inform Paddy about would still have materialised, and thus this breach was not the factual cause of the injury. Even if he would not have proceeded, the risk here was not created by the breach but was present regardless and notwithstanding how the operation was performed.[4] However, as Lord Steyn accepted in **Chester** after referring to the academic work of Prof. Honoré,[5] situations which Paddy finds himself in cannot be fitted within normal causation principles, but policy and corrective justice support vindicating his personal autonomy. Otherwise, the duty owed would be stripped of its content and would, in Lord Hope's view in **Chester**, be particularly, useless, for a patient like Paddy who

[6]In the latter part of this sentence, use the facts from the question to identify Paddy with the reasoning of Lord Hope, to make your application stronger as well as, again, showing an in-depth knowledge of the judicial reasoning which impacts on this point.

[7]Refer to *Chester* to reinforce your argument that legally the breach should be seen as the cause of an actionable injury, i.e. the lost autonomy.

[8]Your aim here is to just briefly raise the possibility reflecting your awareness of the similar facts between Paddy's situation and that in *St. George*. This also shows that you understand the point by applying it in dismissal of the potential argument by the Centre.

[9]Make sure that you reinforce that the success of any action brought by Paddy would be solely for this injury.

cannot say what they would have done if they had been properly advised.[6]

Therefore, while it could be argued that factually the injury was not caused by the breach of the duty to warn, as Lord Hope highlighted, the injury was caused in the legal sense. It is on this basis that there would not appear to be any issues regarding remoteness of damage, namely that the injury was a kind, type or class that was reasonably foreseeable (**Wagon Mound No. 1** [1961] A.C. 388). The injury suffered was the failure of the new liver to be accepted by Paddy's body, the risk of which, as in **Chester**,[7] was exactly what he should have been informed of by Dr. Done.

Finally, Paddy should be advised that there does not appear to be any defences which the Centre could rely on to counter any claim. The only possible argument[8] would be that his alcoholism put him in a position whereby he needed treatment and therefore, this behaviour makes him contributorily negligent. However, following **St. George v Home Office** [2008] E.W.C.A. Civ. 1068, as this was a lifestyle choice made prior to the creation of the duty of care, it cannot be considered for the purposes of reducing any compensation.

In conclusion, while there may be causation issues in Paddy's situation, there has been a clear breach of the Centre's duty to inform Paddy of the operation's risk. This denial of personal autonomy should, on the basis of cases such as **Chester and Sidaway**,[9] mean that Paddy would have an action for this loss.

✓ Make your answer stand out

- Explain in a bit more detail the issue of vicarious liability.
- Make sure that you clearly distinguish the two potential breaches by the Centre of their duty of care to Paddy.
- Make more reference to academic opinion on the issue of causation and informing patients of risks. A selection of articles are referred to in the opinion of Lord Steyn in *Chester*.
- Draw on the dissenting opinion of Lord Hoffman in *Chester* to give balance to your argument. He expands on this in 'Causation' L.Q.R. 2005, 121 (Oct): 592–603 which is also worth reading in relation to wider issues of causation.
- Add some of the reasons why loss of chance as in *Gregg* is held to be non-actionable.

> **!** **Don't be tempted to ...**
>
> ■ Get into too much of an in-depth discussion on whether a lost chance should be an actionable claim. As the law stands it is not, show that you are aware of the differing views in cases such as *Gregg* but remember that this is a problem question on the whole of negligence and not an essay on that specific issue.
>
> ■ As with the other questions so far in this chapter, avoid explaining about the history of the development of the duty of care.
>
> ■ Gloss over aspects of negligence which are not in issue, all must be referred to.

? Question 4

Owing to a recent flurry of burglaries in the area, a group of local residents decided to form a neighbourhood watch team. The purpose of the team was to set up a patrol around the area to act as a deterrent by approaching people who looked up to no good and to contact the police at the first hint of any criminal activity.

One of the members, Brandon, had that day gone away for the night and having realised he had left a downstairs window open sent a text to Mac, a friend but non-member, asking him to close it for him. However, Mac was busy getting ready to go out and thought there would be nothing to worry about as the neighbourhood watch patrol would go past Brandon's house regularly and it was only one night.

That evening, it was Keith's turn to do the patrol. Keith had already worked a long day at the factory where he was employed and so was tired. As he approached Brandon's house he saw someone climbing through the window but wanting to just get home to watch TV he did nothing, thinking it was just someone who had locked themselves out.

The next day, Brandon returned home to see his house had been burgled with all of his belongings taken. The burglar has never been caught.

Brandon now seeks your advice as to whether he could bring a claim against Mac or Keith as he holds them responsible for what happened.

> ## Answer plan
>
> ■ Set out the general position regarding omissions and deal with Mac's potential liability first.
>
> ■ Consider if there is an assumption of responsibility by Mac towards Brandon which warrants imposing a positive duty to act.
>
> ■ If so, assess whether the duty was breached and confirm the other elements of negligence.
>
> ■ Assess the potential liability of Keith on the same basis.

Diagram plan

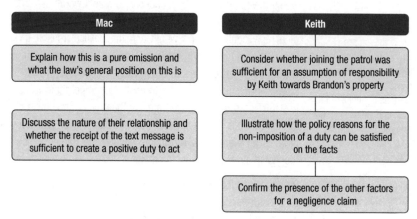

A printable version of this diagram is available from www.pearsoned.co.uk/lawexpressqa

Answer

The issue to determine is whether Brandon has a claim in negligence even though Mac and Keith have not performed any positive acts. This is important as usually the law only permits this in limited situations and thus if they do not fit those, Brandon will be left without redress for his loss. It will be argued that Mac does not owe a duty but Keith may well be held liable.

As indicated, the general position in negligence is that a duty of care will not be imposed in relation to omissions (**Smith v Littlewoods Organisation** [1987] 1 A.C. 241). It is clear that in relation to Mac that this is a case of a pure omission as opposed to being a failure to act as part of a wider positive course of conduct, such as not stopping at a red light, which will carry a duty.[1] Mac has received the text message but clearly omitted to do anything about it and so this is the former category and within the general rule. However, exceptions to this position were outlined by Lord Goff in **Smith**. Of these, the most likely to be applicable is that Mac assumed responsibility for Brandon's property. Brandon could argue that by asking Mac to close the window and highlighting the present danger a duty should be imposed. However, Brandon should be advised that this is unlikely to be accepted as there was no confirmation by Mac that he would

[1] The point here is to show that you are aware of the distinction between the two, and using the facts confirming what we are dealing with here. This is important as the law does impose duties in the latter type of situation.

do so. Had Mac done so, then a duty would be present, as Brandon would have had trust and confidence in Mac's words, which would justify a finding of an assumption of responsibility. In the absence of a reply confirming he would act, the political reason given by Lord Hoffmann in **Stovin v Wise** [1996] A.C. 923 for not imposing a duty for omissions is not addressed. This reason is that it is a greater invasion of a person's freedom to compel them to act than it is to require them to take care of others when they have chosen to embark on a course of conduct.[2] This can only be justified when there is an element of proximity between the parties which their friendship alone is unlikely to create.

Brandon should be advised, however, that he may be more successful in a claim against Keith. While, again, this is a case of a pure omission, the reason for the greater likelihood of success is that Keith is a member of the neighbourhood watch patrol and was meant to be keeping an eye out for burglars that night. By accepting this role, Keith assumed responsibility towards those residents who are covered by the patrol, which includes Brandon. As such, the political reason stated above is overcome; he has volunteered to act and failed to do so.[3] The moral reason advanced by Lord Hoffmann for not imposing a duty is also satisfied. This is based on the idea that there could be an indeterminate class of potential defendants in an omission situation, raising the question of why it is justified to pick out the actual defendant for liability. However, here, as he was performing the patrol that night, it is morally right to pick out Keith for liability over others.

Those factors which suggest an assumption of liability also suggest that the tripartite **Caparo** test[4] for imposing a duty is satisfied here. It is clearly foreseeable that if Keith omitted to approach the person climbing through the window, at the time of widespread burglaries, harm could be caused to the property in question. While it was stated in **Smith** that mere foreseeability is not sufficient to create a duty to prevent criminal acts by a third party, the facts indicate that the key requirement of proximity exists between Brandon, as a resident under the patrol's remit, and Keith who was undertaking the patrol. These factors combined, by addressing the policy concerns for imposing a duty, mean that it would be fair, just and reasonable to impose a duty on Keith.

[2] At this point you are explaining why someone that Brandon wants to make a claim against is unlikely to succeed. As the point of the question is to advise him on the law, you have to make sure you state the reasons why he would not have a claim. If you imagine him in front of you, he would be asking why not, so tell him.

[3] Whereas before you were highlighting how the reasons were not satisfied, now you need to use the facts to show how they have been overcome, as this is what will justify the courts imposing a duty on Keith.

[4] The presence of an assumption of responsibility will generally warrant imposing a duty of care; however, the same facts would also generally satisfy the *Caparo* test. A negative finding of an assumption of responsibility does not preclude reference being made to *Caparo* and so it is worth you highlighting it here to reinforce why you feel Keith is likely to owe a duty in this situation.

As it seems likely that Keith will owe duty of care, Brandon now needs advising as to whether the rest of the elements for a claim in negligence are satisfied.[5] By not doing anything when he saw the person climbing through the window, it would seem apparent that Keith failed to reach the standard of care expected of a reasonable man: the likelihood of harm was increased and thus Keith should have approached the person, or at least contact the police, as that was part of the patrol's remit.

'But for' this breach, Brandon's loss of property would also not have occurred. If he had approached the person and/or called the police, the incident would have been prevented or the person apprehended and, therefore, the causal link required is established. While usually the deliberate wrongdoing of a third party will be deemed an independent cause of the loss (**Weld-Blundell v Stephens** [1920] A.C. 956) exceptionally, where for example the duty in question is to prevent that third party from doing the wrong, as here, it shall not be classed as an intervening act (**Dorset Yacht Club v Home Office** [1970] A.C. 1004). The scope of the duty also means there is not any issue of remoteness. Here the loss suffered by Brandon is stolen property and so it is of a type that was reasonably foreseeable as required by the **Wagon Mound No. 1** [1967] 1 A.C. 617.

6By this stage of your answer, if you have time, you could name the defences but it is not necessary. As they are clearly not applicable to Keith, there certainly is no need to discuss them in detail. Therefore, by treating them like this you show that you understand the full extent of them, which is more important than showing that you simply know them.

Brandon should be advised, however, that if successful, any compensation received may well be reduced on the grounds of contributory negligence. This is because he was aware of the danger of being burgled by leaving his window open, as shown by his text to Mac. However, it is unlikely that any of the full defences[6] to a negligence claim can be relied on by Keith.

In conclusion, Brandon should be advised that he is unlikely to succeed with any claim against Mac, as this is a situation of a pure omission which the law does not impose duties for generally. Owing to the lack of proximity between the two, the policy reasons for the law's approach are not surmounted. However, Keith's position in the patrol is likely to have created an assumption of responsibility which justifies a duty being imposed on him. As the other negligence factors are present, this means that a claim against Keith should succeed.

Make your answer stand out

- Expand on the basis why the law is reluctant to impose duties of care for pure omissions.
- Read B. S. Markesinis (1989) 'Negligence, nuisance and affirmative duties of action', 105 L.Q.R. 104 and refer to this is support of your arguments.
- Explain in more depth, drawing on the cited case, the issue of intervening acts and why they will not break the chain of causation.

! Don't be tempted to …

- List every exception to the rule; just highlight the ones which are most applicable: otherwise, you risk indicating that you do not fully understand them.
- Focus entirely on the duty issue because of the prominence of the omission issue in the question. To obtain the highest marks you will need to address the question in full which, here, is to advise Brandon on a claim in negligence as a whole.

? Question 5

Morris had been unemployed for several months and so recently passed his driving test in order to aid his chances of finding a job. Subsequently, he obtained an interview which he had to drive to. The mixture of driving and the prospect of the interview made Morris feel quite nervous. On his way there he suffered a large anxiety attack during which he overran a red light and struck Siobhan at high speed as she was crossing the road using a pedestrian crossing. Siobhan was rushed to St. Leonard's hospital where her condition was stabilised after being diagnosed with internal bleeding, a collapsed lung and multiple bone fractures. Part of her post-op care was undertaken by a junior nurse Rebus who, as it was his first day, forgot to check the records to establish whether Siobhan was allergic to anything before administering any medication. As a result Siobhan was given medication which she was highly allergic to and she consequently suffered a massive heart attack and ended up paralysed.

Advise Morris and the hospital as to their respective liability, if any, for these injuries.

Answer plan

→ Discuss how Morris owes Siobhan a duty of care.

→ Consider the impact of the anxiety attack and whether this was breached.

→ Highlight how if Morris's duty was breached there would be no causation issues for the initial injuries.

→ Evaluate whether the actions of Nurse Rebus constitute a *novus actus interveniens* and give rise to a separate action against the hospital.

→ Explain how any compensation will be quantified.

Diagram plan

Confirm the duty owned by Morris

↓

Evaluate the impact of the anxiety attack and whether his duty was breached

↓

Confirm that the breach would have caused the initial injuries

↓

Discuss whether the activities of Nurse Rebus are an intervening act

↓

Go through each element of negligence in relation to the hospital

↓

Confirm the over all position of liability

A printable version of this diagram is available from www.pearsoned.co.uk/lawexpressqa

Answer

The issue regarding Siobhan's situation concerns the interrelationship between the acts of Morris and the hospital and the concept of new intervening acts. This is important to determine as it will impact on the level of liability which may be imposed on both parties. It will be argued that as the action of Nurse Rebus was an independent event it will break the chain of causation with regards Morris's liability.

[1]Remember, as with previous answers where a precedent exists, there is no need to talk about *Caparo Industries plc v Dickman* [1990] 2 A.C. 605.

Firstly, as a motorist, Morris owes a duty of care to pedestrians such as Siobhan (**Bassett v Victoria Wine Co** (1958) W.L. 18557).[1] The question is whether this duty to Siobhan was breached. The standard of care to be exercised is that of the reasonable competent driver regardless of their level of experience and, therefore, it is irrelevant that Morris was newly qualified (**Nettleship v Weston** [1971] 2 Q.B. 691). The fact that Morris hit Siobhan 'at high speed'[2] after going through a red light suggests a clear breach. However, Morris's situation is complicated by his anxiety attack before the accident, as this could be classed as a disabling event affecting his level of care and skill. Reference should, therefore, be made to **Mansfield v Weetabix Ltd** [1998] 1 W.L.R 1263, where a driver suffered a medical condition which impaired his driving ability and led to a crash,[3] which is arguably[4] what happened here. The court held that there was no reason in principle why a person should not be deemed negligent where the disabling event was gradual, as opposed to a sudden event, provided they were unaware of the condition. Therefore, if Morris's attack was a sudden condition which came out of the blue and which he was unaware that he might suffer, he would not have breached his duty. However, this is likely to rest on the speed of the attack and the duration to the impact with Siobhan. At the onset of the attack it is likely Morris would have realised that something was happening and so should have pulled over. Obviously, if he was speeding prior to the attack and before he went through the lights, he would be in breach notwithstanding how sudden it was.

Morris should be advised that he may be deemed to have been negligent if the anxiety attack happened gradually.[5] Ultimately, to determine this issue, more information would be required. If Morris knew he suffered from such attacks, particularly as we are told he was feeling nervous while driving, and he felt one coming on yet continued to drive, then on the basis of **Mansfield** he would be negligent. If on the other hand, the attack slowly built up gradually impairing his driving and he had no reason to suspect he suffered such attacks then, again on the basis of **Mansfield**, it is unlikely he will be held negligent. Although, again as with a sudden attack, this may well rest on the issue of duration as even if Morris had never suffered an attack, once it gradually started he should have appreciated some danger and pulled over. Morris should be advised that, depending on the full facts, it is quite likely he will be held in breach of his duty.[6]

If Morris is held in breach of his duty,[7] he should be advised that it is clear that the breach caused the initial injuries suffered by Siobhan. Applying the standard 'but-for' test from **Cork v**

[2]Make sure that you highlight that you are using the facts of the question to substantiate your point.

[3]State enough of the facts, to highlight the connection with Morris's situation, but do not go into a full-blown account.

[4]Strictly speaking, from the facts we do not know for certain that this was definitely the case and so you should not write this sentence as if it was.

[5]As you have identified two scenarios, split them up into separate paragraphs in order to maintain the clarity of your answer.

[6]When you have given a range of potential options remember to give some indication as to which is the likeliest from the known facts. Remember the essence of the question is to advise someone as to what is likely to happen.

[7]As there is an element of doubt whether there was a breach, reflect this in your choice of words.

Kirby Mclean on the balance of probabilities 'but for' Morris's negligent driving, he would not have hit her and caused those injuries. These injuries are also of a type which was reasonably foreseeable (**Wagon Mound No. 1** [1961] A.C. 388) thus not too remote. Further, as we are told Morris went through a red light at a pedestrian crossing which Siobhan was crossing, he would seem to have no valid defence.

The issue, however, is the extent of Morris's liability and whether he will be liable for the subsequent injuries. In negligence the defendant is liable for the damage caused by his breach. While it could be said Siobhan was only in the hospital because of Morris's alleged[8] negligence, an act by a third party can be said to break the chain of causation. For the court to find this the third party act must not be a natural and probable consequence of Morris's own act (**Knightly v Johns** [1982] 1 All E.R. 851) or a foreseeable act (**Lamb v Camden L.B.C.** [1981] Q.B. 625). In applying this we are told that the heart attack was caused by an allergic reaction to medication administered by Nurse Rebus and, therefore, from the injuries sustained in the collision. Medical negligence could be said to be a foreseeable occurrence but does not automatically break the chain of causation. It can do so, though, where the treatment was so grossly negligent so as to be an irresponsible treatment to the injury initially caused (**Webb v Portsmouth Hospitals NHS Trust** [2002] P.I.Q.R. P8). Failing to check a patient's allergies before administering treatment is far below the standard of care to be expected by a medical professional[9] because of the obvious danger of a reaction, as in Siobhan's case. Morris should, therefore, be advised to argue that Nurse Rebus's actions were a new intervening act[10] and thus he is not liable for these subsequent injuries.

Naturally, a hospital vicariously[11] owes a duty of care to all patients for the acts of its staff (**Cassidy v Ministry of Health** [1951] 2 K.B. 343) and, as discussed above[12] this seems to have been breached. The facts also indicate that this breach caused the allergic reaction to occur and thus there appear to be no issues surrounding causation or remoteness. Therefore, the hospital, which has no defence, would be liable in negligence for Siobhan's paralysis.

To conclude, Morris should be advised that he faces being held liable for damages reflecting the initial injuries suffered by Siobhan. The

[8]By calling it 'alleged', you maintain consistency with your previous discussion.

[9]This is obviously the language to be used when discussing breach. You need to use it here because it is only a highly negligent breach of duty by the hospital which will break the chain of Morris's liability.

[10]You could use the Latin phrase if you know it but this will suffice.

[11]This should be an obvious and on the facts unarguable point, but remember to address it for completeness. Part of your advice should be to advise against whom any claim will be made.

[12]Normally, you would establish the duty first but in this instance it makes sense to show the negligence on the part of the hospital, as this is crucial to there being an intervening act for the purposes of Morris's liability.

chain of causation regarding Siobhan's condition was broken by the intervention of Nurse Rebus and so the hospital should be advised that they would be liable for the subsequent injuries. As these acts and the resulting injuries are more independent than concurrent, the Civil Liability (Contribution) Act 1978 will not apply (**Rahman v Arearose Ltd** [2001] Q.B. 351) and each party will be liable for the amount of compensation quantified to reflect the harm that they individually caused. However, Morris should be advised that the quantification of his amount of compensation will not be curtailed by the subsequent tort if it would have resulted in any future, ongoing losses by Siobhan (**Baker v Willoughby** [1970] A.C. 467).

✓ Make your answer stand out

- Support your discussion of whether Morris breached his duty to Siobhan with reference to academic articles such as B. McDonald (2005) 'Blameless?', P.I.L.J. 35 (May): 15–17.
- Indicate how the junior status of Nurse Rebus and his inexperience is irrelevant on the basis of *Wilsher* v *Essex Area Health Authority* [1988] A.C. 1074.
- Discuss in more detail the issue of quantification of damages and mention the criticisms of the approach in *Baker* by the House of Lords in *Jobling* v *Associated Dairies* [1982] A.C. 794.

! Don't be tempted to ...

- Although this question involves medical negligence, do not feel the need to get into a full discussion of cases such as *Bolam* and *Bolitho*. By this stage of your answer, your time is likely to be nearly up and so you should concentrate on completing the answer which you risk not doing by going into those cases. The breach is quite evident here and so such a discussion is not really necessary.
- Explain at length how a duty is owed in both cases; simply state this is the case and provide an authority to support the point.

Psychiatric injury

How this topic may come up in exams

Psychiatric injury is an aspect of negligence concerned with mental harm which has been caused through the negligent act of another. However, it has its own specific criteria for establishing whether a duty of care is owed. For these reasons it is a common exam question in its own right, separate and distinct from the more normal questions on negligence and physical injury. You must ensure that you are familiar with the different rules for establishing liability and the distinctions that the law makes between the different categories of individuals within a problem question. The law has also been heavily criticised with various proposals offered regarding reform. This also makes this topic equally favourable with examiners as an essay question.

Attack the question

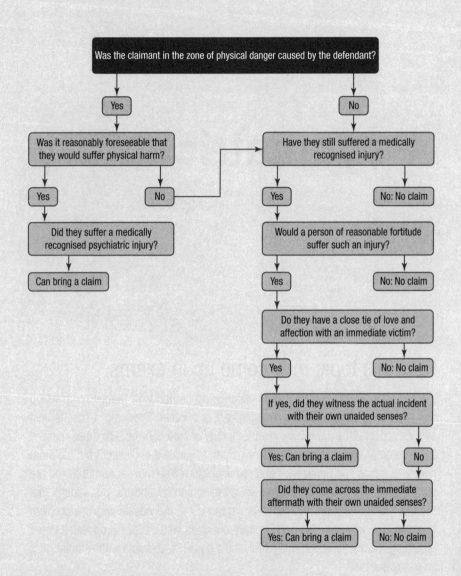

Question 1

'The law in relation to psychiatric injury is "in a dreadful mess"' S. Todd (1999), 115 L.Q.R. 345 at 349

Evaluate the approach taken by the courts in establishing liability for psychiatric injury with reference to academic opinion as to the state of the law.

Answer plan

→ Define psychiatric injury.

→ Explain the distinction between primary and secondary victims.

→ Explain the different control mechanisms for secondary victims assessing whether the law is 'in a dreadful mess'.

→ Explain some of the reform proposals and discuss whether they are better.

→ Conclude by summarising what state the current law is in and whether any reform proposals will help.

Diagram plan

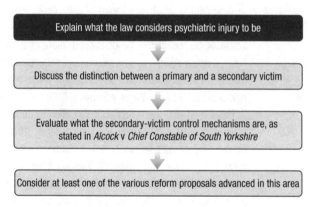

Explain what the law considers psychiatric injury to be

↓

Discuss the distinction between a primary and a secondary victim

↓

Evaluate what the secondary-victim control mechanisms are, as stated in *Alcock* v *Chief Constable of South Yorkshire*

↓

Consider at least one of the various reform proposals advanced in this area

A printable version of this diagram is available from www.pearsoned.co.uk/lawexpressqa

Answer

The statement requires discussion as to the current state of the law in relation to negligently inflicted psychiatric injury and whether it is 'in a dreadful mess'. This area is emotionally charged, raising serious

[1]As the Law Lords have repeatedly affirmed the need for control, a good answer will need to explore what their reasons are for having them. These can then in turn be assessed to see if the policy is right.

[2]This indicates straight away that you are aware of the wider issues relating to this area and that you are also aware of the implications of stating the law is in a mess, i.e. that something needs to replace it.

[3]By referring to judicial comment you will demonstrate your authority for the statement.

[4]This is included to weigh up the merits of the requirement in order to avoid being too descriptive.

[5]State the justification for the distinction, although it is criticised by the Law Commission, it is important to state why it exists.

moral questions for the administration of justice, as many claimants fail owing to the type of victim that they are categorised as. The different judicial approaches to different categories of victim will be assessed with the various control mechanisms evaluated in order to assess their merit.[1] It is argued that the current criticisms of the law are justified and that reform is needed.[2]

The first issue to consider is what amounts to an actionable psychiatric injury. The claimant must suffer a medically recognised psychiatric injury because, as Lord Denning noted[3] in **Hinz v Berry** [1970] 1 All E.R. 1084, English law does not compensate for mere grief or sorrow. Therefore, unlike with physical injury a threshold of psychiatric harm is required. This distinction is because, as Lord Steyn in **White v Chief Constable of South Yorkshire** [1999] 2 A.C. 455 highlighted, expensive expert witnesses are required to establish the exact nature of psychiatric injury, which causes time and cost implications for the administration of justice. Although it is questionable whether this is a sufficient reason for treating psychiatric injury differently, lesser conditions such as mere grief should not warrant liability.[4]

In determining whether a claim is actionable, the law categorises people as either primary or secondary victims. Although the Law Commission has called the distinction 'more of a hindrance than a help', it exists in order to limit the number of people who could bring a claim.[5] Primary victims must be exposed to a reasonably foreseeable risk of physical injury (**Page v Smith** [1996] 1 A.C. 155). Lord Lloyd in **Page** held that there was no justification in treating physical and psychiatric injury differently for such victims. Therefore, provided physical injury was foreseeable the claimant would be successful even if psychiatric injury was not. This treatment for primary victims is acceptable as they have been placed in direct danger. However, an individual who cannot satisfy this will be deemed a secondary victim and must, first, be of 'customary phlegm' (**Bourhill v Young** [1943] A.C.92), and then overcome the control mechanisms from **Alcock v Chief Constable of South Yorkshire** [1992] 1 A.C. 310 to succeed. These act as an arbitrary barrier to bringing a claim under the guise of whether the injury was a foreseeable result of the defendant's act and put such victims in a far less favourable position than primary victims.

[6]By setting out the policy justifications here you provide the context from which to assess the mechanisms.

Before outlining these mechanisms, the policy considerations which underpin them as outlined by Lord Steyn in **White** require discussion.[6] Primarily, there is a judicial desire to prevent a flood of litigation by permitting a wide class of individuals to make a claim. This combines with the need to avoid imposing disproportionate liability as the negligent act may only have been a momentary lack of concentration. Therefore, this is justifiable on the basis of fairness to the defendant. The final consideration was that the prospect of compensation may act as a disincentive to recovery. Stapleton (1994a) calls this as a well-intentioned desire to protect the claimant's condition deteriorating through the stress of a trial. However, this is doubted by Teff (1998)[7] who argues there is little evidence to support the assertion; therefore, it would seem hard to sustain an approach based on this consideration.

[7]In exams include citations for academic opinion but save time by abbreviating it; if it is a book, as with Stapleton, then just put the year.

The first control mechanism[8] is a need for a close tie of love and affection with an immediate victim of the incident. In **Alcock** it was held that there is a rebuttable presumption of such a tie between a parent and child, and spouses. The defendant should reasonably foresee injury to these groups but not necessarily others such as siblings who would have to show evidence of their closeness. This creates uncertainty and is more likely to cause deterioration in a claimant's condition.[9] Weir (1992)[10] argues this risks causing 'embarrassment' to claimants who face cross-examination on their closeness, and contradiction by investigators.

[8]The control mechanisms should be the key part of your answer and where you should focus your time. Ensure that you refer back to the premise of the quote to assess whether the mechanism leaves the law 'in a dreadful mess'.

[9]This relates the criticism of the mechanism back to the policy justifications for imposing them.

The second mechanism is that the claimant was present at the incident or its immediate aftermath. **McLoughlin v O'Brien** [1983] 1 A.C. 410 extended the aftermath temporally forwards and spatially away from the scene, thus covering seeing the person in hospital. This alleviates some strictness by not insisting on the claimant being at the scene but is also another arbitrary line drawn by the courts. In **McLoughlin** the claimant arrived two hours later while the bodies were unclean, yet in **Alcock** relatives who arrived later, having travelled further, were denied a claim.[11] It is also questionable whether the result would have been the same if the bodies had been cleaned in **McLoughlin**. The issue is far from clear and again reinforces the statement that the law is in a mess.

[10]Try to vary your sources of academic opinion to illustrate your wider reading, rather than relying on the same academic.

[11]By highlighting a different result in another case you reinforce the idea that the law is inconsistent and unsatisfactory.

[12]Again, as with the other paragraphs, it is important to balance the discussion by stating what the reason for the mechanism is first before you provide any criticism of it. If you personally feel that the mechanism is justified, write the reason after the criticism so that the answer reads more strongly.

[13]By using a judge from the main case you give the argument more force than if it was just an academic; as the judges decided the law and if they are not happy with it, it leads in to a discussion as to reform.

[14]Depending on the time that you have left in your exam, you could go into more depth here.

[15]Depending on the number of proposals that you discuss, ensure that you state which one you prefer to round off your discussion.

The final mechanism is that the psychiatric injury was a result of directly perceiving the incident or aftermath with one's own senses. While similar to the second mechanism, it requires that the injury result from the sudden impact of witnessing the event and not from some gradual exposure. This can produce inconsistent results. No claim will stand if the injury is caused immediately by being informed, by a third party of, say, the death of a child. The basis, according to Lord Keith in **Alcock** appears to be a lack of proximity and because English law has never allowed for recovery in this way.[12] However, if the claimant arrives at the mortuary in sufficient time, they will have a claim. This is hard to justify; if it is reasonably foreseeable that a parent would suffer injury as a result of witnessing an incident, surely it is a foreseeable occurrence from being informed of the incident.

Even within the judiciary the consensus is that the law is unsatisfactory, with Lord Oliver in **Alcock**,[13] unable to defend the law 'as either entirely satisfactory or as logically defensible'. This has led to widespread calls for reform, notably from the Law Commission. A significant aspect[14] of the Commission's proposals was to remove the second and third mechanisms owing to the unjust results they can bring; the first mechanism would be retained in amended form. A conclusive, automatic statutory presumption of closeness was proposed for the existing groups but widened to include siblings and cohabitants. Those not within the list would still have to prove their closeness under the common law. If adopted, the floodgates would still be prevented from opening by retaining some control but in a more logical and fairer way.

To conclude, it is submitted that the statement describes the law correctly. Reform is not only desirable but a necessity in order to ensure justice to victims of negligence. The Commission's proposals would vastly improve the situation while still maintaining control over claims.[15]

✓ **Make your answer stand out**

■ Discuss the policy reasons for having more control mechanisms for secondary victims seeking a claim.

■ Evaluate whether these policy reasons are justifiable control mechanisms.

■ Contrast the position with claims for physical injury.

■ Ensure that you discuss the implied issue of the question, i.e. reform. Although the question does not expressly state that you should discuss this aspect of the topic, it is implied by the quote that reform is needed. By not discussing reform you would still pass the question but by including reform you would show that you understand the wider issues surrounding the area.

■ Demonstrate your own original views on the issue and which reform proposals you favour.

! **Don't be tempted to …**

■ Have an excessive focus on academic opinion as to the state of the law. The question says to make reference to it and it is clearly an important aspect, but the main thrust of the question is asking you to analyse the judicial approach to the area, which requires a focus on the policy factors influencing their decisions.

? Question 2

Malford Football Club was due to play at home to their local rivals, Shadwell Athletic. The match has a history of crowd violence and there are rumours of a prevalence of counterfeit match tickets; however, a reduced number of police were present. Elements of Shadwell's hooligan group, the 'Shadwell Army', started to attack Malford fans outside the entrance to the Main Stand. In the absence of the police, Malford fans rushed to enter the Main Stand, which was already full because of the counterfeit tickets, resulting in a crush.

Jobi is watching the game at home; his younger brother Tommy is at the game and sits in the Main Stand. After not hearing from Tommy, Jobi rushes to the hospital to see if he is there. Two hours after seeing the incident on TV, Jobi is informed that Tommy has been killed and is asked to identify the body. Owing to the number of patients, Tommy's body has not been cleaned up; upon seeing Tommy, Jobi suffers a nervous breakdown.

Tamas is outside the ground in the middle of a group of fans being attacked. Although Tamas avoids physical injury, upon witnessing the violence, he goes into shock and subsequently undergoes a personality change.

Advise Jobi and Tamas whether they could make a claim for psychiatric injury against the police who have acknowledged they had insufficient men at the ground to control the crowd.

Answer plan

→ Jobi – establish that he is a secondary victim and then work through each control mechanism in turn and apply to the facts of the question.

→ Tamas – identify that he is most likely to be a primary victim and discuss whether he has suffered a medically recognised psychiatric injury.

Diagram plan

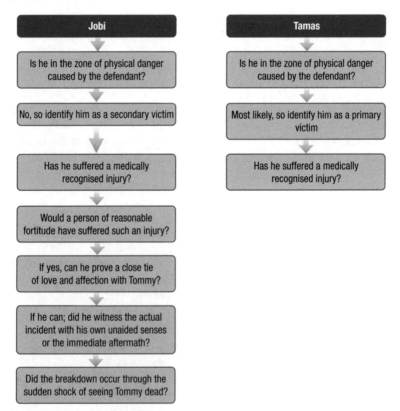

Jobi

Is he in the zone of physical danger caused by the defendant?

No, so identify him as a secondary victim

Has he suffered a medically recognised injury?

Would a person of reasonable fortitude have suffered such an injury?

If yes, can he prove a close tie of love and affection with Tommy?

If he can; did he witness the actual incident with his own unaided senses or the immediate aftermath?

Did the breakdown occur through the sudden shock of seeing Tommy dead?

Tamas

Is he in the zone of physical danger caused by the defendant?

Most likely, so identify him as a primary victim

Has he suffered a medically recognised injury?

A printable version of this diagram is available from www.pearsoned.co.uk/lawexpressqa

Answer

The issue to advise Jobi and Tamas is whether they have satisfied the criteria that the law requires in order to bring a claim for negligently inflicted psychiatric harm. They should be advised that where a claimant suffers psychiatric injury but was not in any physical danger, policy-influenced control mechanisms are imposed to limit when a duty of care will be owed by the defendant. This is important as a successful claim cannot be brought against the police without fulfilling the criteria, even though they have suffered injuries. It will be argued that on the facts Tamas is likely to be successful in his claim while Jobi may face more difficulty.

In regard to Jobi's claim for the nervous breakdown that he suffers, he should be advised that, following **White v Chief Constable of South Yorkshire Police** [1999] 2 A.C. 455, in order to qualify as a primary victim he must have been placed in physical danger through the defendant's negligent act or at least had grounds to reasonably fear for his physical safety. As Jobi was not at the ground, this is not satisfied, therefore, Jobi should be advised on the law for secondary victims as governed by **Alcock v Chief Constable of South Yorkshire** [1992] 1 A.C. 310. Notwithstanding the control mechanisms within **Alcock**, Jobi must first have suffered a medically recognised injury which occurred despite being of 'customary phlegm' (**Bourhill v Young** [1943] A.C. 92). A nervous breakdown would satisfy this requirement although we do not know if he is of reasonable fortitude.[1] However, on the basis that he is of customary phlegm Jobi needs now to be advised as to the **Alcock** control mechanisms.

[1] Although 'customary phlegm' has been used before, phrasing it in this way for the second time will help demonstrate your understanding of what is meant.

The first of these is that the claimant has a close tie of love and affection with an immediate victim of the incident, which in this instance is Tommy. This is required, as the claimant's injury must be reasonably foreseeable to the person who caused it to warrant liability. This mechanism seeks to prevent an excess of claims and liability which is disproportionate to the conduct concerned. Jobi should be advised that such closeness is presumed between spouses and parent and child, but under **Alcock** siblings will not automatically be regarded as being sufficiently close. Therefore, Jobi will have to demonstrate evidence that he was sufficiently close to

[2]The fact that it is Jobi who rushes to the hospital, and there is no mention of any parents, raises a suggestion that this may be the case but do not assume anything definite either way.

[3]Because in the last paragraph it was not established whether the necessary closeness is present, you will need to phrase your next sentence in this way to explain why you are proceeding to the next control mechanism when the claim may well have already failed.

[4]A brief account of the facts is required to lay the basis for arguing that Jobi's case is more like *McLoughlin* than *Alcock*.

[5]It is vital to use the facts within the question to support the argument being advanced.

[6]Although there is the option of discussing the *Alcock* mechanisms in any order, it is advisable here (as opposed to, say, after the point of medically recognised injury), to deal with this one following the proximity in time and space, as the question suggests that the injury was caused by the shock of seeing the unclean body in the hospital and, therefore, it follows better from discussing how he needs to see the body with his own senses.

Tommy, which may be difficult as shown in **Alcock** itself. However, Lord Ackner acknowledged that such closeness will be determined on a case-by-case basis and, therefore, the fact that Jobi is only Tommy's brother may not prevent Jobi successfully claiming. Factors which may help would be evidence such as perhaps Jobi raising Tommy in the absence of any parents;[2] if this cannot be done, then Jobi's claim would fail.

On the basis that Jobi can prove a sufficiently close tie with Tommy,[3] the next issue to advise on is whether he has sufficient proximity to the incident in time and space. This means that Jobi must have been at the incident in person. This may be an issue for Jobi as initially he only sees an incident on TV, which under **Alcock** is not sufficient. However, Jobi should be advised that **Alcock** endorsed the idea of coming across the immediate aftermath of the incident with one's own senses (**McLoughlin v O'Brien** [1983] 1 A.C. 410) as being sufficient. Although in **Alcock** the claimant who identified his brother-in-law at the mortuary some eight hours after the incident was held not to have witnessed the immediate aftermath, Jobi should be advised that his situation is more analogous to the actual case of **McLoughlin**. In that case the mother was told at home of a crash involving her family, two hours after it had happened. Upon arriving at hospital, she was informed that one of her children was dead, which, together with seeing the extent of the injuries to the rest of her family, caused her to suffer psychiatric illness.[4] Therefore, as Jobi saw Tommy in the state that he would have been in at the stadium, having not been cleaned up as in **Mcloughin**, and this was only two hours after the actual incident,[5] it would appear that Jobi has the necessary immediacy to overcome this mechanism.

The final aspect of **Alcock** to advise Jobi on is in relation to the means with which his breakdown was caused.[6] Psychiatric injury must be caused suddenly from the shock of perceiving the incident or the immediate aftermath through their own senses rather than merely being informed by a bystander. Although Jobi is informed of Tommy's death by a third party, we are not told exactly when the breakdown occurs. It appears to have occurred from the sudden shock of seeing Tommy dead, as we are told he suffered the breakdown 'upon seeing' the body. Therefore, Jobi should be advised that only on the basis that he can satisfy the court that he

[7]Again, use the exact wording from the question to strengthen the suggestion that Tamas qualifies as a primary victim.

[8]Raise this point as the facts are inconclusive, and as the law is not clear whether actual danger is needed, you can show your knowledge of this. Use the vagueness of the facts to add to your evaluation.

[9]Having raised two possibilities as to whether Tamas is a primary victim, it is important to come down on one side and explain why as you are advising him and he would want to know.

[10]As the possibility has been raised that he may not satisfy the primary-victim conditions, you should, for completeness, state what the situation would be in that instance. However, as clearly Jobi is the person which the question is seeking to test you on in relation to secondary victims, a repeat of the whole process is not needed.

had a sufficiently close tie of love and affection with his brother would he appear to be able to make a successful claim.

With regard to Tamas, he should be advised that by being in the middle of a group of people that are getting attacked[7] he would appear to have satisfied the condition of being a primary victim. Although it could be argued that by being in the middle of the group he was not in any actual danger owing to the buffer of people around him, this would be dependent on the number of Shadwell fans attacking the group and how many Malford fans were between Tamas and the attackers.[8] However, Tamas should be advised that he is still likely to be deemed a primary victim[9] on the basis that the lack of police controlling the crowd in the street did put him in reasonable danger of physical injury because of the history of violence between the fans.

Tamas should be further advised that the fact that he has suffered no actual physical injury will not be a barrier to his claim, as under **Page v Smith** [1996] 1 A.C. 155, provided it was reasonable to foresee physical injury, it is immaterial if the only injury which in fact occurs is psychiatric and this was not foreseeable. The final issue to advise Tamas on is that the injury he has suffered, a personality change, has been accepted by the courts as a medically recognised psychiatric injury which can give rise to an actionable claim (**McLoughlin**). However, Tamas should be advised that if he was deemed not to be a primary victim he is unlikely to be successful in satisfying the **Alcock** criteria as we are not told of any relationship to an immediate victim.[10]

To conclude, as there appears to be no available defences, Tamas may well be successful in claiming against the police, but Jobi's claim will fail unless he can demonstrate that he was sufficiently close to Tommy.

Make your answer stand out

- Highlight your knowledge of cases by relating the facts of the question to what actually happened in particular cases; this will then strengthen your various argument as you will have actual authority for applying the legal principles in that way.

- Demonstrate the policy rationale underpinning the law on psychiatric injury during your answer. Advise the parties not only as to what the law is but also why, as in this area of law a person, such as Jobi, may not be successful in a claim simply on the grounds of policy. This will also demonstrate that you have a deeper understanding of the topic.

- The question does not ask for any comment as to reform of the law, and in seeking advice an individual will be more concerned with what the law currently is. However, as this area has been heavily criticised, it is beneficial to touch on the issue in your conclusion as this will show that you are aware of developments in the area and have a fuller understanding on the law, how it may change in the future and what the implications would be.

! **Don't be tempted to ...**

- Assume that as Tommy was only Jobi's brother, and we are not told of any other facts, that there could not be a close tie of love and affection.

- Just take it for granted that Tamas will definitely be a primary victim as the facts are not conclusive; ensure that you round off the discussion with what the situation will be if he is a secondary victim.

Question 3

'What rescuer ever thinks of his own safety? It seems to me that it would be very artificial and unnecessary control to say a rescuer can only recover if he was in fact in physical danger. A danger to which he probably never gave thought, and which in any event might not cause physical injury ... I do not share the view that the public would find it in some way offensive that those who suffered disabling psychiatric illness as a result of their efforts to rescue the victims should receive compensation ...'

Per Lord Griffiths, dissenting on the question of 'rescuers', in *White* v *Chief Constable of South Yorkshire* [1999] 2 A.C. 455 at 465

In view of this statement, evaluate the position of a rescuer in a claim for psychiatric injury and whether the law is at a justifiable position.

Answer plan

→ Briefly outline the background to *White* and highlight the decision of the case.

→ Highlight that while rescuers claiming for physical injury are treated favourably this is not the case when the claims are for psychiatric injury.

→ Outline the position of rescuers drawing on the opinions of the majority and evaluate the merits of their reasoning.

→ Contrast the reasoning of the majority with that of the minority.

→ Conclude as to which reasoning is the better view and why.

Diagram plan

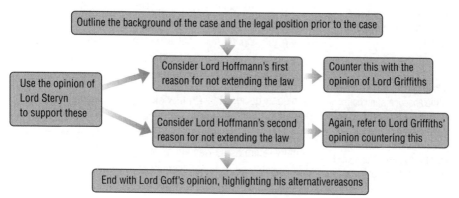

A printable version of this diagram is available from www.pearsoned.co.uk/lawexpressqa

Answer

The issue to address is the merit in the law's current approach to rescuers who, in undertaking the rescue, suffer psychiatric injury. This issue arose in **White v Chief Constable of South Yorkshire Police** [1999] 2 A.C. 455, where the House of Lords reinterpreted existing authority on the matter and created a new control mechanism for claimants to overcome. The rationale behind the majority's decision is evaluated before assessing the merits of the dissenting opinions. It is argued that while within the context of the factual background to the case the position is understandable, overall, the position in terms of legal principle cannot be justified.

[1]By setting this out you have a yardstick from which to determine whether the decision of the case was correct. The history of the case illustrates why the judges formed the opinions that they did.

[2]Obviously, there were two grounds to the appeal, one regarding the duty owed as employee and one on the basis of their rescuer status. As the question is focused on rescuers, you need to focus on just that aspect of the appeal.

[3]It is important to state this, as the absence of authority allowed the majority to come at the matter as they did on policy grounds. It also sets up a contrast to Lord Goff, which can be evaluated later.

[4]As Lord Griffiths' reasons for dissenting on this point are at complete odds with Lord Hoffmann's, raise them as argument against the merit of the majority's view.

In order to make a full assessment of the legal position, it is necessary to briefly outline the factual background from which it has originated.[1] The case originated out of the same incident as **Alcock v Chief Constable of South Yorkshire Police** [1992] 1 A.C. 310. However, whereas **Alcock** concerned the relatives of those that died, the claimants in **White** were the policemen who assisted in the aftermath of the incident and subsequently suffered psychiatric injury. The legal position, following **Chadwick v BRB** [1967] 1 W.L.R. 912, was considered to be that, as with physical injury, rescuers would be in a special position and have a successful claim. The Court of Appeal had allowed the policemen's claims whereas the relatives in **Alcock** were unsuccessful. The defendant appealed, with one ground being[2] that as the officers were not in any reasonably foreseeable physical danger they would have to satisfy the **Alcock** control mechanisms to be successful. The majority, allowing the appeal, held that a rescuer who was not at any risk of physical danger could not be classified as a primary victim and, therefore, must satisfy the control mechanisms.

The majority decided that **Chadwick** was not authority for the proposition that a rescuer was in any sort of special position regarding psychiatric injury.[3] Mr. Chadwick was what would now be considered a primary victim as he was at risk of physical injury. As for whether the law should be extended incrementally to impose liability where a rescuer, in no physical danger, suffers psychiatric injury, Lord Hoffman felt that there were two reasons for saying no. Firstly, it is clearly understood that a rescuer is someone who puts themselves in physical danger. If the term was extended as proposed to cover those who, such as the claimants, provide assistance in the aftermath, then difficulties would arise in distinguishing such a person from a mere bystander. Lord Griffiths disagreed with this analysis,[4] believing that while a distinction is needed between providing immediate help at the scene and treatment once the victim is safe, this could easily be established on the facts of each case. Therefore, Lord Griffiths would have dismissed the appeals and allowed the law to be extended, provided it was still reasonably foreseeable that the rescuer in question would suffer psychiatric injury. This is arguably the better view; while some distinction is required in order to prevent too wide-ranging liability, taking matters on a case-by-case basis allows control to be maintained but also allows flexibility where warranted.

The second reason in Lord Hoffman's opinion was firmly one of public policy. He felt allowing the claims would offend ordinary people in view of the fact that they would become better off than the relatives in **Alcock**. Lord Steyn called such a situation, whereby the relatives lose out while spectators giving peripheral assistance could recover, an 'unedifying spectacle'.[5] In countering this point, Lord Griffiths felt that the public would not find it offensive that people who had actually been involved in the aftermath and, significantly, suffered a disabling psychiatric illness could receive compensation. The important difference was the suffering of such illness as opposed to mere grief and bereavement. In view of the factual context of the decision, it is hard to argue with the concerns of the majority.[6] However, approaching the matter ignorant of the **Alcock** decision and looking at simply the principle to be determined, and the direct facts, it seems hard to disagree with the counter opinion of Lord Griffiths that a case-by-case look at the facts could adequately deal with the matter.

Lord Goff would also have dismissed the appeals; however, his reasoning was different and more forceful.[7] He noted first that Mr. Chadwick did not actually rescue anyone but simply brought aid and comfort. Additionally, he noted that in **Chadwick** there had been some physical danger but this was treated as irrelevant as it was the whole horror of the event which caused his injuries. Each of these factors was important; the first meant that we should not be restricted as to what is meant by a rescuer. The second factor showed that there was no reason to single out for compensation only those who had done rescue acts where those acts were only incidental to the wider incident which, as a whole, caused the psychiatric injury. Lord Goff suggested that insisting that a rescuer be objectively exposed to the risk of physical injury was, in fact, contrary to authority. This meant that the majority were wrong viewing the question as to whether the law should be extended, rather than whether the law should be restricted.[8] In his view, the majority were imposing an undesirable artificial barrier against recovery for foreseeable psychiatric injury. Furthermore, Lord Goff felt that the majority's concern in relation to public offence at certain claimants being seen to be better off which underpinned their opinions were misconceived. The role of tort is to compensate, at the expense of those whom the law deems responsible, those that

[5] If you include some of Lord Steyn's opinion in your answer, although essentially the same, it demonstrates your knowledge of the whole case and supports your argument.

[6] As the majority were so clearly swayed by the factual background to the case and the decision in *Alcock*, it is important to have raised this beforehand. By doing so you give yourself a platform from which to fully evaluate the reasoning given in the case.

[7] Therefore, your answer will benefit from Lord Goff's reasoning being looked at separately from Lord Griffiths'.

[8] It is quite central to explaining Lord Goff's opinion that you highlight the different way that he saw the question to be asked in the case. Therefore, you need to state what the question was in his view in order to fully demonstrate your understanding of his reasoning.

[9] As Lord Goff was basing his opinion firmly on tort principles, you need to provide some explanation as to the underlying principle and function of tort law. This will strengthen your discussion of Lord Goff's opinion and show the depth of your understanding of tort law generally.

have been injured.[9] Some claimants will always be more able to prove the defendants' responsibility than others. This did not warrant restricting their claims; all that should be done is that each claim is measured against the same legal principles. The control mechanism proposed by the majority would equally deny a relative who had attempted a rescue, while the existing mechanisms would defeat a claim by the policemen where they had no more than witnessed the event. It is hard to argue with this reasoning, particularly as it is firmly grounded in principle.

To conclude, it is now settled that a rescuer who is at no risk of physical injury must satisfy the **Alcock** control mechanism to be successful. In reaching this position it could be said that the majority in **White** were unduly influenced in attempting to give solace to the relatives in **Alcock**. From an emotional perspective, the decision is understandable. However, in terms of legal principle, the current position is hard to justify, a point in fact conceded by the majority, and the view of the minority in relation to rescuers is preferable.

✓ Make your answer stand out

- Tailor your answer to suit your view. Therefore, if you actually disagree with the minority in *White*, end your answer with the views of the majority and why they are more justified. This will ensure that your answer finishes strongly.

- Although the question is specifically on psychiatric injury, contrast the position of a rescuer in a claim for psychiatric injury with that of a rescuer suffering physical injury.

! Don't be tempted to ...

- Dwell too long on setting out the factual backdrop to the case and provide too much detail. This is needed simply to illustrate why the majority reached the decision that they did and no more.

- Ignore the opinions of the dissenting Law Lords on the basis that their view is not the law. The question asks you whether the current position is justified and, therefore, in order to do this adequately, you have to evaluate the opposing views provided from the case.

- In particular, do not simply focus on Lord Griffiths from the minority just because the question quotes his opinion. Lord Goff gave a longer opinion based on different reasoning which should be referred to.

Economic loss

5

How this topic may come up in exams

Economic loss is a specialist/restricted situation as to when a duty of care in negligence may be owed. It can come up as an independent question from general negligence or within the sole negligence question. Therefore, consult your course guide to see how you have been taught it. It is equally liable to appear as an essay on the policy of the area or as a problem question consisting of both forms of economic loss (i.e. resulting from negligent misstatements or negligent acts) or focusing on one type. As such you will need to learn the whole area, as well as briefly aspects of breach/causation/remoteness and defences.

◼ Attack the question

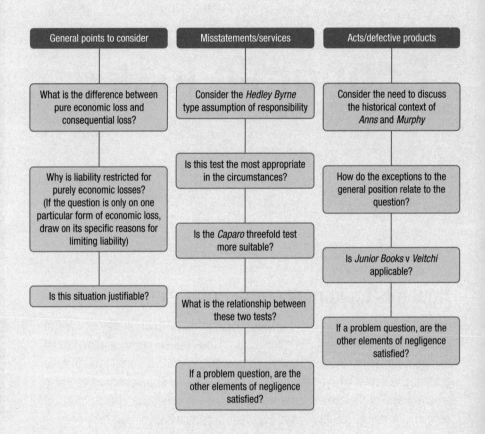

General points to consider	Misstatements/services	Acts/defective products
What is the difference between pure economic loss and consequential loss?	Consider the *Hedley Byrne* type assumption of responsibility	Consider the need to discuss the historical context of *Anns* and *Murphy*
Why is liability restricted for purely economic losses? (If the question is only on one particular form of economic loss, draw on its specific reasons for limiting liability)	Is this test the most appropriate in the circumstances?	How do the exceptions to the general position relate to the question?
Is this situation justifiable?	Is the *Caparo* threefold test more suitable?	Is *Junior Books* v *Veitchi* applicable?
	What is the relationship between these two tests?	If a problem question, are the other elements of negligence satisfied?
	If a problem question, are the other elements of negligence satisfied?	

A printable version of this diagram is available from www.pearsoned.co.uk/lawexpressqa

Question 1

'I do not think that voluntary assumption of responsibility is a helpful or realistic test for liability.' *Per* Lord Griffiths in *Smith* v *Eric S. Bush* [1990] 1 A.C. 831 at 862

Evaluate the merits of the assumption of responsibility test for establishing a duty of care in cases of economic loss.

Answer plan

→ Explain what the test is, exploring how it works and how it has developed.

→ Explore the criticisms levelled at the test.

→ Outline the requirements of the test from *Caparo* v *Dickman* [1990] 2 A.C. 605.

→ Assess whether *Caparo* is a better test, considering any problems that it has.

→ Drawing on *Customs & Excise Commissioners* v *Barclays Bank plc* [2007] 1 A.C. 181, evaluate whether the tests can actually work together to overcome any perceived limitations.

Diagram plan

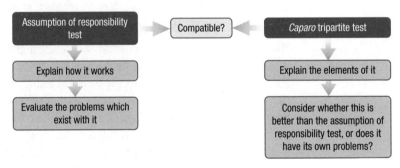

A printable version of this diagram is available from www.pearsoned.co.uk/lawexpressqa

Answer

The assumption of responsibility test deriving from **Hedley Byrne *v* Heller** [1964] A.C. 465 determines whether a claimant has an action for pure economic losses resulting from negligent misstatements. The issue here is whether the test should be used or whether there is a more appropriate alternative, namely the **Caparo** test. It is argued that both have merit and work well together in order to find a duty.

The basis of the test is that the statement maker assumes responsibility towards the claimant, who then reasonably relies on the statement which leads to their loss. This is regardless of the absence of a contractual or fiduciary relationship between the parties. The circumstances are said to be equivalent to a contractual situation, merely lacking consideration.[1] As such, the relationship which exists between the parties is said to be 'special', creating a closeness which is the extra element required to overcome the policy objections to such actions and justify a duty being imposed.[2] In **Hedley Byrne** itself the imposition of a duty was easy to justify. The claimants had directly asked (albeit through their own bank) for the credit reference from the defendants. While there was no contract for its provision, it was reasonable for the defendants to have anticipated reliance on the reference as it was clear why the reference had been requested and, thus, by supplying it they had assumed responsibility towards the claimant in light of this reasonable reliance.[3] The directness of the request supports the proposition that responsibility had been assumed and highlights the merit of the test's application. The concept fits the situation, while avoiding the prospect for indeterminate liability arising from a careless spoken word.[4]

The test has been developed to cover the negligent provision of services (**Spring v Guardian Assurance plc** [1995] 2 A.C. 296). Lord Goff felt that the correct basis of the test is that the claimant entrusts the defendant with the conduct of his affairs. In **Spring** the issue was over the provision of a reference for a job which was negligently provided. The extension has merit as there is still a direct relationship between both parties; however, doubts arise from its continued development. In **Henderson v Merrett Syndicates** [1995] 2 A.C. 145 the reliance was more indirect; A had contracted with B to perform a service for the benefit of C in the knowledge that it was for C's benefit. The reliance, therefore, was less direct than in **Hedley Byrne**. However, the test's application had merit because A's knowledge that C was benefiting from the service attached a closeness which justified the idea that A had assumed responsibility towards C. Lord Goff argued that any criticisms of the test arose in order to prevent the scope of liability extending to an indeterminate class. In **Henderson** this was not an

[1] You need to offer a little explanation here as to why it occurs outside of these situations to fully explain the point.

[2] By including this line by way of explanation, you indicate that you are aware that there are policy reasons behind the law and that it is only because of special circumstances that the law recognises a duty, without having to necessarily get into too much depth as to why. Remember the thrust of the question is on the merits of the particular test and not the merits of imposing a duty generally.

[3] Adding any further facts from the case is not really going to add anything to your answer. What effectively you need to demonstrate through the facts is how the test operates and why this is justified.

[4] By rounding off the paragraph with this line you further acknowledge the key policy concern which Lord Devlin discussed in *Hedley Byrne*.

issue as the knowledge and reliance created an identifiable class which was not indeterminate.

Therefore, the merit of the test is prevalent where you have directness between the parties or at least sufficient knowledge that the statement/ service is being relied on by an identifiable class. Questions over the test's merit arise when the test is not used in these situations. It is hard to explain, when there is a contract between A and B which C does not know about, how A has assumed responsibility for C and C has relied on it. This is seen in **White v Jones** [1995] 2 A.C. 207 where the negligent failure to redraft a will meant that the intended beneficiaries, the claimants, received nothing. Dissenting, Lord Mustill argued that for an assumption of responsibility to exist there must be mutuality between the parties which involves both playing an active role in the transaction, leading to the claim for liability. Such a requirement could be said to actually be present in all of the cases since **Hedley Byrne**, even **Henderson** where, as it were, C had in fact engaged B to contract with A. However, this was lacking in **White**. Lord Browne-Wilkinson suggested that assumption of responsibility referred to the task to be performed, not the legal obligation. The defendant had involved himself in the claimant's affairs and so the case was aligned with previous ones justifying a duty. This is questioned by Murphy (1996) who argues that to create a special relationship the responsibility assumed must be to the actual claimant. This is in line with Lord Griffiths' view in **Smith** who opined that the assumption of responsibility only has any real meaning if it refers to when the law deems the maker of a statement to have assumed responsibility towards the person who acted upon the advice. This questions the test's merits in situations such as **Smith** and **White**, because in Lord Griffiths' view the maker of the statement, if asked, would not consider himself to be assuming legal responsibility for anyone bar the person he contracted with. Lord Griffiths preferred to apply what became known as the **Caparo** test. This requires the claimant and the injury suffered to be foreseeable, proximity between the parties and it being fair, just and reasonable to impose a duty.[5]

However, while the **Caparo** test may have more merit in certain situations, it has been judicially acknowledged that it does not always provide the answer, with Lord Walker stating in **Customs & Excise Commissioners v Barclays Bank** that it merely provides 'a set of fairly blunt tools',[6] and the other judges expressing similar sentiments. Indeed, even in **Caparo** both Lords Bridge and Roskill[7]

[5]Clearly, you will need to outline what the test involves but the actual issue of the question does not make it essential to break down these in depth. You could perhaps do this to make your answer stand out more.

[6]By highlighting a specific quote here you add substance to the general assertion that you are making.

[7]Whereas Lord Bridge's opinion is the most well known from the case, by including reference to Lord Roskill you show a wider and deeper level of knowledge of the case; and secondly strengthen the assertion that you are making about the limits of the test by showing it was more of a widely held view.

[8]Although you have just highlighted some problems with the *Caparo* test, remember the point of the question and see if this test has any merit which might make it better than the assumption of responsibility test.

[9]This allows you to conclude your answer by pulling the arguments for and against each test together. Your aim should be to consider the extent that the two tests can work together in a sensible and coherent manner. If you feel they cannot, you should advance this and suggest what you feel needs to be done to improve the state of the law. If you feel they can, you need to show how this is so.

highlighted how the elements of the threefold test lacked sufficient precision to have utility as a practical test and were, at most, labels describing situations where a duty has been held to exist. However, this vagueness does have some merit in that it allows judges scope to look at the entire circumstances in light of any prevailing policy and determine the matter.[8]

In conclusion, this leaves two tests which can be used and questions as to which should be used and when.[9] The test has merit as a mechanism for establishing the sufficient proximity between the parties which makes it in turn just to impose a duty and, as such, it is simply a means of satisfying the **Caparo** requirements. As Lord Bingham noted in **Customs and Excise Commissioners**, cases are unlikely to have been decided differently if the **Caparo** test had been used. Effectively, both tests are compatible and of equal merit and effectiveness, although each has a more appropriate realm of application. Therefore, Lord Bingham's approach of looking at the whole circumstances in light of policy considerations and then using the assumption of responsibility test as a start before applying **Caparo**, if needed, is the correct and appropriate approach to take.

✓ Make your answer stand out

- Read J. Murphy (1996) 'Expectation losses, negligent omissions and the tortious duty of care', C.L.J. 55 (1): 43–55; and S. Hedley (1995) 'Negligence – pure economic loss – goodbye privity, hello contorts', C.L.J. 54 (1): 27–30 in order to gain some substance for your argument.
- Explain briefly what the policy reasons are which make the law seek to limit when a duty arises for these types of losses.
- Highlight specific strengths and weakness with the individual elements of the *Caparo* test.

! Don't be tempted to ...

- Labour the facts of the case. You need enough to show how the application of the test did, or did not, have merit to that particular situation but that is all.
- To stray into examining in depth the merits of recoverability for economic losses; remember the question is about the specific test used to find a duty.

? Question 2

Henry, a financial adviser, undertakes work for Clown's Bank plc, although he also does independent work for himself. When he is doing work for Clown's Bank he is provided with an office and administrative staff; the bank also has control over the range of financial products he may offer and provide him with basic wage plus bonuses. However, he does have the opportunity to make extra profits from any non-investment products that he sells to the customer and he can determine the level of risk to expose the customer to.

One night in the Ducker and Diver Arms public house, somewhere Henry is known to work out of when he is working late, Henry is approached by Gideon, whom he met through his work with the bank. Gideon explains that he has inherited £1 million and requires investment advice. Henry explains that he has had six pints of strong Belgian lager and so is not really in the right frame of mind and tells Gideon to come to the bank tomorrow. As Henry leaves he shouts back: 'Royal Bank of Wales – that's a company on the up; we'll discuss them tomorrow.'

Thinking that this was Henry's investment advice, and as he has always acted on his advice and never lost out, he decides to save time and rather than see Henry went online and invest the whole sum in Royal Bank of Wales. Two weeks later the Royal Bank of Wales received an urgent government bailout and their shares became worthless, with Gideon losing his investment.

Gideon now seeks to sue Clown's Bank for his economic loss, owing to what he feels was a negligent misstatement by Henry. Advise the bank.

Answer plan

→ Determine whether Henry is an employee acting in the course of his employment for vicarious liability purposes.

→ Evaluate whether there is an assumption of responsibility towards Gideon by Henry by making the statement that he did.

→ Consider the social environment in which the statement is made.

→ Discuss whether, in the event there is no assumption of responsibility, a duty towards Gideon may be found under the *Caparo* tripartite test.

Diagram plan

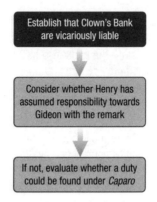

A printable version of this diagram is available from www.pearsoned.co.uk/lawexpressqa

Answer

[1] Your point here is to show that you appreciate the practical consequences for the bank of finding a duty in this situation as they are, effectively, your client. The other task is to give an indication of knowing the context within which the law operates, i.e. one limited on policy grounds, which you can then develop in your main body.

The issue to be determined is whether Clown's Bank vicariously owed a duty of care towards Gideon in relation to his economic losses. Such a finding would be financially significant and, despite the law's reluctance to find such duties on policy grounds, there are instances where one will be found.[1] However, it is argued that while it is possible that they have responsibility for Henry the situation is not such as to overcome the law's policy concerns and warrant finding a duty.

Firstly, it needs to be established whether the bank are in fact responsible for Henry's acts if a duty of care is found. The bank should be advised that they will be vicariously liable if it can be shown that Henry is an employee and was acting in the course of that employment when he made the statement. Henry's employment status is blurred by the fact that he does work independently of the bank as well as acting for them. Historically, whether a person was an employee was determined by reference to the level of control that he was under.[2] However, this did not fully reflect emerging employment relationships, so an economic reality test was developed. This requires looking at the overall situation for evidence of a contract of service – **Market Investigations Ltd v Minister of Social Security** [1969] 2 Q.B. 173. This case proposed a non-exhaustive

[2] You want to briefly show that you know what the test was historically, especially as this is still a consideration, but you should then go on to show how you are aware that this is no longer deemed completely suitable.

list of factors to consider, with control just being one. Others were whether the person provided his own equipment and hired his own staff and their degree of responsibility. Applying the factors to Henry, they suggest that he is likely to be classed as an employee. While Henry has some individual responsibility, he is provided with an office and administrative staff by the bank who also dictate what he can offer clients; significantly they pay his wages and bonuses. Therefore, overall, this suggests that there is a contract of service.

Henry, though, must have been in the course of his employment when he made the statement. However, it occurred in the evening, in a pub, after Henry had been drinking. The test to apply is the close-connection test from **Lister v Hesley Hall** [2002] 1 A.C. 215. This requires the tort to so be closely connected with the employment that it is fair and just to hold the bank vicariously liable. Henry met Gideon through his employment with the bank and the tort is allegedly[3] in making a negligent misstatement to a client regarding a financial investment which is what he is employed to give; the fact that Gideon was told to visit the bank also suggests that the advice was given in his role as an employee. All of this, together with the fact that Henry is known to work late and uses the pub for work suggests that Henry could have been in the course of his employment.

On the basis that the bank could be deemed vicariously liable for Henry's statement, it is important to advise the bank now as to whether a duty of care was owed to Gideon.[4] Generally, there is reluctance to find duties for economic losses. Partly this is because, as Lord Reid observed in **Hedley Byrne v Heller** [1964] A.C. 465, people will often express definite opinions in informal settings, even though recognising that people may be influenced by them; but they do so without the same level of care as if it was a professional setting. As words can spread far and be relied upon by people of whom the maker has no knowledge, it can lead to indeterminate liability to an indeterminate class. Therefore, it held a duty could, in principle, exist but more was needed than for normal negligent injuries. There would need to be an assumption of responsibility by Henry towards Gideon, and then reasonable reliance by Gideon on the statement.

A duty can occur outside of contractual and fiduciary relationships (**Hedley Byrne**) as the assumption with the reliance is deemed to create a special relationship which overcomes the law's reservations.

[3]Remember you have not yet established that there is negligence at this stage.

[4]Even if you conclude that the bank would not be vicariously liable, you need to remember that the main issue of the question is whether a duty of care is owed for economic loss. Therefore, you would still need to go into this but use an opening phrase such as 'On the basis that the bank were...'

The bank should be advised, though, that Lord Reid in **Hedley Byrne** suggested that a special relationship could only arise in a business situation owing to the reasons stated above. Therefore, while the social nature of the incident may still warrant being classed as in the course of his employment it may negate the imposition of a duty of care. The Court of Appeal has, though, found a duty in a situation of non-business advice between friends – **Chaudhry v Prabhakar** [1988] 3 All E.R. 718. In any event the existence of an assumption of responsibility is judged objectively (**Henderson v Merrett Syndicates** [1995] 2 A.C. 145), but a divergence of opinion exists as to whether it refers to the task or actual legal responsibility.[5] In **White v Jones** [1995] 2 A.C. 207 Lord Browne-Wilkinson felt it referred to the task. If this is the case, by making the statement Henry could be said to have assumed responsibility. However, this is questioned academically by Murphy who argues it must refer to assuming legal responsibility to the claimant. On this basis Henry arguably fails this requirement. He has indicated that Gideon should visit him tomorrow in the bank to discuss the investment and also indicates that he has been drinking. These facts could actually also be used to counter any suggestion of even satisfying Lord Browne-Wilkinson's interpretation, as he has not technically given advice.

Gideon obviously relies on the statement, which means that if a duty was found, causation would also be satisfied;[6] however, reliance must be reasonable. The informal context – with Henry leaving a pub, indicating that he has drunk a lot of strong lager;[7] while additionally, only saying they will discuss the investment tomorrow – means it can be strongly argued, especially in light of the sums involved,[8] that Gideon's reliance was in fact wholly unreasonable.

Therefore, while it would seem that the requirements for a duty have not been satisfied, it has been held in **Customs & Excise Commissioners v Barclays Bank plc** [2007] 1 A.C. 181 that the absence of an assumption of responsibility does not prevent resort to finding a duty on the basis of the alternative threefold test. However, while foreseeability is present here and proximity is also arguably satisfied owing to their past relationship, the reasons why Gideon's reliance is not reasonable are also likely to mean that it is not fair, just and reasonable in these circumstances to find a duty towards Gideon.

In conclusion,[9] it appears that on either basis of establishing a duty for economic loss, Gideon is unlikely to be successful and, therefore, the bank will not be liable for Henry's advice.

[5]Reference to this debate in this part of your advice allows your answer to develop into an academic discussion of the law and shows your awareness of differing academic and judicial opinion as to what this element of the test means.

[6]Insert a reference to causation to show that you are also advising in the wider context of negligence as if the bank is to be liable, which is what the question asks you to advise them on, a factor which would need to be satisfied.

[7]Although you have said this a lot, you want to keep driving home the facts which support the view you are expressing. As long as the context is there, this is fine.

[8]In this part of your answer it is all about the application of the facts, so you do not need to write that much here and do not need any great reference to case law.

[9]Although the preceding paragraph may read like a conclusion and the end of your answer, you should just draw both strands of potential liability together and conclude by reiterating that both tests are likely to fail.

✓ Make your answer stand out

- Relate your discussion of the impact of the statement being apparently made in a social context to the issue of whether Gideon is in fact in the course of his employment.
- Include a fuller discussion on whether the other elements of negligence are present to round off your advice to the bank if the bank was deemed to owe a duty.

! Don't be tempted to …

- Spend too long on the vicarious liability element. Show that you have spotted that there is a potential issue there and that you have an understanding of how the law works, but remember that the main thrust of the question is on economic loss. Although at the same time, make sure you do cover all aspects of it.
- Go off on a long tangent with your discussion of what the phrase 'assumption of responsibility' should mean; remember the question is ultimately about advising the bank of their liability and requires application of the law to the facts.

❓ Question 3

Cogmire Builders Ltd contracted to renovate a sports complex for Quay Borough Council who had bought the existing premises after it had closed down. Under the terms of the contract the shell of the building is to be built by Cogmire Builders Ltd, but certain specialist electrical work was carried out by Peter & Sons Ltd. All building operations were solely supervised by a firm of consulting architects, Cleveland Consultants, who were employed by Cogmire Builders Ltd at the request of the Council as they had previously overseen other Council projects and were specialists in this type of work.

On the day the complex was due to open, a fire broke out which was caused by the negligent electrical work of Peter & Sons Ltd, and the complex remained closed for a further two months.

Several months after the complex finally opened, cracks appeared in the floor of the gym. Investigations showed that the floor was not laid properly and could not take the weight of the machines. The sports complex was closed for several weeks while the gym floor was re-laid and reinforced.

Cogmire Builders Ltd has now gone out of business; advise Quay Borough Council as to what action, if any, they may take in common law negligence.

Answer plan

→ State the law's position on economic losses arising from negligent acts of construction and advise the Council why this is the case.

→ Then take each defect separately.

→ Explain the 'complex structure theory' and whether this may provide the Council with an exception to the general position.

→ Discuss the applicability of *Junior Books* v *Veitchi* [1983] 1 A.C. 520 in relation to the cracked floor as an option for claiming the losses from that defect.

→ In doing so, explore the ex-post rationalisation of *Junior Books* as an application of *Hedley Byrne* principle and assess whether this helps.

Diagram plan

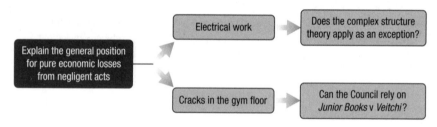

A printable version of this diagram is available from www.pearsoned.co.uk/lawexpressqa

Answer

The issue here is whether the Council has any redress for the economic losses which they have incurred through the negligent construction of the new complex. This area of negligence is one which is tightly restricted on policy grounds, meaning there is little scope for a duty of care to be established. However, there are some limited exceptions and the Council will be advised to two which may be applicable to their case: namely, the 'complex structure theory' for the electrics and the case of **Junior Books** in relation to the gym floor.[1]

[1]As the law is quite firm in its reluctance to recognise a duty in such a situation as this, it is perhaps even more beneficial to highlight early on how you are going to go about arguing your case so the marker knows.

The Council should be advised that the general position is that where someone negligently performs an act, they will not be liable for any losses which result that are of a purely economic nature;

however, economic losses which are consequential to property damage or physical injury can be if a duty was owed and its breach caused such damage or injury. While it may seem that the fire damage and the floor cracks are property damage, they should be advised that the courts see situations such as this as simply a case of purchasing something which is of less quality and, thus value, than what was expected. Therefore, the actual loss is the financial cost of bringing the premises up to the standard that was expected (**Murphy v Brentwood D.C.** [1991] 1 A.C. 398).[2] The rationale for this position[3] was explored in **Spartan Steel & Alloys Ltd v Martin & Co. (Contractors) Ltd** [1973] 1 Q.B. 27 and includes the prospect of indeterminate liability for the defendant, the fact that the nature of the risk being such that precautions could be taken e.g. insurance and the need to avoid undermining contract law. Allowing a tortious claim for a defective product would create a transferable non-contractual warranty. It would also duplicate contract law which provides remedies where a product is not of satisfactory quality or fit for purpose.

In relation to the fire damage, if the Council directly contracted with Peter & Sons, a claim under the contract would arise. If not, the Council may still have an exception to the general position under the 'complex structure theory' which would allow a claim against the electricians. The theory suggests that the different elements of a building can be viewed as distinct items of property and thus if one part damages another part, there would be sufficient appropriate property damage on which to base a claim for economic loss. In the Council's case this would mean that the electrical work is distinguished from the rest of the complex which it damaged through its negligent installation.[4] However, the theory, first mooted in **D & F Estates v Church Commissioners for England** [1989] A.C. 177 as a basis for explaining **Anns v Merton L.B.C.** [1978] A.C. 728, is not an adopted legal principle. The theory received a closer evaluation in **Murphy**, and notwithstanding academic criticism it received some judicial support for its application in limited circumstances. Lords Keith, Jauncey and Bridge[5] stated that the complex part in question would need to have been installed by a sub-contractor. Here, the Council should be advised that if the electricians were sub-contracted by Cogmire Builders they would appear to have a claim. This is supported by the fact that all three gave as an example

[2] It is important early on in your advice to the Council to explain not only what the legal position is, but it also demonstrates that you understand why their situation falls within that position. This sentence shows the marker that you have fully understood the context of the question and grasped the basic principles.

[3] By then going into the rationale for this position and explaining it to the Council, you will reinforce the impression that you fully understand the framework for this area and early on in your answer have obtained a good foundation of marks before you have really got into the question.

[4] After explaining the outline of the theory, illustrate how it transfers to the facts to show the marker what you are thinking before you go on to discuss the merits of the theory in full.

[5] By including all three you show that, while not part of the ratio of the case, it did have majority support.

[6]As the facts indicate that this is a given, there is no need to go into depth as to what is required in these aspects of negligence, but for completeness you should use the facts as stated in the question to support the proposition that a negligence claim can be supported.

[7]Although there is nothing to suggest this is the case on the facts, you should consider it, as, just because one is not expressly mentioned, it could well be the case and so your advice would be incomplete without assessing the implications of one being present.

[8]This is obviously a practical point but important in the context of giving advice as to what action may be taken. Demonstrate that you have picked up on the fact and understand the implication.

of when the theory could apply – negligently fitted electrical wiring which caused a fire.

If a duty is held to exist, as we are told the electrical work by Peter & Sons was negligently fitted and this caused the fire to break out,[6] it appears that the Council would have a claim against them in negligence for the economic losses suffered. The only possible defence they may have is an exclusion clause;[7] however, in view of the danger to life this is likely to be unreasonable under UCTA 1977.

In relation to the gym floor, as Cogmire Builders have gone out of business any potential claim, in contract or tort, would be futile.[8] This leaves only the consultants as possible defendants. This is complicated by the absence of a contract between them and the Council: they were contracted by the builders. As above, the loss is purely economic but the Council may have recourse to the case of **Junior Books** in any claim.

In that case a specialist sub-contractor, specifically chosen by the claimant to be employed by the main contractor was successfully sued when their work, defective flooring, turned out to have been negligently performed. There is a slight factual similarity, therefore, between both instances. This is important as **Junior Books** has been subsequently heavily criticised and seems now confined to its own facts (**Muirhead v Industrial Tank Specialities** [1986] Q.B. 507). In the case, Lord Roskill outlined several factors which created a sufficient degree of proximity between the parties. These included being nominated and specialists in the role they were contracted for. Further, the sub-contractors were solely responsible for the contracted task and knew exactly what was required. As such they knew that their skill and experience were being relied upon by the claimants. While slightly different, the Council should be advised that there is some correlation here. The consultants were specialists in overseeing this sort of work and hand-picked by the Council for their skill and experience. As such, they were solely responsible for overseeing the construction and would have appreciated this and that their expertise was being relied upon by the Council.

The Council should be warned, though, that while the case has not been overruled, it has been criticised at every opportunity by the House of Lords and, therefore, basing a claim on this authority may not be the best course. As the case has been subsequently rationalised on the basis of the **Hedley Byrne** principle of assumption of responsibility, any claim should perhaps be framed on this basis. This requires the Council demonstrating that Cleveland Consultants, in performing their service, assumed responsibility towards the Council who reasonably relied upon their service. This appears supported on the factors mentioned above in relation to **Junior Books**; however, in **Henderson v Merrett Syndicates** [1995] 2 A.C. 145 this explanation of **Junior Books** was doubted. Therefore, any claim for the losses from the cracked floor may prove futile, no matter how it is framed, for the absence of a duty.

In conclusion, owing to the nature of the losses suffered by the Council, their chances of any actions being successful are remote. However, it may be possible to successfully sue the electricians in relation to the cost of restoring the complex following the fire, but the losses from repairing the gym floor will be harder to recoup.

✓ Make your answer stand out

- Advise the Council as to their position regarding any consequential economic losses and explore more why these are more justifiably recovered.
- Include some explanation as to the merits of the rationale for restricting recovery in this area – would it really undermine contract law?
- Include some comparative analysis with other jurisdictions which have not followed *Murphy*.
- Read J. O'Sullivan (2007) 'Suing in tort where no contract claim will lie: a bird's eye view', *Professional Negligence* 23 (3): 165–92; and S. Hedley (1995) 'Negligence – pure economic loss – goodbye privity, hello contorts', C.L.J. 54 (1): 27–30 for some academic opinion on this area of law and the cases which you will refer to in your answer.

! Don't be tempted to …

- Stray into examining in depth the merits of recoverability for economic losses; remember the question is about whether the Council can establish a duty owed to them by either party.
- Focus heavily on the history of recovery in this area and the merits of *Anns*, as it has been overruled and this is a problem question you need to focus on what the law is and how it might be applied.
- Miss out reference to the other aspects of negligence. They are needed briefly for completeness.

Product liability

How this topic may come up in exams

This topic is centred primarily on the Consumer Protection Act 1987; however, the Act did not abolish the common law negligence action. Therefore, you also need to be aware of the narrow rule in *Donoghue* v *Stevenson* and how this applies to manufacturers of defective products. The existence of both actions means that a comparative essay is likely, alongside issues of why the Act was needed. However, the differences between the two actions mean that both will have to be discussed in problem questions in order to assess which claim may be best.

■ Attack the question

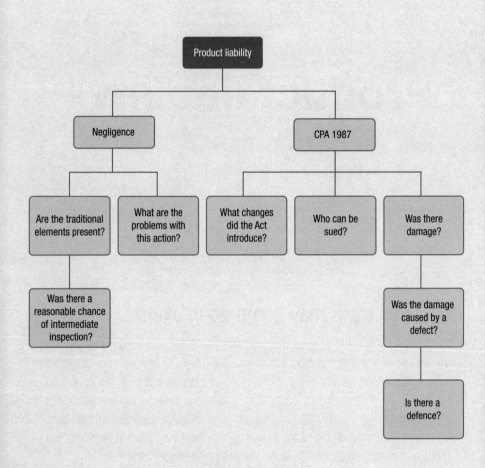

Question 1

'The Consumer Protection Act 1987 was simply an exercise in legislative indulgence to show activity on the part of Parliament. There was no need to burden manufacturers with additional regulation which offers no greater protection.'

Evaluate the validity of this statement.

Answer plan

→ Discuss how the common law provided consumer protection through negligence.

→ Highlight what difficulties consumers faced in negligence.

→ Outline the purpose of the Act.

→ Explain the requirements for liability, highlighting the difference it makes to the common law.

→ Consider if the Act was, therefore, worthwhile or whether it simply created different problems.

Diagram plan

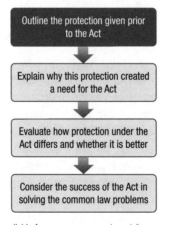

A printable version of this diagram is available from www.pearsoned.co.uk/lawexpressqa

Answer

The issue to assess is whether there was any real need for the Consumer Protection Act 1987 or whether the common law, through the tort of negligence, was satisfactory in offering protection for

[1]Not only is this factually and legally accurate, but by mentioning it here you demonstrate that you are aware of the Act's background and place in the wider scheme of the law. You will also have shown straight away that you have recognised how this relates to the premise within the question: namely, that regardless of the merits of the protection under the Act, it was required.

[2]The question is predominantly on the need for the Act, so briefly set out the basis of a claim in negligence but focus on what the problems were in bringing such a claim. This allows you to argue more whether the Act was actually needed.

[3]Use the limitations of the negligence action to further support why the Act was required and not just legislative indulgence.

defective products. If the Act was not needed and offers no different protection, then it can be said to be an unnecessary burden. It is argued though that the Act strengthens consumer protection and was also needed as part of a wider process of protecting consumers in the EU because of the development of the Internal Market.[1]

Only since **Donoghue v Stevenson** [1932] A.C. 562 have manufacturers been held to owe a duty of care in negligence to the ultimate consumer of their product, where the product is intended to reach the consumer in the condition it left the manufacturer, with no reasonable chance of inspection by an intermediary. Therefore, if this duty was breached by failing to take reasonable care and this breach caused the damage, which was of a foreseeable nature, then in the absence of a defence the manufacturer was liable.[2]

While significant, there are clear limitations to the decision.[3] Firstly, there must not have been a reasonable possibility for the product to have been inspected between manufacture and purchase by the consumer. This means that if a party in the supply or manufacturing chain could have inspected the product and found the defect, then the manufacturer avoids liability. This can be more detrimental depending on the product in question and creates something of a lottery for consumers as they may not know if the goods have been inspected.

The second limitation is that **Donoghue** concerned product manufacture and not design defects. Often the design creates the defect rather than the absence of reasonable care when making the product. Further, where the product has been designed defectively it means there is a greater potential for harm as all of the products are effected, not just a batch. The problem is intensified, owing to causation's importance in negligence. A claimant must show that the design defect is capable of causing the harm in question and then did cause that harm. This difficulty is clearly seen in relation to medicinal drugs and the Thalidomide cases. In negligence claimants do not benefit from hindsight (**Roe v Minister of Health** [1954] 2 Q.B. 66) and must show that at the time the product was put into circulation the manufacturer acted unreasonably.

Following the Thalidomide incidents, arguments were advanced that, rather than a fault-based system, a strict liability regime should be adopted for defective products. This would be consistent with ideas of loss distribution, deterrence and economic efficiency. The

[4]Use this opportunity to show off your deeper knowledge of tort and its underlying principles in order to support why a strict liability should have been introduced. By relating its implementation to tort principles, you strengthen the argument that it is worthwhile.

[5]Although you are now talking about the Act, make sure you show that you know how the two actions relate to each other, seeing as both still exist.

[6]Don't worry that you are somehow changing the question with a sentence such as this. The point is to tackle head-on as to why the Act was passed and refute the suggestion in the statement that it was simply Parliament trying to show it was doing something.

[7]By starting this part of your answer like this, it means that you are relating your discussion back to the statement and shows that you are now dealing with the underlying premise within the statement.

manufacturer is best placed to insure the risk and can then pass this cost on to consumers. To ensure their prices are kept low, greater care would be taken to ensure premiums do not rise.[4] These ideas also chime with the idea that, as the product was created for profit, it is fair to impose the risk on the manufacturer. In any event, the EU took the initiative by passing Directive 85/374/EEC. The Directive's purpose is to harmonise the level of protection offered by all member states by implementing a strict liability regime. It was this, regardless of any other need for reform, which brought about the Act. Therefore, it was clearly not just an exercise in indulgence by Parliament.

Notwithstanding the difficulties faced by consumers, actions in negligence have been retained though.[5] The Act's central aim is to impose liability without fault on the producer of a defective product (s.2(1)). A product is defined in s.1(2) as any 'goods or electricity' and includes a component of a larger product, such as the fan within a laptop, and so is quite wide. The position of the consumer is also aided under the Act by the fact that the product's producer also includes the person who imported the product into the EU, which makes bringing an action easier for consumers rather than them having to sue a manufacturer from overseas. Generally, however, suppliers remain non-liable for the defect unless the conditions of s.2(3) are satisfied. The question is whether the Act, while initiating the EU measures, has also resolved the difficulties faced by consumers and so was worthwhile.[6]

The Act can be justified as a required addition to consumer protection if it does indeed impose strict liability.[7] However, it is arguable from the Act's wording and the early cases that liability was not so strict. Defect is defined in s.3 as being where 'the safety of the product is not such as persons are generally entitled to expect'. Under s.3(2) all circumstances should be taken into account when determining the level of safety that the public can expect. These include the marketing of the product and whether any instructions or warnings regarding use were provided. Further consideration is to be given to how the product may reasonably be expected to be used and the time when the product was supplied. The issue is that, while the Act seeks strict liability, concerns have been raised that determining whether the product was defective allows considerations of fault and so negligence reappears by the back door. This was seen in **Worsley v Tambrands Ltd** [2000] P.I.Q.R. P95 where a warning placed on

[8]There are a number of cases that you could use here. It does not matter which you do use, so long as you include one which illustrates the point that the courts were interpreting 'defect' in a way which was akin to looking for fault. This forms the basis of whether, despite the Directive, the Act was worthwhile or just reiterating the common law position.

the product regarding a small risk of toxic shock syndrome meant that liability was avoided.[8] The courts will assess the sufficiency of the warning, which can be said to amount to whether the manufacturer has been at fault. This negates the Act's purpose and supports the suggestion that it has added nothing to consumer protection; establishing a lack of care would still be required. However, the use of fault-based reasoning was criticised by the Court of Appeal in **Abouzaid v Mothercare (UK) Ltd** [2000] All E.R. D 2436. It was deemed irrelevant whether the defect had come to Mothercare's attention. The lack of negligence did not prevent liability under the Act. The emphasis on strict liability was followed in **A v National Blood Authority** [2001] 3 All E.R. 289 where consideration of the care taken by the manufacturer was excluded; what should be assessed are all relevant circumstances, not all circumstances. This has been criticised as contrary to the wording of both the Act and the Directive. However, it is defendable for giving effect to the spirit of the legislation and providing it with a role distinct from negligence.[9]

[9]As it is implied in the question that the Act serves no purpose, make sure that you include an opinion on this issue.

In conclusion, Parliament ultimately had no choice but to pass the Act in order to comply with EU law. As the Act provides a different form of liability from negligence, especially as interpreted in **A**, the Act should be welcomed as an increase in consumer protection. It circumvents the hurdles which are faced in negligence actions and places the risk on the best placed person to carry that risk – the manufacturer.

 Make your answer stand out

- Discuss briefly the limited scope for liability prior to *Donoghue*.
- Read J. Stapleton (1994b) 'Product liability', *Law in Context*, Butterworths. This will allow you to incorporate material regarding the theoretical basis for strict liability in this area and why this approach was adopted in the EU in light of American experiences. You can then question the merits of strict liability.
- Refer to journal articles on *A*, as, if this case is wrong to adopt such a strict line in relation to 'defect', then we arguably do have a system which considers fault. You can then consider whether there is still enough distinction between the claims to warrant the existence of both actions. For example, look at C. Hodges (2001) 'Compensating patients: case comment on *A* v *National Blood Authority* [2001] 2 All E.R. 289', 117 L.Q.R. 528; and G. Howells and M. Mildred (2002) 'Infected blood: defect and discoverability a first exposition of the EC Product Liability Directive', 65 M.L.R. 95.

! **Don't be tempted to ...**

- Try and cover all of the provisions of the Act. Remember that the main aspect of the question is that there was no need for the Act to be passed. Therefore, you should weight your answer more in favour of the difficulties under the common law position.

- Set out in depth the requirements in negligence. Touch on what they are but, as above, focus on the problems they caused.

- Gloss over the influence of European law in this area. Ultimately that was the reason for the passing of the Act and, so, on a question regarding whether the Act was necessary, it is quite a fundamental point.

? Question 2

Kamui decided that it was time for him to purchase a new mobile phone and so visited his local branch of Handset Superstore, a leading mobile phone retailer. Kamui decided on the latest handset by Nokorola primarily because the salesman told him that it had the longest battery life while also having the shortest charge time, and so would save electricity. The phone cost Kamui £400. The handets are manufactured in Japan and imported into the country by Handset Superstore.

However, the handset had a design fault whereby overheating would occur if the phone was left on charge too long, over five hours. Nokorola knew of this but did not publish the information as the launch of the handset had already been delayed and as the handset could be fully charged within the five hours, which was advertised and so it was felt it would not be an issue.

One day, however, after a long day at work Kamui got home and put his phone on charge but fell asleep after doing so. This meant that the phone stayed on charge for over five hours and overheated which caused the table cloth the phone was on to catch fire. Although Kamui woke in time to get out safely, his house suffered severe fire damage.

Advise Kamui as to what action he may take in relation to the phone and the wider property damage he has suffered, and against whom.

Answer plan

→ Outline the remit and purpose of the Consumer Protection Act 1987.

→ Consider whether the property damage suffered is of a type recoverable under the Act.

→ State what role Handset Superstore and Nokorola will have in proceedings.

→ Evaluate the criteria for establishing liability and identify whether there was a defect with the phone.

→ Discuss whether any defences apply.

→ Consider Kamui's options for bringing a common law claim in negligence under the rule in *Donoghue* v *Stevenson* [1932] A.C. 562.

Diagram plan

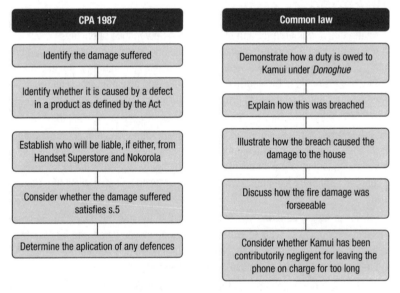

CPA 1987
Identify the damage suffered
Identify whether it is caused by a defect in a product as defined by the Act
Establish who will be liable, if either, from Handset Superstore and Nokorola
Consider whether the damage suffered satisfies s.5
Determine the aplication of any defences

Common law
Demonstrate how a duty is owed to Kamui under *Donoghue*
Explain how this was breached
Illustrate how the breach caused the damage to the house
Discuss how the fire damage was forseeable
Consider whether Kamui has been contributorily negligent for leaving the phone on charge for too long

A printable version of this diagram is available from www.pearsoned.co.uk/lawexpressqa

Answer

The issue to advise Kamui on is the extent that he can recover for the loss of his property which has resulted from the fire, and who he can recover these losses from. This will involve advising Kamui on the provisions of the Consumer Protection Act 1987 as well as the common law tort of negligence. It will be argued that, while compensation cannot be obtained for the damaged phone, the other damaged property will be recoverable under both actions.

Kamui should be advised that Parliament intervened in this area so as to give effect to the Consumer Protection Directive. This saw the passing of the Consumer Protection Act 1987 which aims to protect consumers from defective products and resolve some of the problems which had existed previously in common law claims for negligence.[1] It imposes strict liability on producers of products which cause damage owing wholly or partly to defects within the product (s.2(1)). It is clear that the phone will be a product under s.1(2).

The first issue is whether Kamui has suffered actionable damage under the Act in order to bring a claim. Under s.5(2) the loss of the actual phone is not recoverable as this is purely economic loss to the product itself. However, under s.5(1) damage is recoverable for any other property. This also includes land, which is significant as Kamui's house suffered severe damage so it is not just his personal property which can be claimed for. The amount of property that Kamui can claim for is restricted, though, by s.5(4). This provides that the property must be worth over £275 and so some of his damaged personal effects would not be recoverable.

The question is who is liable for the damage. Nokorola have manufactured the phone and so they would clearly be a producer for the purposes of s.1(2); however, as they may be based overseas it may be easier for Kamui to sue Handset Superstore as the supplier of the phone. This appears possible as s.2(2)(c) state that the liability within the section applies to those who import the product into the EU, which is what they have done. However, as the phone identifies who the actual producer of the product is, a requirement for imposing liability on a supplier such as Handset Superstore is missing. Therefore, any action will just be against Nokorola.

A defect in the phone in accordance with s.3(1) must then be established. The section makes clear that there will be a defect where the product 'is not such as persons are generally entitled to expect'. The section goes on to provide that this includes components within the product and safety in the context of risks of damage to property.

[1] You could legitimately deal with the common law negligence claim first. If this is the approach that you adopt, use a line such as this one to explain why the Act has come into being to offer a parallel form of protection.

[2]Explain why the courts take such an approach and comment on the justification for it, particularly as some authorities have tried to incorporate fault.

[3]In light of what you are writing at this point, reiterate what you see as the defect in the phone to substantiate the point.

[4]Although the defence will clearly not apply, it is worth raising it if only to dismiss it, to show that you are aware it can apply but understand the defence by explaining how it does not apply in this case. The key is to be brief in raising it: you are simply highlighting how it could apply in different circumstances.

[5]Include this to show that you are aware of the distinction between the two actions and to demonstrate why you are discussing this when it seems Kamui may succeed under the Act.

[6]By mentioning this at the start, it ties in with your previous sentence about why it may be worth bringing a claim in negligence while also showing that you know the limitations of such an action.

[7]By wording this in this way, you show that you are fully aware of the differing principles which come out of *Donoghue* and particularly that you understand its direct application to this issue.

Although guidance is given in s.3(2) as to what the public are entitled to expect, it is clear from cases such as **A v National Blood Authority** [2001] 2 All E.R. 289 that a strict line is taken against the producers and efforts are made to remove considerations of fault. This is in keeping with the purpose of imposing strict liability under the Act.[2] In any event, the nature of the defect here, overheating and fire risk,[3] particularly without any manufacturer warnings as to the time the phone should be left on charge means that the phone is certain to be found defective.

It is also apparent that none of the defences contained in s.4 are applicable to Nokorola and so the only possible defence they may have is contributory negligence which applies under s.6(4). If Kamui knew that he was not meant to leave the phone on charge for longer than was required, the defence may succeed and part of his damages would be reduced (Law Reform (Contributory Negligence) Act 1945). This cannot have been the case, though, as we told that all Nokorola have done is stated that the phone can be charged in under five hours, not that it must not be charged for more than five hours.[4]

Although Parliament sought to provide consumer protection, this is supplementary in nature and does not abolish actions in common law negligence. There is no value threshold in such actions and so it provides a useful vehicle to recover for any property which was damaged in the fire, which is under £275.[5] The loss of the phone itself, though, will still simply be regarded as purely economic and is not recoverable (**Murphy v Brentwood D.C.** [1991] 1 A.C. 398.[6]

Firstly, Kamui must show that he was owed a duty of care in relation to the product. This is easily shown as the actual *ratio* of **Donoghue**[7] is that the manufacturer owes a duty of care to the ultimate consumer of their product. This is directly applicable to the relationship between Kamui and Nokorola. Nokorola as the manufacturer owe a duty to take reasonable care in the manufacturing of their phones to ensure that end-users will be safe.

The question is whether this was breached; did Nokorola take reasonable care manufacturing the phone? Even if the part which overheated was sourced from someone else, they must exercise reasonable care purchasing that part and checking it is suitable (**Winward v T.V.R. Engineering** [1986] B.T.L.C. 366). Although

[8]On the facts, there is no real issue of the aspects of causation and remoteness, and there is no real defence available. Therefore, sum these up in the one paragraph, although, if you are faced with a question which does need more details discussion of any of these points, then use a separate paragraph.

Kamui should be advised that the principle of *res ipsa loquitur* does not apply (**Donoghue**), the courts have been willing to infer a lack of reasonable care from the presence of a defect (**Grant v Australian Knitting Mills Ltd** [1936] A.C. 85). The fact that Nokorola knew of the fault and circulated the handset indicates a lack of care.

Causation[8] is also clearly established here, as 'but for' the fault the phone would not have overheated and the fire would not have started. This is especially the case considering that the phone would have not gone through any other inspection process between manufacture and purchase by Kamui which could be said to have interfered with the product. It would also seem obvious that fire damage was damage of a foreseeable type which would occur from the fault. As with damages under the Act, any claim of contributory negligence is unlikely to succeed.

Therefore, in conclusion, Kamui is likely to have a claim under the Act for the damage to his home caused by the fire and any other property of his that was damaged which is over £275 in value. Alternatively, he could claim in negligence and this may be advisable as an additional claim for obtaining property which is under the threshold value of the Act. However, under each action the loss of the phone itself will not be recoverable owing to it being pure economic loss.

✓ Make your answer stand out

- Explain the rationale and merit for imposing strict liability on producers of defective products.
- Consider the distinction made between manufacturing defects and design defects and discuss the different approach to each by the courts, explaining what sort the phone is.
- Explore the problems which exist with each action and make a deeper comparison of the merits of Kamui bringing an action under each.
- Read C. Hodges (2001) 'Compensating patients: case comment on *A* v *National Blood Authority* [2001] 2 All E.R. 289', 117 L.Q.R. 528 in order to obtain some academic criticism of the judicial interpretation taken to the meaning of 'defect' under s.3.
- Discuss the difference between standard product defects and non-standard product defects.

! Don't be tempted to ...

- Spend more time on the negligence action at the expense of the provisions of the Act. Remember that this is ultimately a question on product liability and you are likely to have a question elsewhere dedicated to common law negligence. If you treat the product liability problem question as an opportunity to repeat your answer from that other negligence question, you risk losing out on marks for not fully appreciating the scope of this question. You will also fail to show the full range of your knowledge.

- Try and show that you have more knowledge than you need by reciting parts of the Act which are not relevant, such as the range of defences within s.4. If you cover these in depth it will instead show that you have read the question properly and do not fully understand those provisions.

- Get tied up in the requirements of causation and remoteness unless the facts indicate that they warrant particular discussion. You must mention them, but the weight of discussion should reflect the extent that they are an issue on the facts of the question.

 # Question 3

Piper and Galbraith plc is a pharmaceutical company and has recently produced a new drug, Fiagera, which is marketed as preventing anxiety attacks. The drug was subjected to trials in the UK in line with industry standards and approved by the national regulator. Approval, though, was subject to the drug's packaging highlighting that it should not be used by people suffering epilepsy. However, research in Canada indicated that an ingredient of the drug could cause kidney damage if it was taken for a sustained period. This was published in the *Journal of Canadian Medicine*, which is also available globally.

Manisha had regularly suffered anxiety attacks during her first two years at university. As a result, she visited Dr. Legg who, having never seen Manisha before, prescribed her Fiagera without knowing that she suffered epilepsy. After talking the drug for four weeks, Manisha went into an epileptic shock. However, while also in hospital it was also discovered that Manisha had suffered damage to her kidneys.

Advise Manisha on whether she could succeed in a claim against Piper and Galbraith for her injuries.

Answer plan

→ Start with whether Manisha could claim successfully in negligence for her injuries.

→ Discuss the implications of the drug being prescribed by Dr. Legg and whether this was a reasonable chance to inspect the product.

→ Advise Manisha as to how she could alternatively claim under the Consumer Protection Act 1987.

→ Deal with the epilepsy injury first and consider whether the drug was defective in this regard.

→ Discuss separately the kidney damage and whether the drug is defective in relation to that injury.

→ Consider the possible defence under s.4(1)(e) and the issue of the state of scientific knowledge at the time of the drug's circulation.

Diagram plan

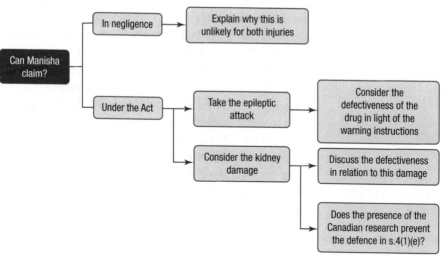

A printable version of this diagram is available from www.pearsoned.co.uk/lawexpressqa

Answer

The issue to advise Manisha is whether she can successfully sue Piper and Galbraith (P&G) for the epileptic attack and the kidney damage following her taking of Fiagera. There are two options

[1]Owing to the facts of the question and the difficulties of bringing such a claim, deal with common law negligence first. This will allow you to end your answer more strongly by discussing the claim which is more likely to succeed. Your answer will read a bit strange if you write about the Act first and the argument that Manisha may succeed and then proceed to talk about an alternative claim which is likely to fail.

[2]While you have not been asked to advise Manisha regarding Dr. Legg, by highlighting this you demonstrate your wider knowledge and understanding of negligence, so it is beneficial but do keep it brief.

[3]Use a sentence such as this explaining why the Act has come about to link the two sections of your answer. You will show that you are aware of the Act's aim as being a response to the difficulties mentioned, as well as developing a nice flow for your structure.

[4]While perhaps not seemingly directly in issue, highlight your awareness of this briefly to show your depth on the subject. This places your discussion of the Act in context.

available to her: one in negligence and another under the Consumer Protection Act 1987. It is argued that Manisha may succeed under the Act for the kidney damage.

Manisha could firstly claim in negligence.[1] Following the specific rule in **Donoghue v Stevenson** [1932] A.C. 562, a manufacturer owes a duty to take reasonable care when manufacturing a product to ensure it is safe when used by the ultimate consumer. However, it would be very difficult for Manisha to succeed in this claim. Under **Donoghue** the duty is only owed when the product is intended to reach the consumer in the same state as it left the manufacturer, without any reasonable chance of intermediary inspection. Manisha was prescribed the drug by Dr. Legg and so arguably there was a reasonable chance of inspection by him. Dr. Legg should have enquired as to whether Manisha suffered epilepsy and thus not prescribed it to her in light of the warning. An analogy could be drawn here with **Evans v Triplex Safety Glass Co. Ltd** [1963] 1 All E.R. 283 where the windshield was fitted by another party. Manisha should be advised that Dr. Legg's failure to do this may mean that she would have a claim in negligence against him under **Bolam v Friern H.M.C.** [1957] 1 W.L.R. 582.[2] Even in relation to the kidney damage Manisha is likely to have problems in negligence owing to the need to prove that, even if P&G failed to take reasonable care in producing the drug, this breach of duty caused her injuries. There could be various reasons for the kidney damage, such as Manisha's lifestyle or whether she was taking any other medicines. This task is made harder by the fact that this is a design defect rather than a manufacturing defect and the courts have been more ready to infer negligence in the latter (**Grant v Australian Knitting Mills Ltd** [1936] A.C. 85). Therefore, Manisha is unlikely to succeed in negligence against P&G.

However, in view of the difficulties with a fault-based system of liability for defective products, a strict liability regime has been implemented in addition.[3] The Act implemented Directive 85/374/EEC, which had sought to introduce strict liability for defective products as a means of ensuring a level of harmonisation for consumers within the Internal Market.[4] It is clear from ss.1(2) and s.45 that the drug will be a product for the purposes of the Act. The fact that Fiagera is made up of different ingredients will not matter as s.1(2) states a product also includes the component parts within an overall product.

It is also clear that P&G will be the producer for the purposes of the Act as they have manufactured the drug (s.1(2)).

The damage must be actionable under the Act which this is, as under s.5(1) damage means personal injury which Manisha has clearly suffered. The question is whether the product was defective. Section 3 defines 'defect' as where the 'safety of the product is not such as persons generally are entitled to expect'. Guidance is given in s.3(2) which significantly states[5] that account should be taken of how the product is marketed and the instructions given. We are told that Fiagera was approved and marketed as not being suitable for epileptics. This causes a problem for Manisha as the first injury she suffers is that of an epileptic attack. Therefore, notwithstanding the strict approach taken when interpreting 'defect' in **A v National Blood Authority** [2001] 3 All E.R. 289, Fiagera was a standard product – meaning it was designed and manufactured as intended. Further, in view of the marketing and that in s.3(2)(b) provision is made as to what may reasonably be expected in terms of the product's use, Fiagera is unlikely to be defective. This is a prescription drug and so it is reasonable for P&G to expect that the drug would not be used by epileptics, especially as this was warned against. Therefore, Manisha is unlikely to succeed for the attack.

However, Manisha has also suffered kidney damage and this was not marketed on the product.[6] Therefore, Manisha needs to be advised as to whether Fiagera was defective in relation to this injury. The issue in relation to this is that under s.3(2)(c) the courts should take account of the time at which the product was put into circulation. At this time, the trials had not shown that it could cause kidney damage. There was evidence from Canada that this would be the case. Further, this information was available globally and so as a pharmaceutical company it is arguable that P&G should have known of this. This is supported by the strict approach endorsed in **A**. The public would expect Fiagera to be safe, especially seeing it had undergone a trial. Therefore, the drug could be said to be defective. Manisha's problem, though, is that even if defective it must, on normal causation principles, be shown to have caused the kidney damage. Therefore, it must be shown that 'but for' the taking of Fiagera Manisha would not have got kidney damage.[7] It is difficult to say whether this was the case and a lot will rest on the conclusiveness of the Canadian research.

[5]When discussing this guidance, focus on the aspects which are most relevant to the facts of the question and ensure that you apply them to the facts. This will keep your answer structured and relevant. If you just spell out all of the points, your answer will become descriptive and not read as well.

[6]As the drug is more likely to be defective in relation to the kidney damage, you should deal with this separately from the epilepsy. This will aid your structure by making it clear that you have identified two separate issues.

[7]If you covered causation in more depth previously when dealing with the action at common law, then you can just refer back to it here. Make sure you do not repeat yourself.

[8]You could learn the section in full and quote that, but as it is quite long it may be better to paraphrase it. This will also show that you understand what the section means, as you can write it in your own words.

[9]Although following *A* the matter is not likely to be interpreted generously; by highlighting that the claim is likely to succeed even on a generous view, it strengthens the argument that the defence will fail.

If the drug is deemed defective and causation shown, Manisha should be advised that the Act does contain defences. The most significant is within s.4(1)(e). This concerns development risks. The producer's knowledge must not be such that a producer of the same product might be expected to have discovered the defect while the product was under his control.[8] Therefore, there is some overlap with whether the drug was defective. The question is whether a reasonable producer of the same product would have known that the defect existed at the time. While criticised as diluting the strictness of liability under the Act, it was approved in **Commission v UK** [1997] 3 C.M.L.R. 923. However, even if generously interpreted it is unlikely P&G would satisfy this as, arguably, a reasonable producer would keep up to date with the latest scientific research.[9] Further, the journal was published before Fiagera was marketed and as it is a global publication it was accessible, which is what is necessary (**Commission v UK**).

Therefore, Manisha will be successful in claiming for the kidney damage under the Act, provided she can satisfy the issue of causation, which may not be easy as shown in **X v Schering Health Care Ltd** [2002] E.W.H.C. 1420. The drug is unlikely to be deemed defective in relation to the epilepsy.

✓ Make your answer stand out

- Explore the debate further around s.4(1)(e) and the corresponding part of the Directive and the extent to which the section is compatible.

- Explain in more depth the distinction made in *A* between standard and non-standard products.

- Consider the merits of strict liability over fault–based negligence and particularly the approach taken in *A* for interpreting the Act. In furtherance of this, look at C. Hodges (2001) 'Compensating patients: case comment on *A* v *National Blood Authority* [2001] 2 All E.R. 289', 117 L.Q.R. 528; and G. Howells and M. Mildred (2002) 'Infected blood: defect and discoverability, a first exposition of the EC Product Liability Directive', 65 M.L.R. 95.

- Discuss the prospect of P&G being jointly liable with the national regulator that approved the drug.

! Don't be tempted to ...

- Ignore either of the possible claims in favour of solely talking about the other in depth. As the question does not set any limits, you need to discuss both. Even if you do not do so because you feel that claim is futile, it may look like you did not realise there is a chance of the claim. At the very least raise it to dismiss the possibility of success.

- Get into a discussion of loss of a chance and *Gregg* v *Scott* [2005] 2 A.C. 176 with regards any chance of the kidney damage occurring.

- Merge your discussion as to both injuries, as arguably the outcome will be different and so you may find you compromise the clarity of your argument.

- Set out all of the defences within s.4 unless you can make the case for them being relevant; otherwise you will use up valuable time without gaining any real benefit.

Vicarious liability

How this topic may come up in exams

Vicarious liability is an important topic as there could be an element of it in a question on any other topic, with varying degrees of emphasis. However, it can also be examined on its own. Where this is the case, it is more likely to be an essay with questions focusing on the justification for imposing liability on a third party who did not commit the tort. Therefore, as well as knowing the mechanics of how the doctrine works, you will need an in-depth knowledge on the policy and theoretical reasons for and against it.

■ Attack the question

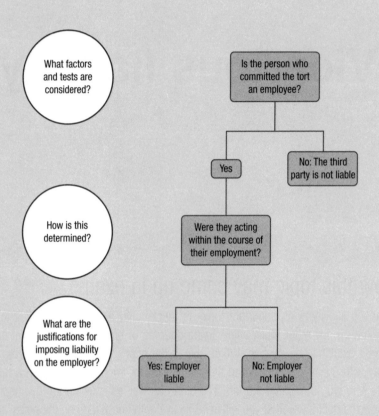

Question 1

'A further concern must lie with the doctrine of vicarious liability itself. Since *Lister* v *Hesley Hall Ltd.* [2002] 1 A.C. 215, the courts have adopted a generous approach towards liability finding conduct as varied as sexual abuse by a warden of a children's home, to a vengeful knife attack by a bouncer outside a nightclub, to be "within the course of employment" (see *Lister* and *Mattis* v *Pollock* [2003] 1 W.L.R. 2158).' P. Giliker (2006) 'The ongoing march of vicarious liability', CLJ 489 at 492

Critically evaluate the justification for vicarious liability particularly in such cases as these.

Answer plan

→ Explain what the doctrine is.

→ Evaluate the justification behind shifting liability in this way.

→ Discuss how the courts currently impose liability under the doctrine.

→ Consider the merits in this approach and whether its application is at odds with the purpose of the doctrine.

Diagram plan

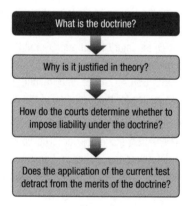

A printable version of this diagram is available from www.pearsoned.co.uk/lawexpressqa

Answer

The issue arising from the quote is whether the courts are applying the doctrine of vicarious liability too liberally since **Lister**. If this is the case it raises questions as to its continued justification as it could be going beyond its purpose. However, it is argued that the current application has a desirable level of flexibility which correlates to the doctrine's original justifications.

The doctrine is used by tort law to shift the burden of liability from individual tortfeasors to their employer even when the latter is free from fault, and as not directly breached any duty owed to the claimant. Therefore, it is a form of strict liability which places a burden on business, which could prove unduly restrictive, with negative economic impacts while distorting ideas of corrective justice. However, the doctrine has several justifications. It gives effect to the principle of loss distribution so that the claimant is able to obtain compensation from a party who has the funds to actually pay it. While perhaps detrimental to an innocent employer, the rationale is that the employer is taking the benefits of that employee's work and thus should carry the risks of his activity. They will also have insurance cover while the actual tortfeasor may be a proverbial man of straw. This leads to additional theories of tort[1] which underpin the justification for the doctrine: namely, economic efficiency and deterrence. The employer's business costs increase the more compensation they pay, as their insurance premiums rise. This increases the cost of their products/services, making them less competitive.[2] As such, there is a strong deterrent factor in ensuring that their employees do not cause injury to others. Overall the doctrine is based on 'social convenience and rough justice' (Lord Pearce, **ICI Ltd v Shatwell** [1965] 656 A.C. 686), and in light of these factors there is a clear justification for the existence of the doctrine.[3]

Notwithstanding these justifications, liability is not automatically imposed on the employer.[4] The courts ask two questions in order to determine the matter and ensure that its application sticks to its rationale. The first reflects the justification for placing liability on employers, and is whether or not an employee actually committed the tort in question.[5] This can be a grey issue because of the prevalence of independent contractors; therefore, as modern employment practices changed and more professionals entered employment from private practice, alongside technological developments, the modern approach applies an economic reality test (**Market Investigations Ltd v Minister of Social Security** [1969] 2 Q.B. 173) which, while still considering control, requires an assessment of factors such as whether the tortfeasor hires his own help and provides his own

---

[1] By setting out the theoretical justification for the doctrine first, you can establish whether any issues are at this level or simply ones of application by the courts.

[2] Discuss the practical impact of the doctrine, as it is against this which its justification must ultimately be judged. If it causes firms to go out of business, the doctrine could be argued as being objectionable on policy grounds.

[3] As you will have discussed several reasons justifying the tort, use a judicial or academic quote to pull them all together and sum up the rationale for the tort.

[4] By introducing the requirements in this way you are tying them in to the justification argument which you have just considered. If liability is automatic, it could be argued this is unfair in light of the detriment it could cause employers.

[5] When you cover the requirements for shifting liability, tie them to the initial justifications to determine where any problems lie and perhaps more strongly support the doctrine by showing that its application correlates to its rationale.

equipment. This overcomes the issue of control which existed histori-cally, while giving a fair assessment of who should be considered an employee, and justifies shifting liability.

Following this, the employee must also have been acting in the course of his employment when he committed the tort. Naturally, the employee must be in the time and space of their employer at this time, or at least a timeframe reasonably connected (**Ruddiman & Co v Smith** (1889) 60 L.T. 708. This is generally easy to determine with issues arising in terms of whether the conduct, while in the time and space of the employer, was actually part of his employment. A new test for determining this was provided in **Lister**, the 'close connection' test. The question to ask is whether the employee's tort was so closely connected with his employment that it would be just to hold the employer liable. It may seem hard to see where the connection is in such instances as **Lister** and **Mattis** where the conduct is clearly illegal; however, Lord Steyn[6] stated in **Lister** that the tort was 'inextricably interwoven' with his duties. The warden was charged with caring for the children, while, as Lord Millett highlighted, he had been entrusted with responsibility for discharging the duty of care owed by the employer to the children, which he clearly failed. This link warranted liability and not simply the fact that the employment created an opportunity for committing the tort; which is why it was stated that liability would not have arisen if the gardener was the tortfeasor. There is concern that the test offers no exact guidance on what is a sufficient connection and why liability is shifted (**Dubai Aluminium Co. Ltd v Salaam & Others** [2003] 1 A.C. 366), which Giliker argues is due to a lack of uniform formulation of the test among the opinions in **Lister**. From a practical perspective, employers cannot obtain adequate insurance to pay compensation when they do not know the scope of the cover needed. This could cause significant economic difficulties for firms as they may end up uncovered or the premiums become too expensive, reducing their competitiveness and their financial health: all for an act which was not of their doing and even expressly prohibited. This is hard to defend and goes against the doctrine's rationale, removing its justifications. If the doctrine operates arbitrarily, it loses legitimacy and its rationale can be questioned. Indeed, Longmore LJ in **Maga v Birmingham Roman Catholic Archdiocese Trustees** [2010] E.W.C.A. Civ. 256 did this, asking whether it is simply to ensure

[6]In *Lister* no test of uniform language was adopted, so it is important that you identify which judge you are referring to as this can help show that you are aware of that fact.

someone can pay or to encourage employers to exert more vigilance over employees.

[7]Never be afraid to take an opposing view to that in journal articles that you have read or that of the judges; provided that you substantiate your answer and show why your view has strength, you should gain more marks.

[8]As above, have the courage to consider whether the issues that are suggested as being detrimental are in fact so. This allows you to really evaluate the merits of the arguments relating to the doctrine justification.

However, these concerns suggest that the justifications are at odds and require one overarching justification when in fact arguably, as Salmon and Heuston argue (Heuston and Buckley 1996), there never has been. The stronger view[7] is that while terms such as 'fair and just' are vague they allow flexibility to develop and apply the doctrine to new situations such as in **Lister**, while being mindful of the need for fairness to both parties. Assessing all of the facts of each situation and weighing them against the doctrine's justifications ensures liability is justly shifted when necessary so as to ensure appropriate compensation for claimants. Any uncertainty could instead be viewed as a positive virtue[8], forcing employers to ensure employees are competent and undertake appropriate and regular checks, which strengthen the deterrence principle through principles of economic efficiency. While employers may be unable to foresee all acts of employees, they do have a degree of control on events by employing the individual, and an understanding that they may even be liable for illegality. This simply requires them to perform adequate risk assessments, which is surely good practice.

Therefore, the doctrine remains as justified today, even in situations such as **Lister**, and gives effect to the foundation principles of tort by ensuring that tortious conduct is corrected through compensatory payments and spreading losses to those who are most able to bear them, and for the other policy reasons which make this fair.

✓ Make your answer stand out

- Ensure that you have read *Lister* and *Mattis* in order to be able to fully understand why liability was imposed and be able to argue whether this was justified.

- Make sure that you have an understanding of the underlying principles of tort so as to be able to draw on them in this area in support of the argument that you advance.

- Look at Giliker's article in the question and Giliker (2010) '*Lister* revisited: vicarious liability, distributive justice and the course of employment', L.Q.R. 126 (Oct): 521–4 to obtain some academic criticism of the expansion of the doctrine.

- Consider whether any issues regarding the justification of the doctrine are theoretical or merely concerned with its practical implementation by the courts.

! **Don't be tempted to ...**

- Refer to vicariously liability as a distinct tort: this will simply suggest that you do not understand the basis of the concept.

- Try to establish a definitive explanation and justification for the doctrine. Simply outline the basic premise and highlight some of the variety of factors which are advanced in support of it.

- Gloss over the need to discuss the need for an employment relationship, as this is an important first stage in establishing liability. While it may not feature in the quote, it is firmly within the remit of the question as that is framed as the justification for the doctrine as a whole which covers all its elements.

Question 2

'This "close-connection" test focuses attention in the right direction. But it affords no guidance on the type or degree of connection which will normally be regarded as sufficiently close ..' *Per* Lord Nicholls in *Dubai Aluminium Co. Ltd* v *Salaam & Others* [2003] 1 A.C. 366 at [25]

Evaluate the extent to which the 'close-connection test' is appropriate for determining whether tortfeasors were in the course of their employment for the purposes of vicarious liability.

Answer plan

→ Outline what the purpose of the doctrine is and why it is warranted.

→ Briefly mention within that context the need for an employee–employer relationship.

→ Evaluate what the 'close-connection' test is and the purpose it serves.

→ Consider the effectiveness of the test and whether it has distorted the role of the doctrine.

Diagram plan

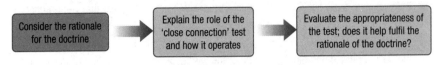

| Consider the rationale for the doctrine | → | Explain the role of the 'close connection' test and how it operates | → | Evaluate the appropriateness of the test; does it help fulfil the rationale of the doctrine? |

A printable version of this diagram is available from www.pearsoned.co.uk/lawexpressqa

Answer

Vicarious liability is the vehicle tort uses to transfer the cost of compensating injured parties from the party responsible to their employer. While there are long-standing justifications for this, the issue is whether the courts' current approach to establish whether the transfer should occur is appropriate or damaging the rationale for the doctrine.[1] It is argued that, while lacking definitive clarity, the test is effective and allows the doctrine to fulfil its purpose in a justifiable manner.

[1]As the question focuses on this specific aspect of vicarious liability, make sure that you highlight in your introduction that you appreciate this. The task is to stay disciplined and not stray into a broader-based answer.

The doctrine imposes strict liability on the employer, irrespective of the fact that they have not directly inflicted the claimant's injury and even if caused solely through the act of the individual employee. It can be seen as a form of distributive justice ensuring compensation is forthcoming but spreading the loss on to shoulders which are more able to bear the loss. This is justified by the law[2] as the employer should be protected by insurance and can also absorb costs by passing them on to consumers through price increases. There is also, therefore, a deterrent factor in ensuring that their staff are competent and continually trained to remain so, as this will make the employer more economically efficient with better quality products/services and thus more competitive in the market place. Another justification is that as the employer is taking the benefit from the conduct underway when the tort was caused, morally they should also carry the risks.

[2]If the doctrine does not have a justified theoretical basis, then there really is no argument that the test should not apply. Therefore, this is the foundation upon which you must build your answer. Briefly set out why the doctrine should apply and then you can concentrate on the merits of the practical application of it.

For the doctrine to come into operation, two requirements must be satisfied. Firstly, reflecting the fact that partial justification for shifting liability is that employers should carry the burdens as well as benefiting from those undertaking acts on their behalf, it must be an employee who actually commits the tort in question.[3] This is decided by the economic reality test (**Market Investigations Ltd v Minister of Social Security** [1969] 2 Q.B. 173), which requires an assessment of factors relating to the economic relationship of the parties, while additionally, as was historically the case,[4] considering the level of control exerted over the individual.

However, the second requirement is arguably the most significant and controversial. This is that the employee must have been in the course of their employment when they committed the tort.[5] Again, as the purpose of the requirement is wedded in the justifications for the doctrine, those justifications can only have merit if the employer is in his employment at the time of the tort.[6] Otherwise, too heavy a responsibility is placed on employers if they are responsible for acts done outside of their time or for their benefit (**N v Chief Constable of Merseyside Police** [2006] E.W.H.C. 3041). The doctrine itself would fall into disrepute. Previously, judicial discussion of this requirement focused on[7] whether the act was authorised or not and, if it was an authorised aspect of their employment, whether it was performed in an authorised manner. This was based on the proposition that acts relating to the scope of employment which were prohibited would not carry liability, but a breach of a prohibition as to the manner of performing an authorised act would be within the scope of the doctrine (**Plumb v Cobden Flour Mills Co Ltd** [1914] A.C. 62). This caused complications in disputes regarding what was the actual scope of employment and whether the act in question was outside it or not, notwithstanding that the scope of employment should be looked at broadly (**Rose v Plenty** [1976] 1 W.L.R. 141). Such a determination was particularly difficult to make with regards to intentional wrongdoing.[8]

In **Lister** a children's home was held vicariously liable for the sex abuse by a warden who was an employee. Clearly, he cannot be said to be performing his authorised employment in an unauthorised way let alone be expressly permitted.[9] It was a

[3] While the focus is on the 'close-connection' test, and you should not stray from that, there needs to be some context provided. As the test is concerned with whether the *employee* is in the course of their employment, you ought to briefly explain that there needs to be an employee for the doctrine to operate.

[4] As this part is not a big aspect of the question, use this phrase to indicate that you understand that the test used to be based on control without having to discuss it in depth.

[5] By starting this section with a sentence such as this, you reinforce and justify why you have just briefly discussed the issue of how to determine whether the tortfeasor is an employee.

[6] By stating the purpose of the requirement at the start, you tie this part of your answer to your earlier section and you have the foundation for assessing the merits of the test.

[7] While the test is the current authoritative approach to the issue, you should consider what it replaced in order to assess whether the move was justified.

[8] By ending with this statement, you highlight one of the problems with the old approach and flow straight into explaining what happened in *Lister*, a case on intentional wrongdoing.

[9] This links the case to the problems identified in the previous paragraph.

[10]All the judges gave opinions, so clearly identify whose analysis you are explaining.

clearly illegal act. Lord Steyn[10] felt that his duties as a warden were 'inextricably interwoven' with what he did; there was an undertaking by the employer to care for the boys and they were abused in their time, and on their premises creating a close connection. It was just a question as to whether it was 'fair and just' to impose liability on that basis. It was not the opportunity given by the employment that warranted liability but, as Lord Hobhouse stated, a relationship had been assumed between the claimant and the employer which imposed duties on the latter. The warden had been entrusted to perform that duty of care and instead breached it.

[11]The point here is to reiterate your understanding of the principal issue of the question and signal, therefore, the key stage of your discussion.

The question, therefore, is whether the close-connection test achieves its purpose or is its formulation in **Lister** detracting from the justifications of the doctrine.[11] Giliker (2006 and 2010) has repeatedly argued that the lack of definitive formulation of a test is causing problems for lower courts, a view seemingly reflected by Lord Nicholls in **Salaam**. Giliker suggests this allows the doctrine's application in inappropriate areas. Clearly, the test is vague and has created uncertainty which is rarely useful. This uncertainty leaves employers not knowing what acts will result in their liability. This could increase litigation as parties equally feel they have a chance of success, particularly when they are intentional illegal acts. At the very least it impacts employers' ability to obtain insurance, which removes one of the factors which is said to make the transferring of liability fair.

However, taken collectively the opinions in **Lister** are reconcilable. Lord Hutton agreed with Lord Steyn, and there is little difference in the language used by Lords Hobhouse and Millett. Although, strictly speaking, adopting different language, they can be reconciled: by entrusting the performance of the duty to the warden it created a sufficient connection to make it fair and just to impose liability. All emphasised the need for a causal link which, as Lord Clyde noted, went back to Salmond's first account of the doctrine. It could be said that the test provides flexibility, allowing a full consideration of the facts and an evaluative judgment made as against the underlying principles of compensation, deterrence and loss distribution while drawing on precedent where applicable. Indeed this was the approach accepted by Lord Nicholls in **Salaam** owing to the wide variety of situations in which the doctrine may operate. He therefore saw an appropriate way through the issue highlighted by the question.

The concern expressed by Giliker regarding the lower courts can thus be overcome. Lower courts are arbiters of fact. Once they have established the full facts of what the employee's duty was and how the tort was committed they have the scope to determine, in light of the doctrine's purpose, whether the two are sufficiently close. If they are, the requirement maintains the necessary justifiable link to the employer to give effect to the doctrine's rationale.

✓ Make your answer stand out

- Learn each opinion in *Lister* and quote the different judges' reasoning to support the argument that they are reconcilable.
- Consider some of the arguments used in the Canadian case of *Bazley* v *Curry* (1999) 174 D.L.R. (4th) 45, SC (from which the House of Lords took the test) to show a broader understanding of its merits in applying to situations such as *Lister*.
- Ensure that you always relate your arguments in relation to the test back to the theoretical purpose that this aspect of the requirement for vicarious liability is meant to serve.

! Don't be tempted to ...

- Broaden your answer to a deal in detail with the wider aspects of vicarious liability; stay focused on the 'close-connection' test as the question requires. You will not impress the marker with this wider knowledge and it will suggest that you do not understand the issue of the question.
- Avoid coming down from the fence and making a decision as to the appropriateness of the test. You will have stated arguments for and against and your answer will end weakly if you do not conclude on the ultimate point.

? Question 3

Brett is an uninsured plumber who gets his work from Brogan Construction. Brett is always instructed on what is required for the job and how it should be carried out by the Brogan foreman, although he must supply all his own tools, including a van to get to each job; he can bring his own labourers to a job but he must pay them out of his wages. Brogan's pay Brett a daily rate for any jobs but he receives no other benefits.

Recently, owing to a shortage of plumbing work on offer, Brogan arranged for Brett to do some work with Hacker Heating Ltd in return for a fee. The job involved fitting a new boiler in a residential property, owned by Ted. However, owing to a part turning up late, Brett rushed the installation as it was already past his normal finish time with Brogan Construction and he had a hangover from the night before and wanted to get to bed. The boiler subsequently exploded, killing Ted.

It has been accepted that the boiler was installed negligently and that this caused the explosion; however, Brett has argued that as an employee he should not be held personally liable, while Hacker Heating Ltd argue he was certainly not their employee.

Advise Brogan Construction on whether they could be held vicariously liable for Ted's death.

Answer plan

→ Explain what the doctrine of vicarious liability and why it is important to this situation.

→ Establish whether Brett can be considered an employee of Brogan Construction.

→ Discuss whether Brett is in the course of his employment.

→ Evaluate the implications of the work being for Hacker Heating Ltd.

Diagram plan

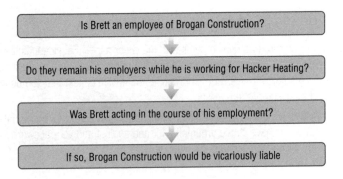

Is Brett an employee of Brogan Construction?

↓

Do they remain his employers while he is working for Hacker Heating?

↓

Was Brett acting in the course of his employment?

↓

If so, Brogan Construction would be vicariously liable

A printable version of this diagram is available from www.pearsoned.co.uk/lawexpressqa

Answer

[1]Although it is not going to need discussing as the doctrine can apply to all torts, it is worth confirming that you are aware of what tort Brogan Construction could be vicariously liable for.

[2]As you have to advise on their potential liability, you will be referring to them a lot, so abbreviate the name.

[3]This means that straight away you have identified the key aspect of the topic to be addressed without straying into irrelevant material.

[4]BC would naturally argue they did not do anything wrong so why should they be liable therefore; in a question such as this explain why the issue of liability even arises to illustrate that you understand the theory behind the doctrine.

[5]You need to state enough to show that you understand the basis for the doctrine, while not deviating from a structure which the question warrants.

[6]The point here is to show that you know what the purpose of the requirement of employee status is, but you need to remember to frame your explanation in the context of giving advice to a lay party, i.e. BC.

There is no issue that compensation for Ted's death is due under the tort of negligence;[1] the matter to be resolved is simply whether Brogan Construction (BC)[2] will have to pay this under the doctrine of vicarious liability. This rests on whether Brett is actually an employee of BC.[3] It is argued that while they may have some liability they should be able to successfully argue that Hacker Heating (HH) should be the predominant contributor of any compensation.

BC should be advised that the reason they face potential liability is that the doctrine operates[4] to shift losses so that they are borne by those who are best able to do so. As employers will have insurance and also benefit from their employees' actions, it is deemed acceptable for them to run the risk of their malfeasance and compensate any injuries caused through the work.[5]

This explanation forms the basis of the requirements which need to be met for an employer to be liable. The first is naturally that the tortfeasor is an employee. If they are not, there is no justification behind the transferring of liability.[6] Traditionally, this is determined applying the control test (**Short v J & W Henderson Ltd** (1946) S.C. (H.L.) 24). This is significant as the factors considered are the employer's power to select who does the work, their right to control the method of work, the paying of wages and their right to suspend or dismiss the individual. Applying this to Brett, we can see that BC do choose what work he does and dictate how it is performed. While we do not know the details regarding the last point, they do pay Brett his wages. Therefore, in all, Brett would seem to be their employee.

However, the control test is no longer the sole factor to determine a person's employee status. Reflecting changes in working practices and technological developments, it was felt that simply looking at the level of control was not appropriate. Instead a range of economic factors are also considered – the economic reality test (**Market Investigations Ltd v Minister of Social Security** [1969] 2 Q.B. 173). This requires, among other factors, an assessment of who provides the equipment and whether the person can hire helpers. On these factors, Brett seems more of an independent contractor as we are told he brings his own equipment and pays labourers from his own wages; contractors are also quite common in this field. If Brett is a contractor, the doctrine would not apply and BC would avoid liability but there are other economic factors which suggest Brett is an employee. Although not told definitively the facts regarding these, it seems Brett has no management responsibility and other than wages has no opportunity of profiting from the sound management of his task. Therefore, while it is possible Brett is not an employee, taken as a whole, particularly the element of control exerted over his work, it is quite likely that he is.[7]

[7]While the issue may be unclear, you do need to offer some advice on Brett's status; otherwise you are not really answering the question which is to advise BC. Highlight what you feel is the key factor which may swing a decision to support your opinion.

On the basis that Brett is an employee,[8] the next issue to advise BC on is the fact that at the time of the tort Brett was working for HH. Under **Mersey Docks & Harbour Board v Coggins & Griffith (Liverpool) Ltd** [1947] A.C. 1, the permanent employer of the employee remains liable even after lending them to another firm. From the case, the decisive factors will be whether BC still pays Brett's wages and can still dismiss him, as well as how long Brett was sent to HH and how complex any machinery to be used is. In relation to the latter two points, Brett was only there to install a boiler and this was within his usual work for BC. As HH paid BC a fee for Brett's services, it is unlikely that they paid him as well; in view of the short duration and nature of the job BC should be advised that the facts suggest that they would remain liable for Brett's work.

[8]Reflect the fact that it is uncertain by framing the opening sentence like this. Even if you do not feel Brett is an employee, you still need to continue to this section on the transfer issue as clearly this is a key part of the question; if you just stop with the previous section, there will be significant aspects of the question and topic which you will not have demonstrated any knowledge of.

However, BC could benefit from **Viasystems (Tyneside) Ltd v Thermal Transfers (Northern) Ltd** [2006] Q.B. 510 where the Court of Appeal held dual vicarious liability could exist in a situation such as this. Liability could be joint or several, with the contributions to be made by each side being determined by the Civil Liability (Contribution) Act 1978. Indeed the facts are similar to those that Rix LJ gave for when liability is likely to be shared. However, **Viasystems** maintained that where one party has absolute control of the employee they will remain solely liable. Here, while we are told Brett was always told how to perform each job by the BC foreman, they would not have been present at Ted's house. Further, HH are a heating firm and so would have detailed knowledge of how to install boilers. This would suggest that any control over how Brett performed the job was more likely exerted by HH. Ultimately, Brett rushed because he was hung-over and wanted to get home; HH let

Brett work hung-over, and therefore, it was within their control to prevent Brett working that day on the boiler regardless of whether BC's foreman instructed Brett how to install it. Therefore, it can be strongly argued that while Brett may have been an employee of BC, if indeed he was, HH had the sole of control of him while he was lent to them for that job. This would mean that BC avoid liability, or at the very least have a much reduced share, with HH being liable for the remaining compensation.

[9]Do not forget this aspect of vicarious liability, as without it the previous discussion is irrelevant. While it seems apparent it will be satisfied, you do still need to touch on it to firmly show that you do in fact know it and can apply it.

However, in any event Brett needed to act in the course of his employment.[9] Clearly, as a plumber engaged to install a boiler, the negligent act was within his employment. The installation took place after Brett's normal finishing time, but while the tortious act must be performed within the authorised employment time, it is clear that Brett extended his day in order to finish the job and so will be classed as still within his employer's time (**Ruddiman & Co. *v* Smith** (1889) 60 L.T. 708). The fact that Brett would not be authorised to install a boiler negligently will also not suffice as there is clearly a close connection between the act and his employment (**Lister *v* Hesley Hall Ltd.** [2002] 1 A.C. 215).

Therefore, the potential vicarious liability of BC will turn on firstly whether Brett is deemed to even be an employee of theirs. Even if he is, owing to the fact that at the time of the act some, if not all, control of his work was in the hands of HH, BC should only, at most, be liable to contribute a part of any compensation under the Act, with HH contributing the rest.

✓ Make your answer stand out

- As control is still a significant factor for cases of transferred employees, cover the control test in a bit more depth than you would other vicarious liability problem questions.
- As there are not as many concrete facts to definitively apply in this question, draw on facts from similar cases and judicial reasoning from those cases to support the arguments that you do advance.
- Explain using the judgment of May LJ in *Viasystems* why dual vicarious liability had not been used previously and consider its merits.

! Don't be tempted to ...

- Make a definitive statement of fact as to Brett's employment, as the facts are not definitively conclusive; do assert a reasoned opinion, though, as to whether he is likely to be an employee.

- Get into a full discussion as to the 'close-connection' test. You will need to reference this but remember the focus of the question is on the employee part of vicarious liability.

- Set out a full account of the tort of negligence, as the presence of the essential requirements are not an issue in the question. The issue is vicarious liability.

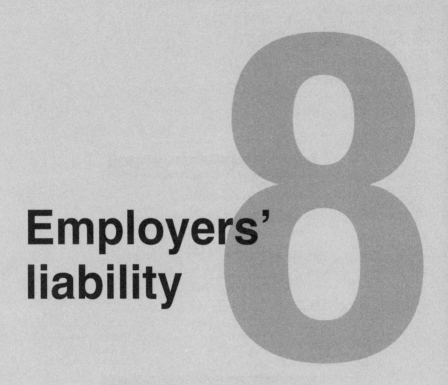

Employers' liability

How this topic may come up in exams

Although this is another offshoot of negligence, it is again a specific application covering injuries caused by the claimant's colleagues, equipment or the system of work imposed by the employer. Naturally, there is an overlap with vicarious liability but this area is distinctive in its own right. Problem questions are more common than essays but you should check carefully how this area is dealt with on your course in relation to vicarious liability and the extent that breach of statutory duty is covered alongside the common law duties.

Attack the question

Common law duty

- Were the competent staff employed?
- Where the workplace and associated tools and equipment reasonably safe?
- Was a safe system of work in operation?
- If no, was the breach the same as the cause of the injury?

Employer's liability

Are any defences applicable?

Statutory duty

- Does the statute expressly permit or exlude damages in tort?
- If silent, can the court construe the wording as giving a remedy in tort?
- Is the duty owed to the particular claimant?
- Was the statutory duty breached?
- Was the breach the cause of the injury suffered?
- Is the injury one which the statute intended to prevent occuring?

A printable version of this diagram is available from www.pearsoned.co.uk/lawexpressqa

❓ Question 1

Kirkbride Manufacturing Ltd is an engineering company which produces a range of tools for the construction industry. Jerome has worked for the company since he turned 16, 5 years ago. Jerome has always had a reputation for conducting practical jokes around the factory; even though a couple of people have suffered injuries as a result of some jokes it has always been put down to his age with the held belief that he will grow out of it one day, particularly as he was a very competent and skilled worker. However, one day he rolled a lead pipe across a walkway as Fang was coming past. Fang was carrying several boxes, as the factory's trolley was broken. This meant she could not see the pipe and so she tripped, with the boxes landing on her and causing a dislocated shoulder.

Upon hearing Fang's scream as she fell, Karl, who was filing the end of a screwdriver on a machine bought from a reputable firm, looked up. As he did so the screwdriver lost contact with the machine's filing wheel which should have caused it to stop spinning. However, owing to an electrical fault in the machine, it did not and as Karl turned to resume his work he caught his hand on the wheel and severed a finger. The machine had recently undergone an inspection by Chris and a licensed individual but the defect was too latent to be picked up during the check.

Advise Chris, the owner of company, as to his liability for these injuries.

Answer plan

→ Explain what the non-delegable duties are and why they were created.

→ Identify which duty is in issue with regards to Fang's injury.

→ Assess whether this has been breached by Chris and whether the breach caused the injury.

→ Consider the possibility of any defences applying.

→ Repeat this process with regards to Karl's injury.

Diagram plan

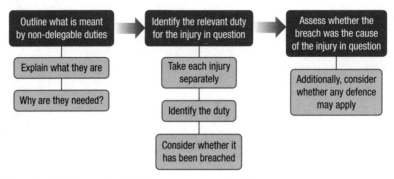

A printable version of this diagram is available from www.pearsoned.co.uk/lawexpressqa

Answer

[1]By discussing this in your introduction, you show that you have correctly identified what specific issue of tort the question is addressing and have not mistakenly read the question as one on vicarious liability.

The issue to advise Chris on is whether his company will be held personally liable in negligence even though he was not directly at fault for the injuries. This will involve advising Chris of an employer's non-delegable duties which are owed to all staff, which ensure that employers cannot escape liability by insisting that responsibility for the duty of care in question had been delegated to another employee to discharge.[1] It is argued that the relevant duties of providing competent staff and adequate equipment[2] have been breached.

[2]Identify what specific non-delegable duties are in issue. This, and the previous point, will help create a sense of anticipation in the marker that they are about to read an answer which is on the right track.

Chris should be advised that at common law a series of non-delegable duties have been developed by the case of **Wilson and Clyde Coal Co. v English** [1938] A.C. 57. These duties include providing competent staff, adequate plant and equipment, a safe place of work, and a safe system of work, and apply to each employee personally (**Paris v Stepney B.C.** [1951] A.C. 367). These were required to reflect the socio-economic and technological developments of the industrial revolution and the increasing use of potentially dangerous machines in the workplace.[3] Historically, as no insurance system was in place, the courts were reluctant to burden emerging businesses with civil liability claims. However, as the insurance system developed, and indeed became compulsory (Employer's Liability (Compulsory Insurance) Act 1969), in light of the increased dangers it became untenable for employers to simply

[3]What you want to do here is to show that you know the duties and understand why they are needed. This will allow you to explain to Chris why the law may see it as justifiable that he be held liable.

claim they had delegated their duty to a competent member of staff whom they had hired with care.

The first duty which the company will be alleged to have breached is in not providing competent staff. Although we are told Jerome was skilled and competent in his work, the duty extends further than just competency in doing the actual task that the employee is employed for. As such, it covers situations which may not fall within the 'course of their employment' aspect for the purposes of a claim using vicarious liability.[4] This can be seen in **Hudson v Ridge Manufacturing Co.** [1957] 2 Q.B. 348 when, as with Jerome, the employee in question tripped another up, causing them injury. Again similarly, in **Hudson** there was a history of the employee conducting practical jokes and indeed he had been reprimanded several times. The company was held liable for not exercising reasonable care to bring the jokes to an end. This is obviously significant for Chris and the fact that Jerome has never been reprimanded despite causing previous injuries suggests that Chris is even more likely to be found in breach of this duty. It could also be used to support a finding that Chris did not ensure the workplace was safe.

From the facts it is clear that there are no causation or contributory negligence issues. While historically there may have been a defence of *volenti* in that Fang assumed the risk of working alongside Jerome, this clearly defeats the modern thinking as to employer's liability and thus would not be worthwhile pursuing.[5]

The next issue to advise Chris on is that of the faulty machinery. It is another duty of an employer that they provide adequate machinery and equipment for their employees. This requires reasonable care to ensure that reasonably safe equipment is used and kept in reasonable condition. Chris may argue that he has discharged this duty as best he could in relation to Karl's injury. The machine was purchased from a reputable source and had been recently inspected with no defects found. Under **Davie v New Merton Board Mills** [1959] A.C. 604 this would have been sufficient and Chris would not be held liable as he could not be said to have delegated the duty to another, having inspected the machine himself. Further, it would seem that the latent nature of the defect meant there was no way of noticing the development of the fault. However, this decision has been overturned by the Employer's Liability (Defective Equipment) Act

[4] This allows you to show not only that you have knowledge of vicarious liability but also that you have an understanding of the relationship of the two and when each is more applicable.

[5] This allows you to show that the defence has applied in the past and can still be used in some circumstances, but illustrate your understanding of the area by using the theory you discussed earlier to show why it would not succeed here.

[6]Clearly you need to learn this section; however, rather than learning it word for word, learn it in your own words. This will allow you to write the provisions quicker while also demonstrating that you have understanding of the section as well as knowledge.

[7]As you are now moving into some specific application of the requirements under the section, put these in a separate paragraph in order to add some clarity to your answer and ensure the answer is easy to read.

[8]Remember you are advising Chris of his potential liability; while you need to give the possibilities, he would expect an indication of what is the likeliest scenario, so offer one.

1969. The statute provides in s.1 that any negligence is attributable to the employer where they have provided equipment for the purpose for their business and a defect in the equipment causes injury to an employee operating the equipment in the course of their employment, where the defect is in fact the fault of a third party.[6] The section was designed to address the perceived imbalance resulting from **Davie** and make it easier for employees to obtain compensation, as otherwise their only route was a claim against the manufacturer who may be out of business or, increasingly, based overseas.

The section does not automatically impose liability on Chris.[7] It does seem apparent that the injury was caused by the defect, as if it had stopped as it should have it would not have occurred. However, the defect must still, on the balance of probabilities, be due to the fault of the manufacturer. Notwithstanding the passing of the inspection, we are told there was an electrical fault in the machine, as opposed to an electrical fault in the factory, and therefore this suggests that it was a manufacturing fault. Naturally, this will need to be proved: and if it cannot, Chris would avoid liability but if it can, as is more likely,[8] Chris would be liable for Karl's injury. The amount that Chris may be liable for, though, could be reduced on the basis that Karl's own negligence contributed to the injury. Karl has not looked before continuing his work and presumably this type of machinery would make some noise while in use. This would mean that under the Law Reform (Contributory Negligence) Act 1945 a proportion of compensation, reflecting this negligence, would be deducted. Chris should be advised that the courts have indicated a reluctance to find contributory negligence against employee factory workers (**Caswell v Powell Duffryn Associated Collieries Ltd** [1940] A.C. 152) but this was in relation to a breach of statutory duty, at a time when contributory negligence was a full defence. As this is a common law duty, some reduction is quite likely.

To conclude, Chris should be advised that the common law imposes duties on employers to ensure the safety of those carrying out their work, and thus from whom they are benefiting. By not preventing Jerome's practical jokes, he has failed to employ competent staff for his other employees to work alongside. In addition, while not his own fault, he has a piece of defective machinery in use in the factory. As a breach of both duties resulted in injuries being suffered by his employees, he will be held liable, albeit with some reduction possible in relation to Karl.

✓ Make your answer stand out

- Highlight how there may be statutory duties which Chris' company may be in breach of and indicate that you are aware of that aspect of the area (but see below).

- Include a bit more on the difference between liability under this area and vicarious liability. On this point see J. Murphy (2007b) 'The juridical foundations of common law non-delegable duties' in Neyers *et al.* (eds), *Emerging Issues in Tort Law*, Hart.

! Don't be tempted to ...

- Turn the question into one on standard negligence: it is specifically about the non-delegable duties that an employer has.

- Go into detail about the non-delegable duties which are not within the focus of the question, as you will merely be describing everything you know and not advising Chris on the specific issues.

- Go into depth on potential liability for breach of a statutory duty, as no statute is present in the question. You will have no grounding to base your discussion on, so again it will detract from the analysis of your answer. Just raise it briefly as a possibility but no more.

❓ Question 2

Fleetwood Mechanics Ltd is a garage providing mechanical repairs for all types of automobiles. As such, they are subject to the (Fictitious) Automotive Engineering (Protection of Workers) Act 2010 which was passed after a series of accidents involving mechanics. This provides in section 1 a list of safety equipment which must be supplied to mechanics and includes eye goggles. Section 2 also provides that all safety equipment supplied to any workers must comply with British safety standards and have an appropriate safety certificate. Section 3 states that a breach of sections 1 and/or 2 will result in a fine.

However, at the time the legislation was passed the garage was struggling financially so Otis, the company owner, chose not to purchase goggles with a British safety certificate as these were more expensive. Instead, he purchased some from another country with less rigorous safety standards. One day, Ray, wearing the goggles supplied by Otis, was working on an engine fitting a new mount, however, when taking out the old bolts, one became lodged in the mount. Ray managed to force it loose but in doing so it flew up striking him in the eye. As the goggles Otis had bought were not of sufficient safety strength, it cracked the lens and blinded Ray.

Also that day, Dobie was working near the entrance of the garage sorting out a tyre delivery. However, the way he had stacked the tyres meant he had narrowed the entrance. Booker was driving a car into the garage for a service but the entrance was now too small and tight to enter so he hit the tyres which fell onto Dobie leaving him with broken ribs.

Advise Otis of his company's liability for the injuries to Ray and Dobie.

Answer plan

→ Consider whether the Act may give rise to damages in tort.

→ Discuss how this statutory duty was breached and assess causation.

→ Evaluate whether Otis has also breached his non-delegable duty to Dobie regarding a safe place of work.

→ Determine whether Dobie has been contributorily negligent for his injuries.

Diagram plan

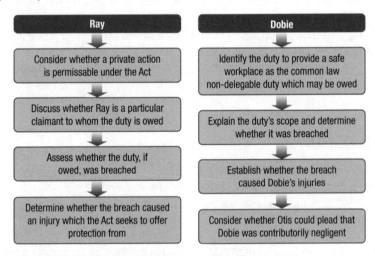

A printable version of this diagram is available from www.pearsoned.co.uk/lawexpressqa

¹This indicates that you have identified the area of tort covered by the question.

²This shows that you have seen that both aspects apply and in relation to which injury.

Answer

Although Otis was not the direct cause of both injuries, the issue which arises is whether he will still be liable as their employer¹ for breaching a statutory duty to Ray and a common law duty of care to Dobie.²

The first issue is whether the Act permits a civil remedy. If so, then it would simply be a case of establishing whether the elements of breach and causation are satisfied. Alternatively, the Act may expressly exclude civil liability. From the sections provided we are not told and in fact most statutes are silent on the matter. In this situation, Otis should be advised that there is no general notion that civil liability arises (**Lonrho Ltd v Shell Petroleum Co. Ltd (No. 2)** [1982] A.C. 173). Instead the courts exercise their discretion in interpreting the Act to determine the matter.

[3]Structurally, it is always important to state and explain the general rule first and then explain how there may be exceptions to it. Then, as you go on to state the factors which create the exception, ensure that you apply them to the facts.

Lonrho held, that while the ultimate question was identifying whether the Act had the purpose of giving civil remedies, other factors should also be considered. Generally, if the Act provides for penalties, this should be construed as not conferring a right. However, **Lonrho** identified exceptions to this general proposition,[3] one of which was where the Act was enacted to protect a particular class. We are told that the purpose of the Act was to protect mechanics after a series of accidents, therefore this seems satisfied. This is supported by **X v Bedfordshire C.C.** [1995] 2 A.C. 633, although this case also stated that it must additionally be shown that Parliament intended to grant a private right of action on members of the protected class.

[4]This naturally follows on from the preceding sentence, but deal with this aspect in a new paragraph to enhance the clarity of the arguments. Simply use a sentence such as the preceding one to create a flow from one paragraph into the next.

Where the Act is deemed to have 'social welfare', the intention to create a private right will not exist (**Phelps v Hillingdon L.B.C.** [2001] 2 A.C. 619). In relation to this Act, while it is aimed at the welfare of mechanics this is a far narrower class and not society at large as in cases such as **Phelps**. Arguably, it is unjust if an Act aiming to prevent injury to a class did not allow injured class members to seek a civil remedy.

[5]Don't dwell on this point as it is not of primary relevance, but provide an example to illustrate your point.

[6]Be careful not to sound repetitive. You are just building on the general point that you made earlier. You could alternatively deal with this point at the time of first raising the general proposition.

One reason why the Act may do this is if it expressly provides for an alternative remedy, or a better alternative exists elsewhere.[4] The latter could be where the duty is placed on local authorities whereby the claimant would have recourse to administrative law remedies.[5] This is not the case for Otis, and the more significant issue is the fact that section 3 states that a breach will result in a fine. This shows a remedy is within the Act; however, as **Lonrho** states, if the Act is specifically for the protection of a class a civil action may still arise.[6] A fine is unlikely to go to the injured mechanics unless it goes to a central fund akin to the Motor Insurance Bureau to pay victims. If this is not the case, then the mere imposition of a fine would not mean it is inappropriate to give rise to a civil action, and indeed where the situation relates to workplace safety a more generous approach is adopted (**Ziemniak v ETPM Deep Sea Ltd** [2003] E.W.C.A. Civ. 636). Notwithstanding these considerations, the process has been criticised for ultimately coming down to the courts making a policy decision on the merits of the case. However, there would not seem to be any policy reasons for denying a claim and, on balance, it is likely that the duty would give rise to a civil action.

If the matter is actionable in tort, Ray must overcome several other considerations. However, it is clear that of these Ray is certainly, as a mechanic, owed the duty and also that this was breached, as we are told that Otis bought goggles that were cheaper and not compliant with British safety standards. There does not seem either to be any issue of the breach causing the injury, as we are told that the bolt cracked the goggles Ray was wearing because they were of insufficient strength. On the basis that a British standard pair would not have cracked, it is clear that 'but for' failing to supply the right goggles, as the duty requires, the injury would have been avoided. Finally, as the Act specifically mentions supplying goggles, it is clear that eye damage was an injury which the Act sought to protect mechanics from. Otis should be advised that he will not have a defence, as even if the act is not construed as strict liability Ray cannot be said to have assumed the risk or contributed to the injury in any way himself as he was wearing what was supplied.

In relation to Dobie's injury, it is clear the Act does not deal with this situation. However, Otis should be advised that as an employer he also has a series of non-delegable duties towards each of his employees personally (**Paris v Stepney B.C.** [1951] A.C. 367). These are non-delegable in the sense that responsibility for discharging the duty owed cannot be delegated to someone else.[7] They ensure that the claimant is able to prove an action against someone, and that that someone is able to pay compensation which the employer is able to do, as insurance is compulsory under Employer's Liability (Defective Equipment) Act 1969. The duties were set out in **Wilson and Clyde Coal Co. v English** [1938] A.C. 57 and are to reasonably ensure competent staff, adequate plant and equipment, a safe place of work and a safe system of work.

The relevant duty here[8] is whether Otis has provided a safe workplace, as Dobie was injured after the entrance to the garage

[7]While this aspect of the question is the subsidiary issue, do not miss the opportunity to earn more marks by providing some evaluation and showing an insight into the depth of your knowledge.

[8]As previously, create a flow between the paragraphs: separate out this aspect of your question into one paragraph on the nature of the duty and a second on the application of the duty to facts.

[9]On these facts this is highly relevant, so make sure you explain the scope of the duty's application.

was narrowed by the tyre wall. The duty is concerned with ensuring the employer takes reasonable care to create a safe environment and this extends to entrances[9] (**Ashdown *v* Samuel Williams & Sons Ltd** [1957] 1 Q.B. 409). From the facts, Booker crashed through the tyres because the entrance was narrowed, suggesting the duty was breached. It is apparent if the duty was breached it did cause the injury, as the falling tyres broke Dobie's ribs as they hit him. However, while this may seem harsh on Otis as the danger was created by Dobie himself, this does mean under the Law Reform (Contributory Negligence) Act 1945 a reduction in Dobie's compensation may be made to reflect any contributing negligence on his part. By stacking the tyres in the entrance so as to restrict it and then continuing to work behind the stack, Dobie has indeed been negligent.

[10]As you will have already concluded each injury as you dealt with it, you just need a short overall conclusion here just to round off your answer.

Therefore, in conclusion, Otis should be advised that he is likely to be found liable for both injuries as he breached his duties owed, although the compensation payable to Dobie could be reduced.[10]

✓ Make your answer stand out

- Consider whether the injury to Ray may also be a breach of the common law duty to provide reasonably safe equipment and/or a safe system of work, particularly if you feel the injury may not be actionable in tort under the Act.
- Discuss in a bit more depth why Ray could not be said to have voluntarily assumed the risk of injury.
- Include a bit more on the difference between liability under this area and vicarious liability. On this point see J. Murphy (2007b) 'The juridical foundations of common law non-delegable duties' in Neyers *et al.* (eds), *Emerging Issues in Tort Law*, Hart.

! Don't be tempted to ...

- Turn the question into one on standard negligence, or vicarious liability: it is specifically about employer's liability for breach of statutory duty and one specific non-delegable duty.
- Go into detail about the non-delegable duties which are not within the focus of the question, as this will just make your answer come across as a description of everything you know and you are not advising Otis on the specific issues.

Question 3

'To a person unversed in the science or art of legislation it may well seem strange that Parliament has not by now made it a rule to state explicitly what its intention is in a matter.'

Per Lord du Parcq in *Cutler* v *Wandsworth Stadium Ltd* [1949] A.C. 398 at 410

In light of this statement evaluate the court's approach for determining whether Parliament intended a remedy in tort for a breach of statutory duty by an employer.

Answer plan

→ Outline the leading case of *Lonrho Ltd* explaining its importance.

→ Discuss the general rule from the case.

→ Highlight the exceptions regarding when a remedy will be deemed to exist.

Diagram plan

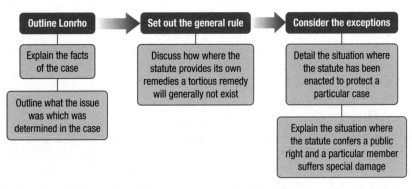

A printable version of this diagram is available from www.pearsoned.co.uk/lawexpressqa

Answer

The issue to discuss is the rules which the courts have adopted in order to determine when someone will be burdened with civil liability towards another private individual in tort when they have breached a statutory duty. These rules are important because as the quote suggests the matter is generally far from clear from the statute in question. This means that how the courts choose to interpret the statute and the factors which they consider when doing so is vital to any outcome. While the courts have consistently held this to be a matter of construction, it is argued that the actual decision in each case is influenced by policy considerations.

The leading case which sets out the framework of how the courts will approach the issue of construing Parliament's intention in relation to providing a private remedy in tort is **Lonrho Ltd v Shell Petroleum Co. Ltd (No. 2)** [1982] A.C. 173. The case concerned large losses suffered by Lonrho when it complied with a sanctions regime created by the Southern Rhodesia Act 1965. The subsequent legislative orders made it a criminal offence to supply oil to Rhodesia and outlined the punishment for non-compliance.[1] However, Lonrho's competitors did not comply with the order, which was the reason for Lonrho suffering losses. The question was whether, in the absence of an express provision of a civil remedy, the legislation could be construed as doing so.[2] Lord Diplock, giving the opinion for the House, noted it had been held since **Cutler v Wandsworth Stadium Ltd** [1949] A.C. 398 that the matter was one of construction of the legislation. His Lordship then proceeded to set out the process for undertaking such construction.

The starting point is always what the legislation states; however, as the quote by Lord du Parcq in **Cutler** shows,[3] Parliament regularly fails to the expressly cover the issue in the drafting of the legislation. Therefore, the general rule which has been developed by the courts and which was endorsed by Lord Diplock is that where the Act creates an obligation and specifies the manner for enforcement of that obligation, then the obligation cannot be enforced in any other way. This means that, where the legislation provides for a set of criminal sanctions in respect of a breach of the duty contained within the legislation, the duty cannot also be enforced in tort. The rationale for this is that Parliament has clearly considered the issue of enforcement and remedies for a breach and while not expressly ruling out a tortious action has expressly opted for another form of enforcement.[4] The same is also true where the breach of the statutory duty will give rise to remedies in administrative law.[5] For example, where the duty under the legislation is placed on a public authority, then an action in judicial review will exist. The courts thus see this action as the preferred

---

[1] Include this point in your outline of the facts, as the presence of the criminal sanctions was a factor which influenced the court's decision. Mentioning it now will tie in with your discussion of this factor later.

[2] Do not go into the exact details of the case. Remember: your aim here is just to set out the fact that this is the leading case and what the issue is.

[3] This allows you to relate your answer to the quote in the question, which in turn allows you to use the plea in the quote as the basis of your conclusion.

[4] It is important to explain the reasoning behind this. Use this reasoning as the basis of your analysis as to whether it is right for the courts to deny a party the chance of obtaining compensation.

[5] Include a discussion of this, as not all statutes will provide for criminal sanctions and so it is a different factor within the debate. This also allows you to get into the treatment of public authorities and discuss whether they should be protected from tort actions because of the possibility of administrative law remedies.

action rather than subjecting the public authority to a tortious action which could lead to a depletion of public funds for the operation of that authority. The authority will also see the costs of its operation rise, as they will need to take out insurance to cover the chance that a tortious action may lay against it. This threat of litigation can act as a stifling effect on the authority and so is considered against public policy.

However, in **Lonrho** two exceptions were cited by Lord Diplock. The first is where the statute is passed to protect a specified limited class, as opposed to the public generally. In determining this, the purpose of the statute is important. Just because a specified class is referred to, it does not automatically follow that it was passed for their protection. An example of this is **Cutler**[6] whereby the Betting and Lotteries Act 1934 provided that space be provided at dog tracks to bookmakers. However, it was held that the purpose of the Act was not to protect the livelihood of bookmakers but simply to regulate proceedings at dog tracks. Therefore, as Lord Browne-Wilkinson stated in **X v Bedfordshire C.C.** [1995] 2 A.C. 633, for the exception to apply it must be shown that the statute imposed a duty on someone for the protection of limited class and that Parliament intended to give members of that class a tort action for a breach of the duty.

The second exception is where the statute creates a right to be enjoyed by the general public. However, while this may seem contrary to the first exception, the crucial point is that then one of the public suffers 'particular, direct and substantial' damage (*per* Brett J in **Benjamin v Storr** (1874) L.R. 9 C.P. 400), which is different from the publicly generally. However, where these are welfare statutes implementing social policy, the duty is naturally going to be placed on a public authority. This brings into play the considerations discussed above regarding whether another branch of the law already provides a more suitable remedy, such as administrative law.[7] The right conferred under the duty is part of a wider public policy and not simply a private matter between the authority and the individual, and this is why there is a strong requirement to show damage beyond that suffered by others before the individual tortious right will arise. In **O'Rourke v Camden L.B.C.** [1998] A.C. 188, Lord Hoffmann also noted that the wide discretion given to authorities under such social welfare legislation means that Parliament would have been aware

[6]Using an example at this point demonstrates your knowledge of that case but also strengthens your explanation of how the exception operates and what is required for it.

[7]By stating that the previous material applied here you will not need to repeat that part of your answer. The marker will already have read your points on the matter. This allows you to then focus on additional points which relate directly to this exception.

[8]It is beneficial to highlight this, particularly if you are adopting the argument that this answer does. If you have time before you start your conclusion, you could use this point as the basis of a penultimate paragraph and explore the positive impact that policy can have in more detail.

[9]Obviously, if you are criticising how something works, you should offer an opinion on how it can be rectified. This is particularly important if there are published proposals for reform, as otherwise it may indicate your lack of knowledge.

there could be errors of judgment and thus unlikely to see these lead to tortious liability.

Therefore, while there is a clear general rule, the exceptions to it create uncertainty in the matter. This uncertainty arises because there is no set formula as to when a case will be deemed to be within the exception and because of the heavy influence of public policy factors. This is why Williams (1960), among other academics, has dismissed the process as fiction, one of looking for something which is not there. While this helps employees in industrial situations (such as cases under the Factories Acts), it could be said to be unfair on the employer and creates an artificial liability.[8] The reform proposals[9] of the Law Commission should be adopted and so a presumption of a civil right will exist unless the Act contains clear words to the contrary. This will force Parliament to fully consider the implications of imposing a duty under the legislation and decide what the consequences of a breach should be. This will create certainty and reduce the financial burdens of litigation and insurance, particularly in light of the growing number of regulatory statutes which create duties on parties.

 Make your answer stand out

- Read academic articles such as that by Glanville Williams (1960) 'The effect of penal legislation in the law of tort', 23 M.L.R. 233 to obtain some depth as to the criticisms of the current process.

- Look at Law Commission (1969) Report No. 21, 'The interpretation of statutes' to be able to provide a fuller explanation of what they proposed.

- Contrast these arguments by also reading R. A. Buckley (1984) 'Liability in tort for breach of statutory duty', 100 L.Q.R. 204, who argues that the Law Commission reform proposal would not have resolved all of the problems of the process.

- Explore further how policy can be seen as the basis for finding a civil action in industrial cases and consider whether this is fair.

! Don't be tempted to ...

- Get tied down in the specific facts of *Lonrho*. Remember you are just setting up the issue to discuss by mentioning the case. There were other issues in the case which are relevant to your discussion.

- Go into detail about the other questions which the court must consider after determining whether the Act in question permits a civil action in tort. You could touch on these at the end, but remember that the question is focused on the issue of construction of the statutory wording.

- List a whole load of case examples where a tort action was found to exist or not. Stick to what the rules are for dealing with the issue and what factors are considered. You need to evaluate these using case examples where necessary to support your argument. An excessive amount of facts from cases will have a negative impact on your structure.

Occupiers' liability

How this topic may come up in exams

This topic is an extension of the tort of negligence. However, it has its own self-contained statutory framework governing when a duty will arise, and so you need to be careful to recognise whether a problem question is concerned with normal negligence or occupiers' liability. In the question look at premises which are controlled by one of the parties. Although the situations when the duty of care arises differ, some aspects are the same, notably causation and remoteness. The Acts do not have many sections, but what is needed is located in specific subsections so ensure you know these. Problem questions are more common than essays. However, when the question is an essay, it tends to focus on whether the legislation is necessary and/or whether it achieves the right balance between the parties in terms of burden and protection.

■ Attack the question

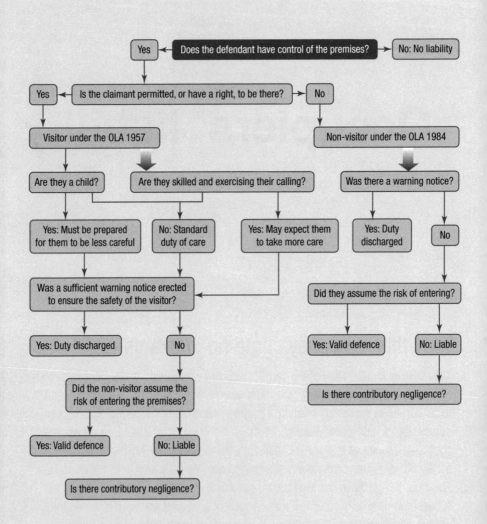

❓ Question 1

Hubert has gone to his council-owned local park with his 7-year-old brother, Cornelius. One of the main attractions of the park is an outdoor swimming pool at its centre.

Owing to the hot weather, and the fact that it is quiet, Hubert decides to have a swim; as children are not allowed in the pool, he tells Cornelius to wait where he is while he does so. However, after five minutes, Cornelius becomes bored and noticing a newly installed playground goes off to play on the slide.

Owing to financial restraints, the council had to build the slide cheaply. They employed the firm who tendered the lowest amount – Cowboy Construction Ltd. Because of the financial restraints, the council did not check to see the quality of their previous work and took at face value their claim that they had in fact undertaken such a project. Cowboy Construction Ltd had actually never built children's playgrounds and so made up what they were doing as they went along. This meant the slide was very unstable which an adult would have appreciated. When Cornelius reached the top, the extra weight sent the slide crashing down, resulting in Cornelius suffering a broken leg.

Advise the council as to their potential liability under the occupiers' liability legislation.

Answer plan

→ Identify the status of Cornelius and which Act applies to him.

→ State what the extent of the duty of care is under the Act.

→ Consider whether this is modified owing to Cornelius' age.

→ Evaluate the significance of the danger being created by an independent contractor.

→ Consider if the council may have any other defences to Cornelius' claim.

Diagram plan

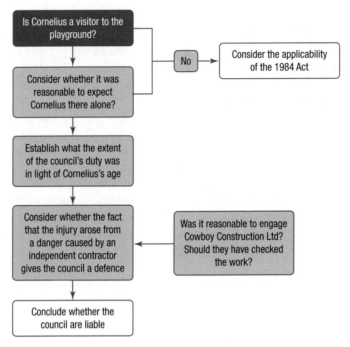

A printable version of this diagram is available from www.pearsoned.co.uk/lawexpressqa

Answer

[1]Do not wait to show that you have identified which Act is most relevant to the facts.

[2]Show early on that you appreciate the purpose and the scope of the Act and use this to provide the context to the issue which you have identified.

[3]Similarly, show that you know what the key issues in the Act are in relation to the question.

The council require advice as to the applicability of the Occupiers' Liability Act 1957[1] to the current situation. The applicability of the Act is important as it imposes liability for controllers of premises towards those who are injured while on those premises, and provides for greater care towards children.[2] It will be argued that the council will have owed Cornelius a duty of care and that they are unlikely to be able to rely on the work of the contractors[3] to discharge this duty.

Liability under the Act is only imposed on occupiers of premises. While not defined within the Act, it has been held to mean the person who has such control of premises that they should realise that want of care on their part may lead to injury to those coming to the premises (**Wheat v E. Lacon Co. Ltd** [1966] A.C. 552. As

[4]While this may seem an obvious point, it is important that you advise the council on it and establish that they will be the occupier for the purposes of any claim. By doing so you also show that you have knowledge of the point.

the council own the park, and therefore, the playground, they would clearly have control of the premises.[4]

The first issue to establish is whether Cornelius would be owed a duty under the Act, creating a claim. For this he would need to be classed as a 'visitor' to the premises. This term covers anyone who is permitted by the occupier to be on the premises. The fact that we are told that the playground is for children and is within the park suggests that, in the absence of any age or entry time restrictions which are broken by Cornelius, he would be deemed to be an invitee and thus a visitor under the Act (s.1(2)).

As the council are likely to owe a duty of care, they need to be advised next on the extent of that duty. Under s.2(2) this is to take such care as is reasonable in the circumstances to ensure that Cornelius is safe while using the playground in a manner which is permitted. As we are told that Cornelius was using the slide in the normal manner, there is nothing to suggest that he was using the playground in a way which would take him outside of his permission for being there.[5] Therefore, as the slide was unsafe for normal usage, it is clear that the council have breached their duty to ensure Cornelius's safety while using the playground.

[5]It is important that you illustrate this; otherwise, your argument is unsubstantiated on what could be a key point in assessing the council's liability.

[6]Where the facts are too vague to give a more concrete answer as here, discuss both possibilities and if need be tell them that more information is needed. Remember they are your client, so this would be a valid comment rather than giving them an inaccurate picture. You should give them some idea, though.

The council might argue that the danger of the slide would have been noticeable to an adult and that Cornelius should not have been there alone. However, two points can be raised against this assertion. Firstly, following **Phipps v Rochester Corp** [1955] 1 Q.B. 450, in such a situation it must be determined whether the council could reasonably have expected Cornelius's unaccompanied presence. More information is needed here and evidence will need to be gathered as to the extent that children did use the playground unaccompanied.[6] If this was the case, the council would need to demonstrate that they took steps to prevent it from occurring. However, displaying notices saying that children must be accompanied at all times may not suffice, as the playground could be deemed as an allurement[7] to children. This would mean that Cornelius would remain a visitor and thus, owed a duty through implied permission (**Jolley v Sutton B.C.** [2000] 1 W.L.R. 1082), even if certain entry requirements were displayed but not complied with. This is because the issue must be viewed in light of s.2(3)(a) which provides that the council must be prepared for children to

[7]You could discuss this above when you discuss whether Cornelius is a visitor. If you do, then take care to ensure that you do not repeat yourself.

[8]You have been given Cornelius's age in the facts for a reason, so use them to build up the strength of your argument.

be less careful than adults. This would relate to not only spotting dangers but also appreciating any warnings. Therefore, as a 7-year-old,[8] they should expect Cornelius not to have noticed that which an adult would. In view of Cornelius's age and the nature of the premises in question, it would seem likely that the council not only owed a duty but breached it, particularly if there were no entry restrictions. In light of the playground being new, guardians are less likely to anticipate any danger as it would be reasonable to expect it would be safe before opening it to children.

[9]Show your understanding of the subsection by paraphrasing the wording, and then to aid your structure break it down into the individual components and apply them to the council in turn.

However, the council should be advised that they may have a defence of having discharged their duty because the injury resulted from a danger caused by an independent contractor. Under s.2(4) the occupier is not to be treated as answerable, without more, for danger where it is caused by the faulty construction work of an independent contractor and it was reasonable in the circumstances to use the contractor.[9] The council should be advised that where the work, here the construction of the playground, requires special skill and equipment which they do not posses, then it will be reasonable to engage the contractor (**Maguire v Sefton M.B.C.** [2006] E.W.C.A. Civ. 560. This would seem applicable to the situation here; however, the council should be advised that the subsection goes on to state that the occupier may also have to have taken reasonable steps to ensure that the contractor was competent for the task, and the work was properly done. This would be a reasonable step here, as it would be clear that failure to check the quality of the work would pose a danger to users of the playground. As we are told that an adult would notice the slide was dangerous and yet the playground was open, it is clear the work was not checked upon completion by the council. This, when combined with the fact that although the council inquired as to their competency they did not verify the information, would suggest that the council will likely be held to have not discharged their duty.

[10]As this is still an aspect of negligence, do not forget to touch on these issues.

In conclusion, the council will have owed Cornelius a duty of care, and their failure to check the competency of Cowboy Construction Ltd and the quality of the work upon completion will result in them being in breach of that duty. There do not appear to be any issues of causation or remoteness[10] and, therefore, the council should be advised that they will be liable for Cornelius' injury. They should be further advised that even if Cornelius was not deemed to be a visitor

[11]Depending on how long you have left, you could include this within your main body and expand upon it.

under the 1957 Act, they could well be liable under the 1984 Act as a non-visitor.[11] The slide was in a dangerous state and they arguably had reasonable grounds to know this, as it had been constructed by a firm whose work had not been checked. There would also be reasonable grounds to believe that unaccompanied children may go on the slide and, owing to the nature of the danger, it was a risk which was reasonable for them to protect against.

✓ Make your answer stand out

- Highlight the possibility of a claim against the council in common law negligence.
- Explain why children are afforded more protection, using some of the judicial comment in *Phipps*.
- Use the facts of the question as much as possible to build and support your argument.
- Use academic opinion from your reading as well to support your interpretation of the facts, particularly where you do not have a case authority, such as with regards to the need for the council to check the work of Cowboy Construction Ltd.

! Don't be tempted to …

- Discuss s.2(3)(b) and the issue of the duty owed to skilled workers; it is not relevant to the specific issue of the question and you would be just be indicating that you have not fully understood the question.
- Avoid alternating between both Occupiers' Liability Acts. If you think that the 1984 Act may be applicable, or want to discuss it for completeness, do so at the end once you have advised the council fully on the 1957 Act or you will lose your structure.

? Question 2

Frank is a singer who is permitted to use the hall of his local social club to practise. Recently his 10-year-old brother, Sammy, came to stay with him. Because Sammy hopes to be a singer when he is older, Frank took him to the social club to let him listen to him practise. The entrance to the social club has a large notice stating that after 6 p.m. no children are allowed inside. Arriving at 6:08 p.m. Frank saw the sign and thought that it would be alright. As they entered, Frank waived to the barman and owner, Dean, who waived back but did not remark on Sammy's presence; it turned out that he did not see Sammy enter.

During his practice, the fire alarm sounded and Dean shouted for everyone to leave the premises, so Frank and Sammy headed for the exit. However, Frank then turned around and said that it would be some kids playing a prank as 'they always do it'. Sammy took his lead from his brother and followed him back to the hall. Wanting to get back to his practice, Frank walked back towards the hall; however, Dean, who had started cleaning the premises before the alarm went off, had left a large puddle of water in the corridor to the hall. Frank did not notice and slipped, severely injuring his back. Sammy panicked and ran for help but in doing so tripped over some loose floorboards near the exit and dislocated his knee.

Advise Frank and Sammy.

Answer plan

→ Take Frank first and establish whether he is a visitor under the 1957 Act.

→ Explain the extent of the duty under the Act.

→ Assess whether Frank does anything to alter his visitor status before he is injured.

→ If so, evaluate whether the 1984 Act is applicable to his situation.

→ Outline the extent of the duty and evaluate whether it was breached.

→ Consider any defences Dean may have.

→ Highlight how Sammy is a non-visitor under the 1984 Act.

→ Repeat the final three points in relation to Frank.

Diagram plan

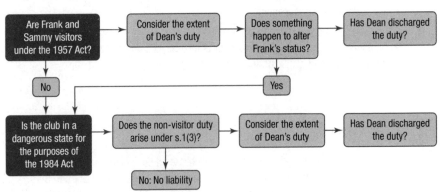

A printable version of this diagram is available from www.pearsoned.co.uk/lawexpressqa

Answer

The issue to be determined is whether Frank and Sammy have an action against Dean for the injuries that they have suffered while on his premises. Both need advice as to any potential claim under either the Occupiers' Liability Act 1957 (the 1957 Act)[1] in relation to lawful visitors to premises, or the Occupiers' Liability Act 1984 (the 1984 Act) which governs injuries to non-visitors.[2] Which Act applies is important, as the law provides far greater protection for visitors. It will be argued that events prior to their injuries mean that both will be viewed as non-visitors to the premises; however, while Frank may be owed a limited duty by Dean, Sammy will be unsuccessful in any claim.

Firstly, it should be established that any action will lie against Dean as occupier of the premises. 'Occupier' is not defined in either statute; however, under **Wheat *v* E. Lacon Co. Ltd** [1966] A.C. 552, occupiers are those with such control over the premises that they should realise that want of care on their part may lead to injury to those coming to the premises; as the owner, Dean would have such control.[3]

Regarding Frank, the first issue to determine is whether he was owed a duty of care under the 1957 Act by being a 'visitor'. This term is also not defined in the Act; however, s.1(2) does provide that it covers the common law terms of 'invitee' and 'licensee'. Therefore, anyone who is lawfully on the premises will be a visitor; this covers Frank as he is permitted to use the hall to practise.

The extent of Dean's duty under s.2(2)[4] is to ensure that he takes such care to ensure that in all the circumstances Frank is safe while using the premises for purposes for which he is allowed. Significantly, this indicates that the duty only extends to ensuring safety during permitted activities. However, Frank suffered his injury after he had been told to leave the hall because of the fire alarm. Therefore, the injury was caused at a time when Frank was not permitted to be there, and so the duty under the 1957 Act will not apply to Frank.[5] Therefore, the 1984 Act must be looked at.

The 1984 Act provides that a duty will be owed to non-visitors for the risk of injury by way of the dangerous state of the premises or

Margin notes

[1] Abbreviate the name of the statutes to save yourself time, but make sure you shorten it to something which still distinguishes the two Acts.

[2] This sentence indicates to your examiner that you have identified the specific area of tort which the question is concerned with straight away, particularly as the question does not highlight this for you.

[3] Make sure that you use the facts of the question to illustrate, and support, your argument as to the position of the parties.

[4] While you should always give your authority for statements of law, it is particularly important in a statute-based tort that you constantly refer to which part of the Act deals with the point in question in order to demonstrate your knowledge and give strength to your answer.

[5] Although the Act is unlikely to apply to Frank, you should still highlight what the duty is to illustrate your knowledge, but keep it brief unless you feel that it would still be applicable in which case you can go into a bit more depth.

[6]Although paragraph (a), and also paragraph (b) within the subsection discuss reasonable belief as an alternative to actually knowing, as the latter is actually the case in the scenario do not feel the need to explain the full extent of the paragraph.

[7]As this indicates you are not dealing with a normal situation, use this to evaluate the situation rather than just assuming Dean will owe a duty.

[8]If you phrase the start of this paragraph like this, it flows better from the previous paragraph and makes sense why you are proceeding when there could be doubt as to whether the duty even arises.

[9]Even though you are not dealing with the 1957 Act directly, try to contrast the positions to show your understanding of each.

by things done on them or omitted to be done (s.1(1)). The danger here was the puddle left in the corridor. Frank should be advised that in order for a duty to be owed under s.1(3), Dean would need to be aware[6] of the puddle, which he would be as he was mopping the floor. Dean would then need to know that Frank was in the vicinity of the danger. As Dean allows Frank to use the hall and waved when he entered the club, he would know that Frank would be using the corridor to get to and from the hall. Finally, the risk of slipping over the water must be one which in all the circumstances he may be reasonably expected to offer protection from. Normally, a wet floor would be such a danger, but owing to the fire alarm the position may be different.[7] It could be deemed reasonable to have just ensured everyone was out of the building rather than erecting a wet floor sign which would be common practice. However, while Dean was mopping, he should have already erected a sign and therefore, regardless of the alarm, it was a risk Dean should have protected against.

On the basis that s.1(3) is satisfied,[8] the next issue is the extent of the duty owed to Frank. Under s.1(4) the duty is to take such care as is reasonable in the circumstances to ensure that injury does not occur through that danger; it is clear that Frank was injured owing to the danger in question. However, this will turn on whether a sign was erected initially. Under s. 1(5) the duty may be discharged by a warning notice, and Frank should be advised that unlike under the 1957 Act the warning just needs to highlight the danger and not ensure safety.[9] The fact that Frank was not rushing back down the corridor suggests that he would have noticed a sign if present. He should be informed that if one was erected and yet he continued down the corridor, Dean could also successfully rely on the defence of assumption of risk within s.1(6). Even if a warning was not provided, Frank's claim may still fail as a warning is not required where the danger is objectively obvious and the claimant is deemed to have assumed the risk under s.1(6) (**Sidorn v Patel** [2007] E.W.H.C. 1248). However, it is questionable whether this danger was objectively obvious, even if equipment such as the mop and bucket were visible. Therefore, Frank should be advised that his claim should succeed in the absence of a warning notice by Dean.

Regarding Sammy, it is clear that as children were not permitted after 6 p.m. his situation can only fall within the 1984 Act.

10From the facts we are told
that Dean did not see Sammy,
so use this to support how
there is no chance of Sammy
being able to argue that he
was a visitor.

Although nothing was said when Sammy entered, any argument based on an implied licence will fail as Dean had not noticed him enter.[10] The dangerous state of the premises, required for a duty to be owed will be satisfied by the loose floorboards near the exit.

In determining whether Sammy is owed a duty under s.1(3), whether it is unlikely that Dean was not aware of the loose floorboards, as their location suggests that their looseness would have become apparent. Their location also means it is a danger from which it is reasonable to expect protection. However, the duty is determined by the reference to the likely presence of the actual non-visitor in the vicinity of the danger at the time and place of the danger to him (**Ratcliffe v McConnell** [1999] 1 W.L.R. 670). Therefore, establishing that Dean had reasonable grounds to know that Sammy was in vicinity at that time will be difficult. As children were not permitted after 6 p.m., it is hard to see how Dean would know that a child would be in the vicinity at the time Sammy was injured. As it was close to 6 p.m., and the danger was at the exit, it could be reasonable to expect children leaving the club to be in the vicinity. This will require evidence of children being in the club beforehand. However, Dean did not know Sammy was in the club, and in any event prior to the injury everyone was told to leave because of the fire alarm. Therefore, notwithstanding that child non-visitors are given more protection than adults ones, Dean would not owe Sammy a duty in this case.

In conclusion, Frank will have a successful claim if there was no warning sign about the warning, but Sammy will be unsuccessful as Dean would not have owed him a duty of care.

✓ Make your answer stand out

- Highlight how they may still have a claim in common law negligence even if unsuccessful under the occupiers' liability legislation.
- Provide some context to the 1984 Act and some depth as to how it differs.
- Use *Donoghue* v *Folkestone Properties Ltd* [2003] E.W.C.A. Civ. 231 to explain the relationship between s.1(3) and (4) of the 1984 Act.

> **!** Don't be tempted to ...
>
> - Go into depth on the common law definitions of the terms, as they are not really issues in the question.
> - Show your full range of knowledge by being too descriptive about both Acts and outlining provisions which are not relevant to the issues.

 Question 3

'Following the introduction of the Occupiers' Liability Acts 1957 and 1984, the previous distinctions made between different entrants no longer exist. All entrants receive a high level of protection regardless of their status.'

Critically evaluate the accuracy of this statement.

> **Answer plan**
>
> → Outline the position that the common law took prior to the 1957 Act being passed.
> → Explain the aim and scope of the 1957 Act, evaluating its provisions and how they are applied by the courts.
> → Analyse the gaps the Act left in the protection of individuals and why there was a need for the 1984 Act.
> → Contrast the scope and provisions of the 1984 Act to the 1957 Act.
> → Evaluate the extent that it fills the gaps left by the 1957 Act.
> → Conclude with an assessment of the validity of the statement.

Diagram plan

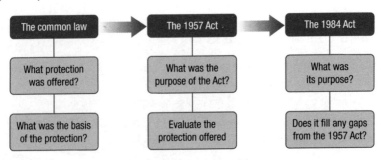

A printable version of this diagram is available from www.pearsoned.co.uk/lawexpressqa

Answer

This issue requires looking at the occupiers' liability legislation of 1957 and 1984 in order to assess whether their purposes have been achieved. Primarily this was to remove the complexities which existed at common law to provide sufficient protection for all. It will be argued that while the 1957 Act did so, it also merely created new issues which required the 1984 Act. However, inequality of protection remains.

Prior to the 1957 Act, the common law imposed a duty on occupiers, the extent of which varied depending on the classification given to the individual injured while on the premises. The classification of entrants ranged from contractual entrants, those on the premises due to a contract with the occupier, to trespassers. In between were invitees and licensees, namely those to whom the occupier gave an invitation or permission to enter the premises. Although similar, invitees were distinguished by having a common interest with the occupier for being on the premises, such as customers. This meant invitees were more protected, which created complexities and caused the Law Commission, in their 1954 report, to call for its abolition as the distinction was artificial.[1]

The 1954 Report led to the 1957 Act which created a common duty of care to be owed by all occupiers. The Act's primary purpose was, therefore, to simplify the law and create certainty as to when a duty would arise and what it would entail.[2] Section 1(2) adopted the meaning of 'occupier' from the common law, namely the person who has sufficient control over the premises so that they ought to realise that a failure of care on their part may lead to injury to another (**Wheat v E. Lacon Co. Ltd** [1966] A.C. 552). The difference was the application of this duty which is owed to all lawful visitors, meaning anyone not a trespasser at common law (s.1(2)). Therefore, the difficulties of ascertaining the category of visitor were generally removed, as was the uncertainty as to what level of duty would be imposed. However, naturally, those trespassers at common law still lacked protection unless the injury was caused from deliberate intentional acts of the occupier or acts which were done with reckless disregard for the trespassers' presence (**Addie v Dumbreck** [1929] A.C. 358. No protection was given from negligent acts, as the view

[1] The point which you should be trying to convey here is the need for the legislative reforms and setting up what the purpose of the 1957 Act was. You will then need to contrast that purpose to the 1984 Act in order to justify the distinction which has been retained later in your answer.

[2] For the purposes of fully answering the question, it is important that you highlight what the Act was trying to do. This is because this will influence your concluding arguments on the state of the law, namely that both Acts sought, on policy grounds, to build in a distinction between the levels of protection offered.

[3]Naturally, building from the previous comments you then need to explain what the policy reason is.

[4]It is important that you evaluate the merits of the Act and its consequences; otherwise, you risk just having a description of it and you will lose the thread of the argument which would otherwise run through your answer.

[5]This is why *Jolley* is a good case to give as an example here; as opposed to other famous cases such as *Phipps v Rochester Corp* [1955] 1 Q.B. 450 and *Glasgow Corp v Muir* [1943] A.C. 448. It allows you to argue whether this was just a pre-1984 issue.

[6]Link the different aspects of your answer together to give the aspect in question more strength.

[7]You could simply move from the previous paragraph into the 1984 Act, but by referring briefly to *Herrington* you demonstrate your awareness of the main impetus behind the need for the Act.

was taken that trespassers came onto the premises at their own risk.[3]

While the 1957 Act achieved its primary purpose of resolving difficulties over whether someone was an invitee or licensee, it simply created a new problem over who was a visitor, especially regarding children.[4] Although no express permission has been given to a child to enter the premises, a duty may be owed if it can be said that the premises allured them on to it so that there was implied permission. This is illustrated by **Jolley v Sutton L.B.C.** [2000] 1 W.L.R 1082, where a rotting boat on the defendant's land was held to be an attractive plaything for children, and in light of its accessibility meant permission to go on the boat was implied. The relative recentness suggests that the 1984 Act has not completely removed the need for the courts to undertake such an exercise.[5] This was the reasoning previously in order to protect people who would otherwise be left without redress. The issue is perhaps complicated by the fact that the term 'trespasser' covered such a wide range of people, from children who had wandered onto the land to those with criminal intent.

The duty applies to all visitors and is to take such care as is reasonable in the circumstances to ensure that the visitor is reasonably safe using the premises for the purpose for which they are permitted to be there (s.2(2)). However, this shows that once the visitor is acting in a manner at odds with their permission for being there, they are no longer protected under the Act. The Act also allows the occupier to alter his duty through contract, albeit now subject to UCTA 1977, and makes some allowance for the type of visitor. Under s.2(3) the occupier can expect those on the premises exercising their trade to guard against the risks associated with that calling. Conversely, they must expect children to exercise less care than adults. Although seeming justifiable, coupled with the readiness to find implied licences for children,[6] it loses justification. A greater burden is created towards people who arguably should not be on their premises, particularly without supervision.

The matter came to a head with **British Railway Board v Herrington** [1972] A.C. 877 where a duty was found towards a boy injured taking a shortcut, through two dilapidated fences, over a railway line. The decision was unanimous but the judicial opinions lacked clarity as to when the duty would arise and its extent.[7] This led to the Law

[8]By explaining the point of the Act, you highlight the inaccuracy of the statement, as it was not intended to offer the same protection as the 1957 Act on policy grounds.

[9]Put these in a separate paragraph so that the analysis and evaluation that you offer previously does not get lost in the detail.

[10]As the premise of the statement is that there is equal protection, take every opportunity to highlight the discrepancy in protection.

[11]Start your conclusion with a definitive statement as to overall answer to the sentiment expressed in the statement and then proceed to summarise why you have reached that view.

Commission producing another report in 1976. Their recommendations formed the basis of the 1984 Act, which provides when a duty is owed to trespassers and sought to achieve a better balance of not burdening occupiers too much in respect of trespassers while offering protection when injury occurs through the fault of the occupier.[8]

Section 1(1) provides that a duty is owed to non-visitors in respect of injuries suffered while on the premises by reason of a danger arising from things done or omitted to be done on the premises. Therefore, the 1984 Act straight away can be seen to afford less protection, as visitors are owed a duty even where the premises are non-dangerous. Even then, the requirements of s.1(3) must be satisfied for the duty to arise.

These are[9] that the occupier is aware of the danger or has reasonable grounds to believe it exists; he knows or has reasonable grounds to believe the other, regardless of lawful authority, is in the vicinity of the danger, or may come within it; and the risk is one which, in the circumstances, it is reasonable to expect him to protect the other from. If satisfied, the duty is to take such care as is reasonable in the circumstances to see that injury from that danger does not occur. There is no duty for injury by other means and so again this duty is of lesser extent than that afforded to visitors.[10]

Therefore, the statement is inaccurate in saying a distinction is no longer made.[11] This distinction between visitors and non-visitors is less acute following the 1984 Act, as non-visitors have more protection than previously and so there is some accuracy in the statement's suggestion. However, this protection is far less extensive than that given to visitors. As such, the premise of the statement that high-level protection is given regardless of the person's status is ultimately flawed.

✓ **Make your answer stand out**

■ Look at both Law Commission Reports:
  – Third Report: Occupiers' Liability to Invitees, Licensees and Trespassers.
  – Report on Liability for Damage or Injury to Trespassers and Related Questions of Occupiers' Liability.
■ Look at some of the provisions such as in relation to discharging the duty, to further show how a distinction is made between the protection offered based on the status of the visitor.

! Don't be tempted to ...

■ Dwell too long on the common law position; simply use it as a foundation to lead into your discussion of the 1957 Act.

■ Go into great depth as to the provision of each statute. The question is focused on you evaluating the difference in the level of protection, therefore, avoid simply describing what each says: instead, contrast the two.

10

Trespass to land

How this topic may come up in exams

Trespass to land is a rather small and uncomplicated area and, as such, means that essay questions are rare. However, you could be asked about the need for the tort and the role it plays in the wider context of how tort protects interests in land. As for problem questions, it is common to find an element of trespass to land combined with other torts such as trespass to the person, nuisance or perhaps even occupiers' liability. Always check to see whether there is an aspect of someone entering another's land without permission or acting in a manner which is inconsistent with their permission.

■ Attack the question

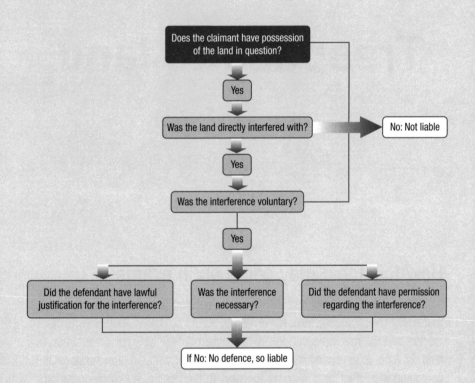

A printable version of this diagram is available from www.pearsoned.co.uk/lawexpressqa

❓ Question 1

John recently bought a large country manor house but, in order to help contribute to the running costs, has decided to allow visitors to enter the estate and view the Japanese water-garden feature. Visitors must pay to enter and are only allowed to enter and exit the through the south gate to the garden. At the gate a large sign states that conditions of entry include no picnics and no taking of photos.

Nicola has paid to visit the garden but as she is about the leave, she sees that there is another gate to the north side which she realises will bring her out nearer her car. As she exits via this gate, it brings her out into an area of grass where John is sunbathing. Outraged at being disturbed, John launches into a verbal tirade at Nicola who runs back through the water garden and the long way to her car.

To make sure that she has left his premises, John wanders into the garden and sees Marina and Charles having a picnic by a fountain with a camera on the blanket. John recognises them as a couple whom he has repeatedly told about the conditions of entry and so demands that they leave.

John goes back to his sunbathing, but is then disturbed by a plane, from the local flying school, flying overhead. John is concerned that this may be a regular occurrence.

Finally, later that evening Chris, Nicola's outraged boyfriend, goes round to the estate. Although he never actually entered the premises, he launched a rock into the water garden. The rock lands in a flower arrangement crushing all of the flowers.

Advise John of these events and what action he may take under the tort of trespass to land.

Answer plan

→ Define what is meant by trespass to land.

→ Establish that John has possession of the land so that he may bring a claim.

→ Examine whether each action complained of was voluntarily directed at the land.

→ Consider any possible justification for the interference.

→ Advise John as to what remedy he should seek.

Diagram plan

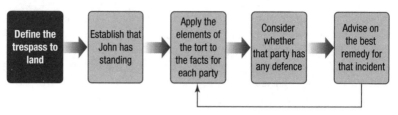

A printable version of this diagram is available from www.pearsoned.co.uk/lawexpressqa

Answer

[1] You will not be expected to put a full reference in your answer but you should try to put some information down, such as the year if it is a book or the journal abbreviation if it is a journal.

The question requires advising John as to several aspects of trespass to land and the potential remedies he may seek as a result to the actions which have occurred. Trespass to land is defined by Winfield and Jolowicz (Rogers 2010)[1] as the unjustifiable interference with the possession of land, and John should be advised that it is actionable without any proof of damage. This is important in this scenario, as apart from the flowers there would not appear to have been any damage to John's land, merely disturbance. It will be argued that John is likely to have an actionable claim against the other individuals but not against the flying school.

[2] Clearly, it would not be much of a question if John did not have standing to bring a claim, but for completeness you should demonstrate your knowledge of the point.

The first issue to be determined is that John can actually bring a claim for trespass.[2] Although a lawful estate is not required, physical presence on the land is insufficient to bring a claim; there must be actual possession. As this is a house which John has purchased and uses for sunbathing,[3] it would appear that John does have possession. John now needs to be advised as to the elements of trespass[4] in order to establish whether he has a claim against each party. As Nicola, Charles and Marina are actually present on the land, they shall be dealt with first.[5]

[3] Use the facts of the question to support why he will have possession and thus standing.

[4] As the question does not have any element of trespass to the person, you can shorten the name of the tort, as there is no need to distinguish it from trespass to the person.

The first element of trespass is that the interference must be direct and immediate. This is clearly satisfied with regard to Nicola[6] as she has been visiting the water garden and was on his land when he confronted her. The next element is that the interference was intentional. Again, this is clearly satisfied as Nicola intended to be in the water garden. John should be advised that, having bought a ticket to enter the water garden, Nicola does have a valid defence

[5] As the aircraft and Chris relate to specific aspects of trespass to land not concerning direct physical contact with the land, deal with them separately.

[6] As Nicola is a more straightforward application of the elements whereas Charles and Marina have a particular focus, deal with them separately.

as a ticket constitutes permission to be in the garden. The issue is obviously whether there is an actionable trespass by Nicola entering the other garden. Clearly, the permission to enter the water garden did not extend to this area as a condition of the contract to enter the garden was that entry and exit is via the south gate only. John should be advised that if Nicola were to argue that she did not, however, intend to trespass on to the grass where he was sunbathing, this would be irrelevant as it must be the act of entry which is intended, which it clearly was as Nicola intended to take a short cut. Even a mistaken entry amounts to trespass (**Conway v George Wimpey & Co. Ltd** [1951] 2 K.B. 266), therefore, as Nicola directly, immediately and intentionally entered the other garden without permission, this would constitute a trespass. Damages would be awarded even though it was a momentary interference.

In relation to Charles and Marina, John should be advised that as with Nicola there is clearly an immediate, direct and intentional inter-ference with his land as they have voluntarily entered the grounds to have a picnic. Although, unlike Nicola, they have stayed within the area for which their ticket allows them, at first glance it would appear that there is justifiable interference as they have a contractual licence to be there. However, John should be advised that where a licence is given to someone, conditions can be attached. This has occurred here as conditions of entry and, therefore, conditions for obtaining a licence to be there, are that visitors to the water garden cannot have picnics and photography is prohibited. The presence of these conditions also indicate that even though Charles and Marina have a contractual licence, it can be revoked without John himself being in breach of contract.[7] As Charles and Marina have broken these conditions, their presence in the garden is inconsistent with their permission to be there and so this will be a trespass. John should, however, be advised that normally where a licence is revoked, the licensee must be given a reasonable time to collect their goods and leave (**Cornish v Stubbs** (1870) L.R. 5 C.P. 334). Thus, there would be no action against the pair unless they took an unreasonably long time to leave. However, as their entry was in breach of the entry conditions, this will be deemed to be a trespass from the moment that they entered John's property. Additionally, as we are told that this is a case of repeated trespass as they continually breach the

[7]Although clearly not an issue of the question, you should show your wider knowledge of the related areas to trespass as you are advising an individual, and in real life this may be an issue for the individual.

entry conditions, John should be advised that for a remedy he may want to seek a permanent injunction rather than just merely damages.[8]

The next issue to advise John on is that of the plane causing him disturbance by flying over his land. John should be advised that there is a property law maxim that a person who owns the land owns the air up to the heavens as well, and as such an intrusion into a person's airspace, even where minor, can constitute a trespass (**Kelsen v Imperial Tobacco Co** [1957] 2 Q.B. 334). However, the right to claim for a trespass of the airspace is restricted at both common law through **Bernstein v Skyviews & General Ltd** [1978] Q.B. 479 and s. 76(1) of the Civil Aviation Act 1982. John should be advised that, provided the plane is flying at a height above that which is required for normal use of the land, there will not be a trespass. This restriction is justified in the interests of the wider society as otherwise civil aviation would ground to a halt and people could not benefit from air travel.[9] John should be advised, however, that under s.76(2), in the event[10] his land has suffered any material damage from something, or someone, falling from the aircraft, he would have an action for that damage.

The final issue to advise John over is the damage to the flowers from Chris throwing the rock. John should be advised that the fact that Chris does not enter his land will not prevent an action for trespass as the longstanding authority of **Smith v Stone** (1647) Style 65 held that throwing a stone onto another's land will suffice. The fact that we are told that Chris did this due to his 'outrage' over the abuse that Nicola suffered suggests that this was clearly an intentional act directed against John's land, which cannot be justified.[11] Chris does not have any defence and so John would be successful in obtaining damages. There would seem to be no reason for an injunction at this time.

To conclude, it would appear that John has an actionable claim for trespass against Nicola, Charles, Marina and Chris, but it is unlikely he will have a claim against the flying school unless the plane was flying at an unreasonable height.

Make your answer stand out

- Show that you are aware that there may be other issues which John should be aware of, such as breach of contract and nuisance.
- Explain in detail how John may get an injunction if he wanted one.

 Don't be tempted to …

- Get drawn into a long discussion over nuisance or privacy issues, as the question tells you just to advise John on trespass to land.
- Just assume that John is eligible to bring an action or gloss over this requirement that needs to be satisfied.

Question 2

'The tort of trespass to land imposes liability on an individual even where the claimant suffers no harm. In view of the many other ways of protecting an individual's interest in land, the tort is not needed and cannot be justified.'

Discuss what is required for liability under the tort of trespass to land and evaluate the need for such a tort.

Answer plan

- → Define what is meant by trespass to land.
- → Explain the role and purpose of the tort and whether it is needed.
- → Outline what the requirements are to establish liability.
- → Assess whether these requirements satisfactorily fulfil the purpose of the tort and are justifiable requirements.
- → Evaluate whether its role could be covered by another tort.

Diagram plan

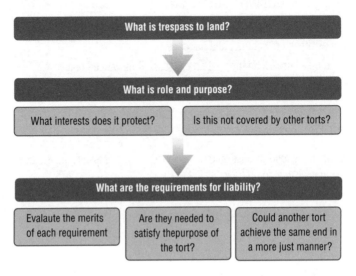

A printable version of this diagram is available from www.pearsoned.co.uk/lawexpressqa

Answer

The issue to determine is whether the tort of trespass to land imposes unjustifiable liability on individuals as they do not need to cause damage to the land for liability to ensue. If the basis of the tort is indeed unjustifiable, then calls for the tort to be abandoned as in the statement have merit. Such a move would be significant as trespass is the only tort protecting land interests which is actionable *per se*. It will be argued that while other torts do offer similar protection, it is the fact that trespass is actionable *per se* which is the justification, as this reflects the fundamental importance of a person's rights in land.

[1]Although you would not necessarily have to go in to detail here as to what is protected, this gives an early indicator that you are aware of the scope of the tort.

Trespass to land is defined by Winfield and Jolowicz (Rogers 2010) as the unjustifiable interference with the possession of land. Therefore, the tort is wider than the lay person's traditional thinking of someone wandering on to their land.[1] The tort exists to protect a person's interest in property arising through possession as opposed to stemming from ownership. The purpose therefore, protection from interference with land, can be seen to be similar to that of the tort of

[2] A sentence along these lines is important in order to tie your answer back to the question and reinforce the impression that you are aware of the full scope of the question. It also naturally leads you into a discussion of the requirements of the tort in your next paragraph.

[3] For each requirement, you need to include a statement either in support of it, or questioning its validity, in order to ensure that you are addressing the issue of the question as to whether the tort is needed. This also makes sure your answer is not purely descriptive as to what the law is.

[4] You could use another case here to demonstrate wider knowledge of the case law, but whichever you use it is important just to refer to one. Avoid the temptation to list several.

[5] Although the question does not ask for a comparison to nuisance, it is the one tort which is similar; however, the important point to note is that the question requires you to look at whether any tort can fulfil the role of trespass. Therefore, a comparison is needed to at least one. Depending on your time, you could draw on a second but do not go overboard with a list of comparisons.

nuisance; however, whereas nuisance is targeted at consequential interference of land such as noise disturbance, trespass is concerned with direct acts such as actually throwing things on to another's land. Therefore, it is clear from the requirements of trespass that its operation and, therefore, applicability to a given situation is unique.[2]

The first requirement in a claim for trespass is that the individual is eligible to make a claim. This is fulfilled by showing that the claimant has an interest in the land and possession of the land (**Mason v Clarke** [1955] A.C. 778). As such, more is needed than mere licence rights or control of the land, although if coupled with exclusive possession this may suffice (**National Provincial Bank Ltd v Ainsworth** [1965] A.C. 1175). This requirement, which is similar to that of nuisance, may face a challenge in the latter tort under human rights grounds, but it is more strongly justified in trespass on the grounds that the whole point of the tort is to protect interference with the possession of the land.[3]

Once it is established that the claimant has possession, the next requirement is that there is an interference which is the result of a direct and intended act. The interference relate to the surface of the land, the subsoil or the airspace and can take many forms: from the obvious entering of the land, to remaining there after one should leave, through to simply placing a stone against a wall (**Gregory v Piper** (1829) 109 E.R. 220). Therefore, this aspect of the tort carries an extremely low threshold. It is the ease for satisfying this requirement which leads to concerns regarding the extent of the tort. These concerns are heightened by the tort not having the check, as in other torts, of requiring some form of damage to result from the interference. This is clearly illustrated in **Gregory**[4] where the interference which was successfully complained of was merely the touching of the claimant's wall by objects which had been placed nearby by the defendant's servant. Arguably, no harm was done at first glance; however, damage could be said to be present by the fact that the protection of a person's interest in property is a fundamental right, as seen in Article 1 of the First Protocol of the European Convention on Human Rights. Therefore, the mere fact that it has been interfered with warrants the imposition of liability and supports the retention of the tort. In the comparable torts some form of damage is necessary for liability to result. While nuisance[16] can require material damage to the land, it is also actionable where the interference relates to the use or enjoyment of the land. Again, at first glance, this seems similar to trespass; however, the important difference is that in nuisance the interference must be substantial, reflecting the fact that there must be some give and take between neighbours (**Sedleigh-Denfield v O'Callaghan** [1940] A.C. 880). Therefore, claimants in cases such as **Gregory**, and **Kelsen v Imperial Tobacco** [1957] 2 Q.B. 334 would be left without redress, as the acts in question were not sufficient to lead to a nuisance. In nuisance, this can be said to be justified as the tort is concerned with consequential interference. This is not the case in trespass which deals with direct and intended acts.[6]

[6]A sentence along these lines leads your answer into the next issue and ensures that the answer flows rather than it being a set of distinct paragraphs on the trespass.

Therefore, these elements of the tort could be said to be the safeguard which warrants the scope of the tort in terms of liability without damage and further justifies the existence of the tort. The interfering act in question must be directed at the claimant's land. This requirement of directness is again a distinguishing factor from other torts which justifies the tort by allowing it to fill a void in protection, which would otherwise exist if the issue was left to just nuisance or negligence which are more indirect in nature. Only one act is required for a claim to arise and, therefore, torts such as harassment, based on a course of conduct, offer no relief from such a situation.

The intention behind the direct act lends further support to the tort. If a person voluntarily and intentionally performs an act which directly interferes with another's land, then surely the law is justified in holding that person to account. Liability is justifiably imposed against that intentional conduct and as such does not need damage to result. Arguably, some harshness flows from this, as the defendant does not have to have intended to interfere with the land in order to be liable. This is illustrated in **Gilbert v Stone** (1647) 82 E.R. 539, whereby the defendant was threatened into entering the claimant's land. As he intended the direct act of entry, liability ensued. Further problems are seen by the case of[7] **Conway v George Wimpey & Co. Ltd** [1951] 2 K.B. 266: here the defendant was liable even where the entry followed a completely innocent mistake.

[7]As the example you are going on to explain is a different issue from that which you highlighted in the previous case, it is fine to draw on another case as it is not a list of cases on the same point.

Therefore, to conclude, the tort of trespass to land can appear harsh in that it is very easy to satisfy the requirements of the tort: one simply needs to intentionally place a foot on another's land without even knowing the land is in another's possession. However, the tort is the embodiment of recognition that the protection of interests in land is a fundamental human right. The simple act of direct interference itself is the damage. If this is not recognised, then all forms of trespass to the person would need abolishing.[8] The purpose and operation of the protection is unique in tort law so as none of the other torts such as nuisance or negligence can satisfactorily protect the same interest in the same circumstances; requiring different elements as they do, further justification is evidenced.

[8]The purpose of this sentence is to indicate that you are aware how this tort sits with the other forms of trespass and that you are aware of the wider repercussions of removing the tort.

✓ Make your answer stand out

- Spread your evaluation of the justification for the tort throughout your answer at each stage rather than just including a passage at the end.
- Make clear what function is performed by the tort and compare whether that function is in fact performed by any other torts.
- Refer your arguments for and against the need for the tort back to the statement.
- Consider whether the defences prevent injustice resulting.

! Don't be tempted to ...

- Write a purely descriptive account of the requirements of the tort; you need to evaluate each.
- Focus on the first part of the question; the second part should have equal weight.
- Just agree with the statement; evaluate its merits and disagree if you feel the tort does perform a unique role.
- Stray into an in-depth discussion of the requirements of the other torts that you mention. Keep more to comparing the role that they play and whether they could perform the function of trespass in a more justifiable way.

11

Nuisance

How this topic may come up in exams

Nuisance problem questions require several different factors to be considered to determine whether a claim has been made out. You will also have to determine whether the nuisance is private or public and whether the nuisance is covered by statute such as environmental protection legislation. In addition, there is the possibility of a question having the potential to explore issues of negligence and the rule in *Rylands* v *Fletcher* as well. There is also a significant human rights impact in this tort, particularly Article 8 of the European Convention on Human Rights and the implications this has for *Hunter* v *Canary Wharf* and the necessity for a proprietary interest to bring an action, which can form the basis of essay questions.

Attack the question

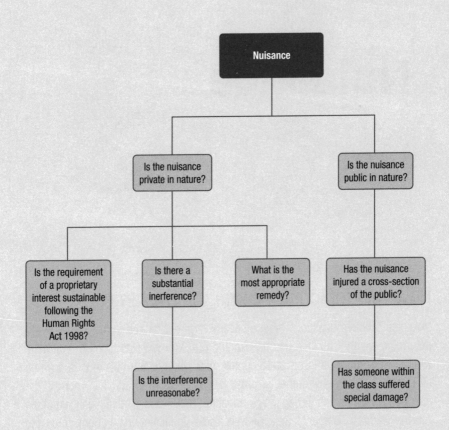

❓ Question 1

Errol has been living in the country mansion that he owns for 13 years. The mansion is a detached property which also includes an area of farmland. Errol's land is next to land owned by Murray. Murray is an American civil war enthusiast who re-enacts parts of the civil war on his land with his friends. Recently, however, Murray grew tired of his job and felt there was money to be made by hosting the re-enactments to members of the public. The events are also combined with lectures on the war to inform people about the history of the war. The events prove to be extremely popular and word soon spreads, increasing the popularity of Murray's business as days out for families. Murray is soon staging the re-enactments several days a week. As a result of this, Errol is subjected to the noise and smell from the guns and cannons going off.

Advise Errol as to his chances of preventing Murray from continuing his actions.

Answer plan

→ Establish that Errol has standing to bring a claim.

→ Determine whether there is a substantial interference with Errol's use and enjoyment of the land.

→ Consider whether this interference is unreasonable.

→ Assess the possibility of Murray having a defence to any claim.

→ Advise Errol on his chances of obtaining an injunction or whether he would have to settle for an alternative remedy.

Diagram plan

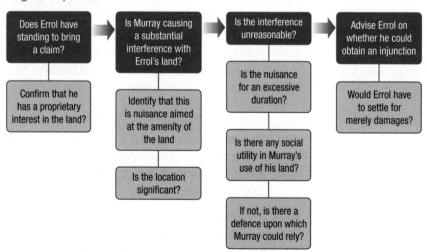

A printable version of this diagram is available from www.pearsoned.co.uk/lawexpressqa

Answer

[1]Show at the start that you have correctly identified the nature of the nuisance.

[2]As you are advising Errol, explain to him what the tort consists of. Again, this will also give an early indicator to the marker that you know how the tort works.

[3]While this may seem obvious, this requirement has been strictly applied and so for completeness you should briefly state it.

[4]Briefly show that you understand what process the law is going through with this aspect of the tort, as this conflict lies at the heart of the tort, before going into your application. This will allow you to demonstrate that you appreciate what the tort is about rather than just what its requirements are.

[5]By adding this, you also show how the tension behind the tort impacts on the application of the requirements for the tort.

[6]By phrasing this in this way, you can show that you know both factors but more importantly that you understand their application by not going into detail on sensitivity, as it does not seem on the facts that it is an issue.

The issue is whether Errol has an action for private nuisance as it appears the use and enjoyment of the land is being diminished.[1] Errol's interest needs balancing with the use by Murray of his land.[2] It will be argued that the requirements of the tort are may be satisfied but that owing to the social function of Murray's activities, Errol may have to accept damages rather than an injunction.

As Errol owns the mansion, he has a proprietary interest in it which confirms that Errol has the requisite standing[3] (**Hunter v Canary Wharf Ltd** [1997] A.C. 655). Therefore, Errol will need to show firstly that the noise and smell amounts to a substantial interference with the use and enjoyment of his land. Errol should be advised, however, that the answer to this question is one of balancing the competing interests of one person's interest in using their land as they wish with that of another to be free from interference.[4] This is a question of fact determined on a case-by-case basis (**Sturgess v Bridgman** (1879) 11 Ch. D. 852).[5] As the interference claimed by Errol does not appear to be based on any particular sensitivity, the factor which will be considered by the courts is the locality of the area.[6] Furthering the idea that there should be some give and take between neighbours, the law looks at the locality where the conduct in question takes place to determine whether interference is substantial. Therefore, noise and smells which occur within an industrial complex may not amount to substantial interference but may do in a residential area. As Errol's location is in the country, it could be said that it is naturally quieter than an urban setting and so the increased noise of cannons going off would be more noticeable. The matter is somewhat complicated as part of the claimed nuisance is the smell. As Errol has a farm on his land, this would presumably create its own smell. While the ammunition used would be smell of a different nature, there is an argument that interference in this form may not be substantial. However, Errol should be advised that, while the smell may not suffice, the noise emanating from Murray's land should be deemed a substantial interference.

Before this amounts to a nuisance, though, the substantial interference must also be unreasonable. Errol should be advised that this involves assessing the seriousness of Murray's interference and then whether his use of his land is reasonable. The first factor to consider regarding seriousness is the duration of the interference. It is perhaps significant that this is not new activity by Murray, and that Errol has only sought action now that the interference is occurring several times a week. Clearly, therefore, the interference is of greater duration which would increase the level of seriousness.

The second significant factor is the objective extent of the interference. As noted, the smell may not be substantial and, further, the extent of this interference may not be as great, owing to the competing smell of the farm. However, as Errol's mansion is a detached country property with farmland attached, it suggests that the smell is travelling some distance. Therefore, if Errol can indeed smell the ammunition from his mansion, this would suggest that the extent of the interference is high. The same reasoning would also apply to the noise from the weaponry and so this appears to be serious substantial interference.

The next issue to determine is whether Murray is a reasonable user of his land. Although liability in nuisance centres on the interference with the claimant's interest in the land being unreasonable, there is, as Lord Goff noted in **Cambridge Water Co. Ltd v Eastern Counties Leather plc**,[7] an interrelationship with whether the defendant's conduct is reasonable. Again, there are several factors to consider for determining this. It does not appear that Murray is acting maliciously and it seems unlikely that the interference could be easily prevented, both of which would lend support the interference not being unreasonable. Additionally, the location where the events are being staged, the countryside, could be said to form the basis of a reasonable use of such land. Indeed, for the activity in question it is arguably essential as the war took place in a rural environment. However, this must be weighed against the fact that while liability for nuisance is strict, and thus not based on the need to take reasonable care not to cause the harm, liability may still arise where the harm caused is reasonably foreseeable (**Cambridge Water**). The harm here is interference with Errol's use and enjoyment of his land from firing guns and cannons. Although this may depend upon some unknown factors such as the exact location of the enactments to Errol's land and the size of the weapons used, this form of harm would be foreseeable as the lands are adjoining.

[7]The actual quote by Lord Goff is not necessarily needed; instead, you just need to refer to the case as the authority for the point that you are advancing.

[8]As this appears to be the main factor and, therefore, your main area of discussion, make sure that you separate it out so that your argument stands out.

[9]You do not know for sure and it may be that they are, so you should place this qualification to your statement for completeness.

[10]As mentioned earlier in relation to sensitivity, by referring to prescription in this manner you show that you know that there is such a defence but that you understand that it is not applicable.

However, a significant factor in relation to Murray is the type of use to which he is putting his land.[8] On the basis that Murray is not acting illegally[9] in staging the re-enactments, there is nothing unreasonable *per se* about his use. In fact, Errol should be advised that what Murray is doing may actually be deemed to be socially useful and, therefore, this will not be an unreasonable interference. This is because the events are popular family attractions as well as appearing to double up as a learning environment by educating people about the war. Errol should be advised that if the court were to adopt this view, the consequence is that an injunction is unlikely to be awarded so as to prevent these activities from continuing, but he may be able to obtain damages for the interference that he is suffering (**Dennis *v* Ministry of Defence** [2003] Env. L.R. 34).

In conclusion, as Errol has not had his proprietary interest interfered with for 20 years, Murray could not claim a defence of prescription.[10] Thus, a court will likely find that Murray has substantially interfered with that interest, and that this is potentially unreasonable owing to its extent and duration. As such, he would be entitled to damages for the difference in monetary value between what his interest was worth prior to the nuisance and its worth following the nuisance (**Moss *v* Christchurch RDC** [1925] 2 K.B.750). While an injunction to prevent further interference may be preferred, Errol may have to settle for damages in lieu of such redress in light of the potential social utility of the use to which Murray is using his land.

✓ Make your answer stand out

- Note any possible alternative claims Errol may have, such as trespass to land or under the rule in *Rylands* v *Fletcher*, if any of the ammunition crosses over the boundary of the property.
- Consider arguments based on Article 1 of Protocol 1 of the ECHR (right to peaceful enjoyment of possessions) which could be used to add strength to Errol's claim, as a court would need to take note of this right when deciding the matter.

■ Try and explain every factor which the court will look at to determine whether the conduct in question amounts to a nuisance; just focus on those which on the facts are most applicable to Errol and Murray. Otherwise, you will lose the structure of your answer and could in fact show a lack of understanding, as they are not all relevant to the question.

Question 2

'Once it is understood that nuisances "productive of sensible personal discomfort" do not constitute a separate tort of causing discomfort to people but are merely part of a single tort of causing injury to land, the rule that the plaintiff must have an interest in the lands falls into place as logical and, indeed, inevitable.' *Per* Lord Hoffman in *Hunter* v *Canary Wharf Ltd* [1997] A.C. 655 at 707

In light of this statement, evaluate the function of the tort of nuisance and assess, with regard to human rights considerations, the merits of this restriction as to who may have an action.

Answer plan

→ Explain the tort's function and what it seeks to protect.

→ Evaluate *Hunter* and explain why the restriction on standing was insisted upon.

→ Consider the viability of this requirement following the incorporation of the ECHR into English law.

→ Assess whether there is a satisfactory way of retaining the essence of the tort with human rights considerations.

Diagram plan

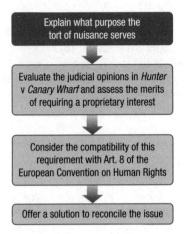

Explain what purpose the tort of nuisance serves

⬇

Evaluate the judicial opinions in *Hunter* v *Canary Wharf* and assess the merits of requiring a proprietary interest

⬇

Consider the compatibility of this requirement with Art. 8 of the European Convention on Human Rights

⬇

Offer a solution to reconcile the issue

A printable version of this diagram is available from www.pearsoned.co.uk/lawexpressqa

Answer

The tort of nuisance offers redress for those who suffer injury to their land; however, because of the firm statements by the Law Lords in **Hunter** *v* **Canary Wharf Ltd** that very purpose means that those who may seek the protection of the tort are restricted and so some individuals succeed while others miss out on redress even though they have suffered the same interference. It will be argued that while the reasoning in **Hunter** has merit, it cannot be sustained in the longer term owing to human rights considerations, and standing should be given to those in residential occupation of the land, perhaps under a new and analogous tort.[1]

[1] As you have just indicated that you are going to disagree with the position adopted by the House of Lords, you should offer an insight into what you propose that the law should be.

Nuisance offers protection to interests in land and can take two forms (**St. Helen's Smelting Co.** *v* **Tipping** (1865) H.L. Cas. 642). Firstly, there is protection from material damage to the land. Claims for such damage are relatively straightforward and involve the defendant's act causing a form of physical damage to the claimant's land. The land itself is damaged and thus it is logical that any claim should be brought by the owner of that land. The second is nuisance producing sensible personal discomfort; the act interferes with the enjoyment of the land: for example, producing noise and smells.

Therefore, it interferes with the enjoyment of all those present on the land, creating an issue as to who will have an action.

This issue came to the fore in **Hunter** where a group of residents claimed nuisance from local construction work. Notably, not all of the residents were householders and included spouses, partners, children and other relations. Their claim initially failed but succeeded in the Court of Appeal where Pill LJ held that, where the claimant occupied the land as a home, there would be a sufficient link to the land to provide standing.[2]

[2]Obviously, this reasoning was rejected by the majority of the House of Lords, but it is worth stating as a point of reference for your answer later on.

Lord Goff rejected the test applied by Pill LJ. He noted that parties may seek negotiations over the matter in order to reach an agreement, but the usefulness of such negotiations require the creator of the nuisance to know who he needs to negotiate with. The usefulness of such arrangements could be diminished if one was needed with everyone who lived in the property. This concern seems fair but, as Lord Cooke highlighted, it could be dealt with by imposing implied authorisation on the homeowner to represent non-owning residents.[3] More persuasively, Lord Goff noted definitional problems with 'substantial link'. While Pill LJ intended his phrase to include the owner's immediate family, he questioned whether it should include lodgers and au pairs who also live there. He then questioned why it would not extend to cover the workplace. A reference point is needed to determine standing; otherwise any individual could bring an action, such as a regular visitor to the house. However, this was overcome by Lord Cooke, dissenting,[4] who argued it was 'weak' to not lay down a rule which was justifiable in relation to spouses and children just because of a grey area as to where the line is ultimately drawn. While the issue may be one of creating legal certainty as well as giving justice to the claimants, this opinion has force in that it could, as Lord Goff observed, be limited quite easily to the immediate family of the homeowner. Other residents could be dealt with on the facts of their case. Lord Cooke further observed that as employees are the concern of their employers, there was no policy basis for allowing the law to extend to non-resident employees.

[3]Although, here, you are advancing the reasons of the majority and why the case was ultimately decided the way it was, you need to subject this reasoning to analysis, and so try to assess the merit of each point you state. You need to look at the flaws directly related to this reasoning before you get on to advancing the specific arguments *for* the alternate view. If you wait until later, your structure will not be as strong.

[4]This needs to be made clear so that the contradictory views make sense.

As the quote illustrates,[5] Lord Hoffman also felt the requirement was needed. However, his view was based on the purpose of the tort being to protect land. He argued it was vital to appreciate that in **Tipping**, while the two forms of nuisance were mentioned, they

[5]Tie this part of your discussion back to the quote in the question.

still amounted to one tort concerned with the protection of land from injury. As such, the basis for an action under the second type was not the nuisance causing personal discomfort; it was because the utility of the land is diminished and, therefore, the land has suffered injury. The tort exists to protect land from injury, and as such it must be the landowner who sues for its injury. He felt that to develop the common law in the manner suggested by Pill LJ would mean distorting the very principles of the tort[6] to fill the gap by moving it away from a land-based tort.

[6]This is why it is really important that you know the purpose of the tort and can explain it, as this was used to justify the majority's decision. If you do not know the theory behind the tort, then you are less able to fully assess the implications and merit of that decision. The tort's purpose is the bar from which you judge the arguments.

In principle, Lord Hoffman's reasoning has considerable merit; however, the consequence is that a non-owning occupier who has their utility of the land diminished is left without a remedy. While such an occupier suffering personal injury as a result of the nuisance may claim in negligence, one suffering distress, discomfort and inconvenience from the act of nuisance has no remedy in that tort. As Lord Hoffman notes, the land's utility is reflected in the amenity value of the land, and the decision denies the existence of any enjoyment of such amenity by anyone bar the owner. However, their individual right remains negated.

[7]As *Hunter* was decided before the incorporation of the Act, it is important that you then move on to consider, regardless of the merits of Lord Cooke's opinion, whether this now acts as a driver for reforming the position adopted by the majority.

The long-term viability of the requirement from **Hunter** is questionable in that, subsequent to the decision, the Human Rights Act[7] was passed and came into force. Importantly, this incorporates the Article 8 right to respect for privacy and family life. The significance of this is that the Article uses the term 'home', and in **Khatun v UK** this was held to be 'autonomous' and not requiring defining domestically. As such, the case arising from the same facts as **Hunter** stated that a proprietary interest was not needed under Article 8. Therefore, anyone whose home is subjected to an actionable nuisance would have a claim. The law's development must give effect to this right (**Douglas v Hello Ltd** [2001] 2 W.L.R. 992), and an insight as to how this was done was given in **McKenna v British Aluminium Ltd** [2002] Env. L.R. 30. Here a striking-out application[8] was rejected on the basis that the claimants, similar in make-up to those in **Hunter**, were said to have an actionable case in light of Article 8. Neuberger J, while not offering any further view of the need for a proprietary interest, was mindful that the claim included a tort analogous to nuisance.

[8]As the case was not a full trial and may appear as a lower court at odds with *Hunter*, you need to provide this context.

It is submitted, in conclusion, that developing an analogous tort based on the interference with the home, actionable by all residents,

9Explain the merit of your
position to demonstrate that
you have thought out the
consequences of such an
approach.

would give effect to Article 8 while overcoming the principle objections of Lord Hoffman to adapting nuisance, and providing redress to non-owning occupiers whose enjoyment of the land is diminished.[9] Either this, or **Hunter** will need to be revisited as there is now a clear divergence with human rights jurisprudence.

✓ Make your answer stand out

- Highlight some of the requirements of the tort to illustrate how they relate to the tort's function.
- Expand on the appropriateness of a negligence claim for people in the position of the residents in *Hunter*, considering whether they fall into a void.
- Give some more insight as to how the analogous tort could look; consider whether it would be an exact replica but with different standing requirements.

! Don't be tempted to ...

- Go on into great detail as to the requirements of the tort, as the focus is on the eligibility criteria to make a claim, not what is required for a successful claim.
- Dismiss the opinion of Lord Cooke in *Hunter* simply because it was dissenting, as it provides material from which to evaluate the merits of the majority's view. He also gives an insight as to how the law could be developed while being kept within reasonable bounds.

Question 3

Gidsville is an estate which is predominantly residential in nature although there are some businesses. However, to regenerate an area on the edge of the estate, the council recently gave planning permission to Prento Petroleum to build a factory on the edge of the estate. The company is a large manufacturer of parts for the oil industry. Having recently won another large contract, Prento Petroleum has had to extend the working day to include shifts up to midnight rather than have the staff work weekends. As a result, the company has employed large numbers of local residents, but the work has generated a large amount of smoke and particularly noise which can be heard over the estate. One of the businesses on the estate, Di Rossi's, an Italian restaurant, has witnessed a drop in trade.

Additionally, Spencer, who works the late shift at the factory, bought a flat opposite Di Rossi's three years ago. However, since he started working the late shift six months ago he has had problems himself with Di Rossi's deliveries arriving at 10 a.m. and waking him up. When he complained, the owner of Di Rossi's, Morgan, pointed out that the deliveries have been turning up at that time for over 20 years and no one has ever complained.

Advise Morgan about any claim he may have for the loss in trade and also about the complaints of Spencer.

Answer plan

→ Identify whether the estate constitutes a sufficient class of people affected by the activities of Prento Petroleum.

→ Establish whether Morgan has suffered special damage so as to make an action applicable.

→ Discuss whether Prento Petroleum can rely on the council's planning permission to defeat any action.

→ Advise Morgan of the claim he faces by Spencer.

→ Evaluate whether the interference is substantial.

→ Consider whether the use of the land by Morgan is reasonable.

→ Advise as to the merits of a defence, if required, based on prescription.

Diagram plan

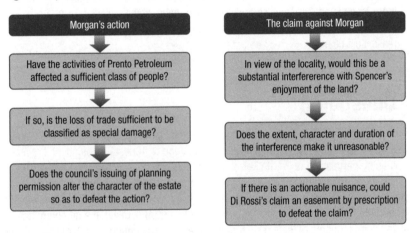

A printable version of this diagram is available from www.pearsoned.co.uk/lawexpressqa

Answer

Morgan requires advice as to the tort of nuisance, owing to the threat to his business from Prento Petroleum and also claims he may face from Spencer. It will be argued that Morgan is likely to be successful in an action for public nuisance against the factory, while his actions are unlikely to be sufficient for any private nuisance claim against him.[1]

Public nuisance requires an act which 'materially affects the reasonable comfort and convenience of life of a class of Her Majesty's subjects' (*per* Romer LJ in **AG *v* PYA Quarries Ltd [1957] 2 Q.B. 169**). Prento Petroleum creating smoke and noise until midnight would affect the comfort and convenience of the residents. However, the area affected must be large enough to constitute a sufficient class. While we are not told the estate's population, the fact that the smoke and noise cover the entire estate suggests that this community would be a sufficient class.

Although public nuisance affects a class of people, an individual can bring an action. However, Morgan must show he suffered 'special damage', which is damage greater than that suffered by others within the class. The damage suffered which would be greater than that affecting the rest of the estate is the loss of custom. Morgan should be advised that while negligence looks less favourably on pure economic losses[2] such as this, a loss of business is sufficient for nuisance (**Benjamin *v* Storr** (1874) L.R. 9 C.P. 400). This particular loss must also be direct and substantial. By analogy with **Benjamin**, the facts here suggest that Morgan satisfies the require-ments for an action. Although, if any of the other business have suffered a loss in trade, Morgan's claim would fail as he has suffered no greater loss than others within the class.[3]

The loss suffered is also foreseeable and so no issue of remoteness exists. Therefore, on the basis that Morgan has suffered special damage,[4] Prento Petroleum will argue that the granting of planning permission authorised any resultant nuisance. While statutory authority provides immunity against nuisance, the position is different with regards mere planning permission (**Wheeler *v* J.J. Saunders Ltd** [1996] Ch. 19). **Wheeler** held that planning authorities have no general power to authorise a nuisance; although they possibly could to the extent that they may alter the character of a neighbourhood through their decisions.

[1] Demonstrate at the start that you understand that both forms of nuisance are applicable to the question and which type relates to each claim.

[2] This may not appear totally relevant but it is an anomaly with the law which has attracted judicial criticism, and so by mentioning it briefly, and in the context shown, you maintain relevance while also showing your knowledge of this point.

[3] As you are giving advice to Morgan and the facts are silent, you must ensure that you explain the situation if this was the unknown factual situation.

[4] As you have ended the previous paragraph with an element of doubt as to the claim, you should start the next part of your discussion in this manner so that it follows on from the previous paragraph.

[5]Make sure that you use the facts of the question to support your argument on this point, as they give a good indication as to what the position will be.

[6]Start with the remedy of an injunction, as this is more likely to be the most desired as well as the least likely to succeed. Therefore, you can finish on the stronger, consolation point that he would at least receive damages.

[7]Start this section of your answer by identifying exactly the issue that Morgan is faced with.

[8]Show that you know how the tort operates.

[9]Even if you have concluded the previous discussion with a view that it is not substantial, the absence of concrete facts means it could be. However, to maintain consistency in your answer, you will need to phrase the introduction of the next point of discussion in a more tentative manner.

Therefore, the question is whether by granting permission for the factory the council have altered the estate's character. Regeneration was a factor behind the decision, so this may be the case; however, we are told that this was just for an area on the edge of the estate, not the whole estate. As Gidsville is predominately a residential area,[5] it is unlikely that the planning permission has sufficiently altered the overall area's character and so the defence will fail.

If Morgan is successful, it is unlikely that an injunction[6] would be awarded to prevent the company's actions completely as this would create unemployment. However, in view of the noise affecting the entire estate, one may be granted to restrict the working times so that work stops earlier. In any event, Morgan would be able to claim damages for his lost trade.

In relation now to the claim against Morgan, the nuisance being claimed is interference with Spencer's use and enjoyment of his land caused by the delivery trucks.[7] The merits of this claim will be weighed, on the facts, against Morgan's right to use his land in a way that he wishes (**Sturgess v Bridgman** (1879) 11 Ch. D. 852).[8] As this only affects Spencer, the action would be for private nuisance and so it must be confirmed that, as the owner of the flat, Spencer would have the necessary standing to bring a claim (**Hunter v Canary Wharf Ltd** [1997] A.C. 655).

The interference must be substantial in nature. Spencer is not using his land in a particularly sensitive way and so the factor to consider is that of locality. While the whole estate is predominantly residential, we would need to know about this particular part of the estate, as what may be a nuisance in one part may not be in another. Noise from delivery vans in a general residential area would likely be substantial; however, a restaurant is unlikely to exist on a general residential road. Further, the fact that Spencer's land is a flat suggests that this could also be above one of the other shops. If so, then noise from the vans is unlikely to be substantial.

On the basis that this is deemed to be a substantial interference,[9] the next issue is whether the substantial interference is unreasonable. There are several factors to advise Morgan but of most relevance are the duration of the interference, its extent and its character. The character of the interference is obviously noise, although it appears it is only an issue because it wakes Spencer up, which suggests that the interference is not an issue otherwise. From the facts, we are told the vans arrive at 10 a.m., although we are not told whether this is daily or how long they stay. Arguably, this is a reasonable time to deliver when most people would already be awake. Further, as delivery vans usually have several stops the noise is unlikely to go on for long.[10] The suggestion that Morgan is a reasonable user is supported by the fact that no one else has complained over a long period and even Spencer has not complained until now. Therefore, even if the noise is deemed substantial, it is unlikely to be unreasonable unless perhaps the noise is excessively loud and goes on for an excessive period. If overall the nuisance is deemed negligible, it will not be actionable against Morgan.

[10]Use your common sense to make informed argument in order to overcome the absence of concrete facts. It is important that you do not just ignore the issue.

However, Morgan should be advised that if the noise is deemed actionable, any claim will likely succeed as he does not appear to have a defence. The only possibility is an easement by prescription. This means that a proprietary interest has been created by long usage (over 20 years). This would be unsuccessful because it is unlikely that noise from delivery vans would constitute an easement, as there is no benefit to the land.[11] Additionally, while the noise has been going on for over 20 years, there was no actionable nuisance during that time as there was no interference with Spencer's land. There would need to be a 20-year period from the time the interference began (**Sturgess v Bridgman** (1879) L.R. 11 Ch. D. 852). The interference has only started since Spencer started working the shifts six months ago.

[11]While being an issue of land law, it is a significant point in relation to the defence against the tort succeeding, and so you should discuss it, drawing on your knowledge of land law.

In conclusion, Morgan should be advised that he should be able to recuperate his losses caused by Prento Petroleum; in relation to Spencer, it is unlikely that the interference from the vans will be sufficient to warrant a successful action.

✓ Make your answer stand out

- If there is deemed to be no special damage, advise Morgan of the possibility of petitioning the Attorney General to bring a relator action on behalf of the whole estate.
- Consider whether the factory may in fact have breached the statutory nuisance provision within s. 79 of the Environmental Protection Act 1990.
- Expand your discussion of Morgan's remedies and consider *Andrae* v *Selfridge & Co. Ltd* [1938] Ch. 1. Although foreseeable, would it be unreasonable in the circumstances to allow the full extent of his losses?

! Don't be tempted to ...

- Litter the second part of the answer with case examples of the factors which are assessed. The important thing is to apply the standard factors to the facts of the scenario. If a case is similar, then refer to it or if it is a specific authority for a point, but otherwise use your time to concentrate on your application.

- Turn your discussion of Morgan's possible defence into a land law answer with regard to whether this is capable of constituting an easement.

The rule in
Rylands v Fletcher

How this topic may come up in exams

While it is a long-standing tort in its own right providing strict liability, the rule is now seen as a subspecies of nuisance dealing with incidents of a one-off escape. As such, while a problem question could consist solely of the tort on its own, you should be aware of the possibility of a nuisance action being present as well, particularly if there is some form of material damage to the land. The development of the tort also means that you could have scope to discuss issues of negligence. As such, make sure you are also able to deal with an essay question concerning the future of the tort and its relevance today.

■ Attack the question

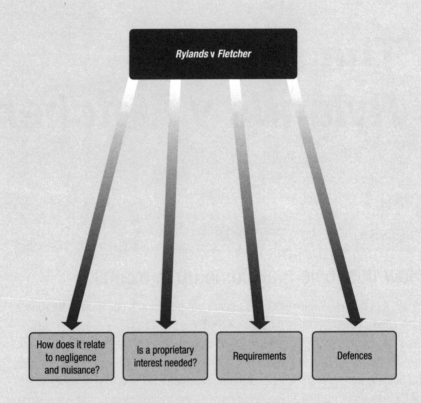

❓ Question 1

Two years ago Cannibal Energy Ltd, a provider of essential chemicals to fossil-fuel companies, acted on a government request to increase energy production through fossil fuels to meet short-term demand, by opening a new processing plant in Templeton on land adjoining a farm belonging to Peck. The company's arrival created vast numbers of jobs in an area that had previously suffered from high unemployment, and the company provided a much needed boost to the local economy.

However, the company's arrival was not without controversy and there have been numerous anti-fossil-fuel protests staged in the town. Earlier this year, in an attempt to discredit the safety of the plant and force the closure of the plant, a prominent and well-known protester, 'Mad' Martin, broke into the plant and vandalised the complex safety system which is part of the production of the chemicals. Consequently, some chemicals escaped by seeping through some minute cracks in the floor of the plant and, ultimately, entered Templeton's water supply.

As a result, Peck suffered the loss of a substantial number of cattle and damage to part of his land after using the contaminated water. The deaths and damage were identified as being caused by the chemicals processed at the plant.

Advise Peck on his chances of successfully claiming for the damage that he has suffered.

Answer plan

→ Establish that Mr. Peck has standing to make a claim.

→ Identify the chemicals as the 'thing' which has been brought on to the land and consider whether this is an extraordinary use of the land.

→ State that the chemicals clearly escaped from the land owned by Cannibal Energy Ltd.

→ Evaluate the forseeability of the harm which would be caused by such an escape.

→ Discuss the potential defence Cannibal Energy Ltd may have as the escape was caused by an act of a third party.

Diagram plan

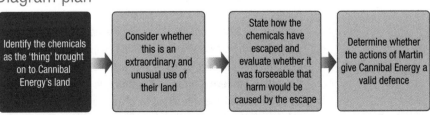

A printable version of this diagram is available from www.pearsoned.co.uk/lawexpressqa

Answer

[1]Show that you know exactly how the tort operates and how it is distinguishable from other torts which concern proprietary interests.

[2]By highlighting this here, you show the person marking your work that you have fully identified all of the relevant issues which need to be discussed.

[3]Before you start to apply the different requirements to the problem, it is worth outlining what the rule consists of.

[4]Paraphrase the rule as stated by Blackburn J to emphasise that you understand the individual parts.

The circumstances surrounding the damage suffered by Peck requires advising him on the rule in **Rylands *v* Fletcher** (1866) L.R. 1 Ex. 265. This tort, while similar to other land torts, offers protection for interests in property which are injured by a one-off occurrence.[1] As such, Peck will be advised as to the elements of the rule and whether the actions of Martin mean that Cannibal Energy has a valid defence.[2]

Peck should be advised that the rule can be stated[3] as requiring a person to bring something on to his land in furtherance of a non-natural use of his land, which if it escaped, would be liable to cause harm. If the 'thing' does escape, then the person is liable for all of the damage which is a consequence of the escape, regardless of their fault in the 'thing' escaping.[4] To bring a claim, Peck needs to show a proprietary interest in the land affected by the escape of the waste and that his property was damaged (**Transco plc *v* Stockport M.B.C.** [2004] 2 A.C. 1). He should be advised that as he owns the farm next to the plant he has such an interest; in addition, his cattle have died and part of the land has been damaged from using the contaminated water.

The first element to satisfy is that Cannibal Energy has brought something on to its land which amounts to a non-natural use of the land. Underpinning the rule is the idea that if the person has voluntarily brought a 'thing' on to their land and kept it there at their peril – here, the chemicals – liability will arise where the 'thing' is not naturally there or the use is 'non-natural'. Originally, this was stated as meaning a special use which brought increased danger and not some use which is proper for the general benefit of the community (**Rickards *v* Lothian** [1913] A.C. 263). This is significant to Peck's case as, while the chemicals bring increased danger, using the land for this purpose has brought a significant upturn to the local economy and so this use could be said to benefit the community notwithstanding what has happened. However, this interpretation from **Rickards** was doubted in **Cambridge Water Co. Ltd *v* Eastern Counties Leather plc** [1994] 2 A.C. 264. Lord Goff stated that the creation of employment, in itself, was not sufficient. The view that benefiting the general community

[5]The important point was that Lord Goff said it was not in itself sufficient. Therefore, as there is another significant practical aspect to the use of the land in this way, this means that it is may not be appropriate to just dismiss the benefits which the plant brings to the area.

was not sufficient was affirmed in **Transco**: the issue is whether the use is non-ordinary. However, there is a government policy of increasing fossil-fuel energy production which requires this chemical being processed.[5] Therefore, when combined with the economic benefits this use of the land may be deemed ordinary. However, there remains doubt as to whether the location of the plant for processing the waste was an ordinary use and so this element is likely to be fulfilled, particularly as this use brings special danger to the land.

[6]While this may seem like it has obviously been satisfied, it still needs to be shown, albeit briefly.

The next aspect of the rule to advise Peck on is that of escape.[6] For a claim to succeed, the 'thing' which the defendant brought on to his land must cross his boundary and enter land not within his control (**Read v Lyons** [1947] A.C. 156). This is clearly seen here as we are told that the waste entered the town's water supply.

[7]Explaining the rationale for this element allows you to build up the level of evaluation in your answer, especially as it has been seen as being a relatively new requirement.

[8]Make sure that you use the facts from the question to support why this case is likely to be different to *Cambridge Water*.

The next issue to satisfy is that the harm caused by the escape must have been a type which was foreseeable. As the rule requires the person to keep the thing at their peril in case it escapes, then, in view of liability being strict, it is just to require that it is foreseeable that damage will be caused.[7] Peck should be advised that while **Cambridge Water** has similar facts and it was not foreseen that the chemicals would get into the water supply, here there are complex safety features in the plant,[8] which suggests that the possibility of damage from an escape was probably contemplated. In **Cambridge Water** it was stressed that the tort is not based on negligence and, therefore, even if the company demonstrates that it took all reasonable precautions to prevent the escape, this would not affect the issue of foreseeability of damage if the escape did happen. When the plant was built, it is unlikely that it was not known that the water supply which supplies Templeton was nearby. As the farm is next to the plant, it must have been foreseeable that the farm would use the local water supply and, therefore, the harm which has occurred – death of animals and damage to the land – must surely be foreseeable, so this appears satisfied. Therefore, it appears, provided the use of the land is deemed an unusual use, that the tort has been made out.[9]

[9]At the end of applying the elements, you should give a mini-conclusion as to whether the tort is likely to be made out in order to explain why there is a need to discuss defences.

However, Peck should be advised that, while liability under the rule is strict, there are various defences to a claim. The defence which Cannibal Energy will rely on is that the escape was an act

[10]These facts are important in determining whether there is any chance that Peck's claim may still succeed and so you need to use them to illustrate why, when it appears the defence is valid, he may still have a chance of success.

[11]Before you end, this is a final opportunity to show your understanding of the relationship between negligence and the rule and whether there is scope for the former to apply in the latter.

of a stranger. The defence applies where the escape is caused by a third-party act, which the defendant has no control over (**Box v Jubb** (1879) 4 Ex. D. 76). This is the case here as the escape was in fact caused by Martin vandalising the safety valves; however, Peck should be advised that this will not necessarily mean that his claim is defeated. We are told that there had been several demonstrations against the plant, with concerns over safety, and that Martin was 'well known'.[10] Therefore, it can be argued that Martin's act could have been anticipated and prevented, creating liability for the company as it was not outside of their control (**Perry v Kendricks Transport Ltd** [1956] 1 W.L.R 85). Conversely, if Cannibal Energy demonstrates that no negligence on its part played a role in the escape, it would likely have a defence. To defeat the claim on the basis that Cannibal Energy is not at fault for the escape may seem at odds with the overall purpose of the tort, but there is some justification where it is a completely independent act of a stranger. However, Peck should be advised that, in view of the comments in **Cambridge Water** about the irrelevance to liability of taking reasonable care, and that in **Transco** negligence was again held not to play a part, even taking reasonable care may not affect Cannibal Energy's liability notwithstanding **Perry**.[11]

To conclude, Peck should be advised that considering the 'thing' in question, and the location of the plant, this would seem to be a non-ordinary use of such land regardless of what benefits it may bring and as such brings the rule into play. While the escape was caused by Martin, his act was arguably something which Cannibal Energy had control over and so the likely defence will probably fail.

 Make your answer stand out

- Explore the extent that fault, or negligence, has become a part of what is a strict liability tort and whether this is a justifiable development.
- Even though it is a problem question, look to include some academic opinion such as P. Cane (1999) 'Fault and strict liability for harm in tort law', in W. Swaddling and G. Jones (eds) *The Search for Principle: Essays in Honour of Lord Goff of Chieveley*, OUP.

Don't be tempted to ...

- Briefly apply the elements and finish the answer quickly. Make sure that you consider potential practical aspects, such as the use of nuclear energy, which may impact on the application of the elements.
- Discuss defences such as act of God or consent, which have no relevance, in order to show that you know them and fill your answer out. Use any time and space you have to include more evaluation of the application of the elements.
- Overemphasise the relationship with torts such as nuisance.

Question 2

'... there is in my opinion a category of case, however small it may be, in which it seems just to impose liability even in the absence of fault.' *Per* Lord Bingham in *Transco plc* v *Stockport Metropolitan Borough Council* [2004] 2 A.C. 1

In view of the above statement, evaluate the requirements for liability under the rule in *Rylands* v *Fletcher* (1866) L.R. 1 Ex. 265 and whether there is a place for the rule in the law of tort.

Answer plan

→ Outline what the rule is and explain the purpose which it serves.

→ Evaluate the different elements of the rule, making sure you explain why that aspect is needed as this will help you determine whether the rule is needed.

→ Consider whether the function of the tort can, and should, be performed by another tort such as negligence or nuisance.

Diagram plan

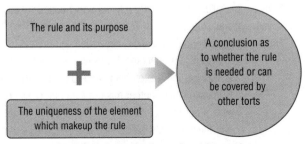

A printable version of this diagram is available from www.pearsoned.co.uk/lawexpressqa

Answer

The rule in **Rylands *v* Fletcher** has provided long-standing liability for a person who damages his neighbour's land through the escape of something which is not naturally present there. However, questions have arisen as to the need for the tort thanks to judicial comments as to its nature and its abolition in Australia.[1] It is argued that the tort, properly understood, serves a distinct purpose which, as the quote suggests, should be retained.

The rule in **Rylands *v* Fletcher** is that where a person brings on to land which he controls something which is not there naturally, and is something which will forseeably cause harm to neighbouring land if it escapes, liability will result where that eventuality occurs. While it is one of a number of torts which protect land, the elements of the rule indicate its uniqueness. The rule targets the defendant's activities, imposing strict liability when they take the risk of bringing something on to their land which may harm another's other's property. This could be said to be a response to industrialisation and the changing nature of land use to encompass more hazardous uses. Therefore, it is different to nuisance which focuses on injury inflicted on the claimant's land.[2] The rule only refers to land which the defendant controls and the focus is on material damage from that land. While nuisance has led to recovery for material damage to the land, the orthodox position is that it concerns amenity interference. Therefore, traditionally there is a clear divide between the purposes of the torts. However, in **Cambridge Water Co. *v* Eastern Counties Leather plc** [1994] 2 A.C. 264, adopting the analysis of Newark,[3] Lord Goff held that the rule was an extension of nuisance, a position endorsed in **Transco**. Arguably, the rapid acceptance of this idea has brought into question aspects of the tort. Historically, owing to the purpose of the rule, no proprietary interest was needed for standing; however, it was stated obiter in **Transco** that this is required. Murphy (2004)[4] suggests that nuisance developed to protect interests in land because of the attachment that land had with social standing, but this was not the reason behind the development of the rule and so it is questionable whether this requirement for standing is warranted which, if correct, reasserts a distinct position for the rule. However, today, the rule exists to deal with one-off escapes of substances from the defendant's land which cause harm.[5]

---

[1] It is worth stating this in your introduction to show your awareness of the context.

[2] As the English position is that the rule is an extension of nuisance, you should early in your answer clearly set out the rule's purpose and how it differs. However, if you are of the view that the rule is justifiably part of nuisance, then do the reverse. Make the case early as to why it is and build your answer from there to then suggest whether there is a role for the rule or not.

[3] Show that you know what the wider reasoning was for Lord Goff's opinion, particularly as it goes to the heart of the question: namely, whether the tort is needed if it is just a part of another tort.

[4] The full citation is below but, as explained elsewhere, in an exam you are unlikely to have time to write the full citation but naturally you must reference your influences. Therefore, give a clear and concise indication of your source.

[5] After your analysis of the purpose of the tort, for clarity and to aid the flow into the elements of the tort you should restate briefly what role the tort serves.

For liability under the rule, the first requirement is that the defendant must bring something on to his land. This in itself does not need to be inherently dangerous, as seen in **Rylands** where the 'thing' was water. The 'thing' must then escape to an area not controlled by the defendant (**Read v Lyons** (1947] A.C. 156). As the 'thing' must be likely to do harm upon escape, one escape is sufficient and so there is a further distinction from nuisance. Nuisance involves looking at factors such as the sensitivity of the claimant and the duration of the interference. Therefore, certain acts may not equate to nuisance but they would fall within the rule. Further, originally it was clear that the damage could be personal injury, although this has changed through the reclassification as an extension of nuisance. Therefore, a return to its roots would further strengthen the need for the tort by increasing its distinctiveness.[6]

[6]At the end of your discussion of each requirement you should try and show how this supports whether the tort has a role to play or not.

The rule was originally stated by Blackburn J in **Rylands** as requiring the 'thing' to not naturally be on the land; however, this was amended in the House of Lords to 'non-natural use'. This was interpreted in **Rickards v Lothian** [1913] A.C. 263 as a use of the land which brings increased danger and is not merely the ordinary use of it. While the additional requirement of not being a use which benefits the community has been doubted in **Cambridge Water**, the essence of the statement was retained in **Transco** where it was held preferable to apply a test of extraordinary and unusual use.[7] Lord Bingham emphasised that this may vary in different times and places; again, while having echoes of the assessed factors in nuisance, it must be remembered that what is being assessed is different. In nuisance it is the interference, whereas under the rule it is the use of the land by the defendant. Further, a use may be extraordinary but reasonable in nuisance, but unreasonableness would not matter under the rule.

[7]What you should be trying to do here is show that you appreciate how the phrase has developed through the case law but without getting too bogged down and losing some of the thrust of your argument.

The next requirement for liability under the rule is that it is foreseeable that harm would occur upon an escape of the thing. This was added by Lord Goff in **Cambridge Water** for the purposes of determining remoteness of damage. The basis for this requirement is within the original rule itself where it talks about the 'thing' being 'likely' to cause mischief. Clearly, while the word was not used, to determine this it must be based upon foreseeability, this then justifies the strictness of liability. Lord Goff also felt it important, in his eyes, to

[8]By stating this you are trying to support the view that the two torts are the same, particularly when the relationship with nuisance was not necessarily needed to decide the point in the case.

[9]While it may seem logical to start with a comparison of the rule to negligence as it is for the latter tort that the rule has been abolished, this is not the case in English law where the rule is classed as part of nuisance. Therefore, you should progress through your answer showing how, in fact, it differs to nuisance, and then show your extended knowledge by considering whether this alternate approach means that the rule is not needed.

reaffirm this point because of what he saw as the similarity between the rule and nuisance, where it is required.[8]

While the English judiciary have increasingly merged the rule within nuisance, Australia has abolished it completely, using instead negligence to cover the same situations.[9] In **Burnie Port Authority v General Jones Pty** (1994) 120 A.L.R. 42 the High Court adopted the idea of a non-delegable duty to be owed by those in control of premises. Its explanation was that over time the scope of negligence had been greatly expanded while the rule's operation had been restricted, so that now the difference between the two was negligible and incidents which would fall foul of the rule would be covered by negligence. However, as Nolan (2005) argues, this idea of fusion is misplaced as the rule is one of strict liability and, therefore, fault does not play a part, unlike in negligence. Further, the reasonableness of the use of land by the defendant, as confirmed by **Transco**, is irrelevant. In support, Murphy suggests that dealing with **Rylands** situations under negligence may also be detrimental to industrial use cases as it will be harder for claimants to prove the necessary standard was breached; also safety compliance certificates may deter people from even trying. Therefore, the rule is best not placed within negligence as its function is clearly distinct.

However, there is nothing necessarily wrong if the rule remains an aspect of nuisance, provided that the rule is not developed restrictively in a manner at odds from the distinct purpose for which it started. However, to ensure this and as arguably there is sufficient difference between the two, it would be best to revert to two distinct torts serving different purposes.

 Make your answer stand out

- To give your answer more academic depth read the following articles D. Nolan (2005) 'The distinctiveness of *Rylands* v *Fletcher*', L.Q.R. 121 (Jul): 421–51; and J. Murphy (2004) 'The merits of *Rylands* v *Fletcher*', 24 O.J.L.S. 643.
- Tie you answer back to the quote by Lord Bingham and consider whether, in fact, the rule should have a wider application.
- Discuss the justification of strict liability; is it right to have liability without fault?

> ! **Don't be tempted to …**
>
> - Go into detail on the torts of nuisance and negligence. The question allows you to judge whether the function of the rule could be performed by these but it is primarily a question on *Rylands* v *Fletcher*.
> - Give just an overview of the rule and its elements; the second part of the question as to the need for the tort must be addressed.
> - Just follow the premise in the quote; the actual question leaves it open for you to adopt whatever view you wish as to the worth of the rule.

? Question 3

LIS Ltd makes insulation products in its factory in Winfieldshire. Roger is employed to work the hot wire machine which is used to cut polystyrene into suitable size blocks. One day while working on the machine, which gets up to extremely high temperatures, Roger received a phone call from his girlfriend whom he had fallen out with that morning. Wanting to patch things up, Roger decided to take the call and got so involved with the conversation that he forgot to turn the machine off while he was on the phone, which lasted about 45 minutes.

Upset by how the conversation had gone, Roger went outside for a cigarette; however, when he returned inside, to his horror he saw that the polystyrene which he had been feeding into the machine had overheated. This had caught fire and, combined with sparks from the machine, had ignited some chemical gas which was stored in the factory. Upon seeing the fire, Roger panicked and ran out without trying to put the fire out but did set the alarm off. The fire destroyed not only the factory but also the neighbouring unit which was occupied by a furniture maker, Weir & Co. Ltd.

Advise LIS Ltd as to its potential liability to Weir & Co. Ltd.

> ## Answer plan
>
> → Establish whether LIS brought something on to its land something which was likely to catch fire.
>
> → Consider whether, if the substance did ignite, the fire was likely to spread to the claimant's property.
>
> → Evaluate whether the fire occurred in the course of an activity which was a non-natural use of the defendant's land.
>
> → Consider the application of the Fire Prevention (Metropolis) Act 1774 and any other possible defence.

Diagram plan

A printable version of this diagram is available from www.pearsoned.co.uk/lawexpressqa

Answer

[1]As you are required to advise as to LIS's liability, you should state what the consequences would be if deemed liable.

The issue to advise LIS on is its potential liability under the rule in **Rylands v Fletcher** (1866) L.R. 1 Ex. 265 for the damage caused by the fire spreading to the neighbouring property. This is important as liability, if found, is strict and will be imposed for all of the damaged caused by the fire spreading.[1] It will be argued that in light of the rule's adaption to incidents of fire,[2] LIS will be liable for the damage suffered.

[2]Give an early indication that you are aware that this situation is not necessarily a direct application of the rule.

[3]While the question is not specifically on vicarious liability, as with issues of standing, it should always be briefly addressed as the company does not appear to have done anything wrong here.

The first issue to advise LIS on is that, while the fire was caused by Roger's inattention as he is LIS's employee and the act occurred during the course of his employment, he was employed to operate the machine safely and did not do so during work time, LIS will be vicariously liable[3] for his actions. It also needs establishing that Weir & Co. Ltd have standing to bring an action against them. LIS should be advised that, while they would have suffered property damage as their unit was destroyed, they also need a proprietary interest in their unit (**Transco plc v Stockport M.B.C.** [2004] 2 A.C. 1). As they operate a business from the unit and are a limited company, it is likely that the occupation would be on a formal footing such as a lease, so satisfying the requirement.

The rule itself provides that where a person brings something on to their land which is a non-natural use of that land, and which is likely to do mischief should it escape, liability will be imposed for the damaged caused as a consequence of the 'thing' escaping. If fire itself had been brought on to LIS's land and escaped into neighbouring land, the application would be relatively straightforward as fire would be something likely to cause mischief upon escaping. The issue here is that no fire was brought on to the land; one was merely

[4]This builds on from what was said in the introduction and shows that you understand the difference between the application of the rule proper and its varied form for fires.

caused and then spread: thus what was brought on to the land did not escape.[4] However, LIS should be advised that the rule can still apply where fire escapes after being caused by a non-natural use of the land (**Musgrove v Pandelis** [1919] 2 K.B. 43), provided a variance of the usual requirements are satisfied.

The relevant principles have recently been restated in **LMS International Ltd v Styrene Packaging and Insulation Ltd** [2006] Build. L.R. 50. The first requirement is that LIS brought on to its land things which were likely to catch fire and kept them in conditions which meant that if they did ignite they would spread to the claimant's land. Here LIS brought the hot wire machine, polystyrene and the gas chemicals which, particularly in the case of the latter, are two 'things' likely to catch fire. Although we are not told of the conditions under which these items were kept, the fact that this was a production factory suggests that significant quantities would be kept there. Additionally, the gas must have been kept reasonably close to the machine for the spark to have ignited the gas. Therefore, the conditions are likely to have been such that, if an item did ignite, there was sufficient other flammable material in the factory to generate a fire which would spread to the neighbouring unit. Obviously, more information would be needed here, and if the converse was established on the facts, there would be no liability.[5]

[5]As you are advising LIS as to its liability, explain with as much certainty as you can what the situation is, including whether LIS would have cause for optimism. Do not just make a definitive statement when the facts are silent.

[6]As doubt has just been raised whether the preceding requirement has been satisfied, you need to phrase the introduction to the next requirement in a way that follows on.

However, on the basis that such conditions are deemed to exist,[6] the next factor to determine is whether this was done in the course of a non-natural use of the land. This factor relates back to whether the things were kept in conditions which were likely to spread, with the words 'non-natural use' referring to whether the 'thing' is naturally there. In **Mason v Levy Auto Parts** [1967] 2 Q.B. 530, a range of inflammable materials kept in a store was deemed a non-natural use of the land. This was based on the quantity of materials, how they were stored and the character of the neighbourhood. As discussed above, the first two of these factors are likely to be equally present and arguably so is the third. The fact that there is a neighbouring property adjacent to the factory does raise questions as to the holding of flammable material in the factory, particularly if the quantities are high.[7] Despite referring extensively to **Transco**, the judge in **LMS International** used the term of non-natural use. Although even on the use of the wording in **Transco**, whether this

[7]Use the facts of the case to support your application of the requirement to the problem and whether it is satisfied by highlighting the similarities.

use is something out of the ordinary in the place and time that it is done, this aspect is likely to be satisfied particularly in view of the similarities to **Mason**.

Lastly, the 'thing' must actually ignite and a fire spread to the neighbouring property. Clearly, this has happened here so LIS should be advised of its likely liability for the damage caused by the fire. Whereas under the rule proper the harm which occurs needs to be foreseeable, this was stated in **Mason** not to be sensible in fire cases as the 'thing' brought on to the land does not escape. While this furthers the debate as to whether this is indeed liability under the rule owing to the differing circumstances between the two situations,[8] LIS should be advised that it is generally accepted that liability is the same under both (Rogers 2010).[9]

LIS should be advised that there are defences to the application of the rule to fire; however, as the fire was not caused by an act of God or by a stranger over whom they had no control, they would not be applicable.[10] The other main defence is s. 86 of the Fire Prevention (Metropolis) Act 1774. This provides a defence where the fire began accidentally. LIS may feel this is the case here; however, LIS should be advised that the word 'accidentally' has been construed restrictively and does not include where the fire began through negligence (**Filliter v Phippard** (1847) 11 Q.B. 347). The facts surrounding Roger's actions suggest negligence in operating the machine by leaving it unattended for so long with material in the machine. In any event, though, the Act has been held not to apply where there was negligence in letting the fire spread (**Musgrove**). As we are told Roger did not attempt to prevent the fire spreading, this would appear to be the case.

In conclusion, LIS should be advised that it is vicariously liable for the acts of its employees in the course of their employment; as Roger appears negligent, LIS will likely be liable for the damage under the rule in **Rylands v Fletcher** in its amended form in relation to fires.

[8]Demonstrate that you have a wider appreciation of the issues and the debate which surrounds the area, and incorporate it into your answer by assessing whether it strictly matters whether it is a pure application of the rule or not.

[9]Show that you have undertaken some wider reading, as well as adding depth to your evaluation, by including reference to some academic opinion on the matter.

[10]By covering the defences like this, you show that you know that they exist but also understand that they are clearly not applicable here, and so you do not waste time giving a fuller account of them.

✓ Make your answer stand out

■ Develop the point as to whether this is in fact an operation of the rule in *Rylands* v *Fletcher* or some form of negligence and consider whether it matters.

■ Consider whether there could be liability under another tort such as negligence or nuisance.

■ Provide more depth as to the application of vicarious liability.

■ Look at A. I. Ogus (1969) 'Vagaries in liability for the escape of fire', Cambridge Law Journal 27: 104, and use the views expressed in the article to support your arguments.

! Don't be tempted to ...

■ Make up facts such as the conditions under which the gas was stored to aid your argument. Advise LIS as to the position based on what you are told and what it could be in the event of further information.

■ Fail to explain what the rule is in its original form, as you need to explain how the requirements for fire have developed from that.

■ Treat the question simply as one of negligence. Where a question involves damage to land and a substance leaving one person's land and entering another's, the question will primarily be on the rule in *Rylands* v *Fletcher*.

13

Trespass to the person

How this topic may come up in exams

Trespass to the person consists of assault, battery and false imprisonment but each component is relatively small in size and straightforward to apply to the facts so it is common for all of them to appear in the same problem question. You need to take the time to check the scope of how you are taught this tort to check whether you can expect other torts alongside it, such as the rule from *Wilkinson* v *Downton* or other forms of trespass. Essays are rarer but when they do arise, they will look at the effectiveness of the tort and its purpose.

Attack the question

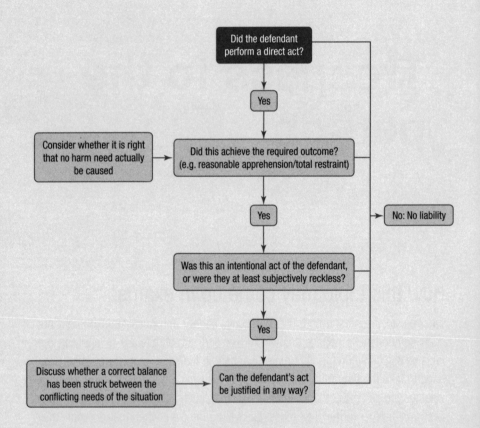

❓ Question 1

Following a government announcement allowing animal testing on a new drug aimed at curing Parkinson's disease, a demonstration was arranged by a group called Save the Apes, Kill a Scientist (STAKAS) in Parliament Square. In order to prevent the demonstration turning violent as in previous STAKAS demonstrations, the police adopted the technique of standing in a line across all of the routes in and out of Parliament Square.

Sylvia, an ice-cream vendor, wanted to cross the square to get to her sales patch but was told by P.C. Hugo that owing to the protest she could not cross the square and would have to go another way. Furious, Sylvia yelled at P.C. Hugo: 'You're just an agent of state control, why are you being such an idiot?' and demanded P.C. Hugo to let her through. When P.C. Hugo still refused, and feeling dejected, she threw a choc-ice in P.C. Hugo's face and walked away.

Shocked by this behaviour, P.C. Hugo shouted back: 'If it wasn't for the Chief Constable being here, you'd get this baton right across your fat gob!'

One of the protesters, in anger at the confinement, threw a brick at the police although it missed its target. Florence, a peaceful protester, saw Beatrice running away from where the brick was thrown and thought Beatrice had thrown the brick. Florence, fearing this would give the group bad publicity, pinned Beatrice down and informed her she was making a citizen's arrest. When the police eventually came over it was established that Beatrice had not thrown the brick and she was released by Florence.

Advise P.C. Hugo, Sylvia and Beatrice as to these instances.

Answer plan

→ Define assault and consider whether Sylvia has committed that tort against P.C. Hugo.

→ Explain the requirements for a battery and apply these to the throwing of the choc-ice.

→ Contrast *Tuberville* v *Savage* and *Read* v *Coker* and determine whether Sylvia was assaulted by P.C. Hugo.

→ Take Beatrice's incident and outline the requirements for a claim for false imprisonment. Consider whether Florence's actions were justified under s.24A of PACE 1984.

Diagram plan

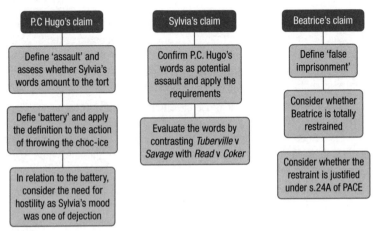

A printable version of this diagram is available from www.pearsoned.co.uk/lawexpressqa

[1] Including this here makes
the introduction to this answer
longer than usual. While you
could deal with this in a second
paragraph before you get into
each incident, it can legitimately
be outlined here. This allows
you to show your understanding
of the nature of these torts and
keep a specific structure to your
answer, dealing with each tort
in turn.

[2] Where you are given a
multitude of instances in a
scenario such as this one,
it is important to provide an
indication of how you will be
dealing with them.

[3] At this stage you have not
established on the facts that
the tort has been made out
while also the facts are not
conclusive: therefore, you
should refer to the matter as
a potential claim.

Answer

The instances which have occurred during the protest give rise to several potential claims under the tort of trespass to the person. This tort comprises of assault, battery and false imprisonment with all three requiring discussion on the facts. The fact that it is these torts in question is significant because each is actionable *per se* without any need to show that the respective claimants have suffered any harm. This is because the interests which the torts are concerned with protecting are bodily integrity and liberty, and thus are deemed to warrant heightened protection from even the slightest interference.[1] Each incident shall be taken in turn,[2] with advice being given to those who have allegedly been the victim of the torts. It will be argued that while P.C. Hugo has a claim for battery, and Beatrice for false imprisonment, Sylvia will be unsuccessful in any claim.

The first incident involves P.C. Hugo, who potentially[3] has a claim for assault and battery against Sylvia. Taking the assault claim first, he should be advised that this is intentionally causing a person to reasonably apprehend the immediate infliction of a battery (unlawful touching). Fear is not required for assault and so the fact that P.C. Hugo is a police officer confronted by an unarmed woman would

[4]Make sure that you use
the direct facts here to
give your assertion some
foundation: otherwise, your
answer may come across as
unsubstantiated speculation
rather than reasoned
argument.

[5]Because this will so clearly
be the case, be more
assertive than for the assault
claim. By explaining that it is
from throwing and hitting him
with the choc-ice you have
also established the basis of
the tort.

[6]Explain why there is a debate
as to hostility. This allows you
to show your knowledge and
analytical skills.

[7]Make sure that you use
a phrase such as this
to emphasise why the
discussion is taking place.

have no bearing on the matter. Although mere words can constitute an assault (**R v Ireland** [1998] A.C. 147), looking at the words at face value there is nothing in them to suggest that Sylvia was immediately about to strike P.C. Hugo and so there would not appear to have been an assault. However, we are told that when Sylvia shouted at P.C. Hugo she did so in a 'furious' manner,[4] which could indicate her gesticulating with her hands. Therefore, if her manner was such that P.C. Hugo did apprehend that she would make contact with him and this was reasonable when objectively viewed, he may succeed in a claim for assault.

The second of Sylvia's actions towards P.C. Hugo appears to be clearer cut. By throwing and hitting him with the choc-ice, Sylvia has committed the tort of battery.[5] A battery is an intentional, immediate and direct act which causes unlawful physical contact with the claimant. In relation to the first factor, even if Sylvia asserts that she did not intend to hit P.C. Hugo when she threw the choc-ice, subjective recklessness will suffice – **Bici v Ministry of Defence** [2004] E.W.H.C. 786. While it could be argued that the contact was made by the choc-ice and not Sylvia, this is irrelevant and there is long-standing authority that an intervening object may be used such as in **Pursell v Horn** 112 E.R. 966. Strengthening P.C. Hugo's claim is the fact that, although Sylvia threw the choc-ice dejectedly as she walked away, this seemingly lack of hostile intent will not defeat a claim. One of the earliest definitions of battery was stated by Lord Holt CJ in **Cole v Turner** 87 E.R. 907 to be 'the least touching of another in anger', which suggests a hostility requirement in order to make the touching unjustifiable;[6] this was certainly the view taken in **Wilson v Pringle** [1987] Q.B. 237. In **F v West Berkshire Health Authority** [1990] 2 A.C. 1, however, Lord Goff explained that using hostility as the qualification for whether touching becomes unlawful ignores the fact that actions such as a slap on the back and non-consensual surgery are both battery yet both lack hostility. Instead, what would take Sylvia's actions outside of the remit of battery[7] is if it could be said to be within the bounds of generally accepted standards of everyday life. It would be very hard for her to argue that throwing an object at someone doing their job, simply because it caused her inconvenience, would be acceptable, and thus this is a battery.

In relation to Sylvia, she may also have a claim for assault. Clearly, the words used by P.C. Hugo indicate a willingness to inflict a battery on her by striking her in the mouth with his baton. However, any apprehension by Sylvia of this occurring would need to be reasonable (**Thomas v N.U.M.** [1986] Ch. 20) and this is where she may have an issue. The fact that a condition is attached to a threat, such as 'If you do not go away now, I will smack you', does not prevent the finding of an assault (**Read v Coker** 138 E.R. 1437). However, this is not what P.C. Hugo has done here. Instead, what his words signify is that he has no intention to actually strike Sylvia because the Chief Constable is present. His words, as in **Tuberville v Savage** 86 E.R. 684, in fact negate any assault and, therefore, it will be held that if Sylvia did apprehend the immediate infliction of a battery, this was unreasonable and therefore no assault took place.

With regard to Beatrice, she should be advised that the tort which she may claim for is that of false imprisonment, where 'false' effectively means unlawful. To be successful it will need to be shown that Florence intentionally and directly caused Beatrice to be totally restrained, within an area set by Florence, who had no lawful authority to do so (**Bird v Jones** (1845) 7 Q.B. 742). It is clear that Florence did completely restrain Beatrice, as she was pinned down until the police established that Beatrice had done nothing wrong. This emphasises that the act was clearly intentional, as Florence thought Beatrice had thrown the brick and intended to detain her until the police arrived. Acting in good faith is no justification for restraining a person's liberty (**Evans v Governor of Brockhill Prison** [2001] 2 A.C. 19); the issue becomes, therefore, whether in view of Florence thinking that Beatrice had committed a crime the restraint was lawful. While a person other than a constable has authority to arrest someone whom they reasonably believed to have committed an indictable offence under s.24A, PACE 1984, it must not have been reasonably practicable for a constable to have made the arrest. There was a large police presence at the protest and so the arrest could have been made by a constable. Furthermore, as the police were not letting the protestors out of the Square, it is unlikely the required condition that the arrest was needed to prevent Beatrice making off is satisfied. In any event,[8] Beatrice should be advised that under **R v Self** [1992] 1 W.L.R. 657, notwithstanding the authority under the section if no offence has actually been committed, as in the situation here, then liability for false imprisonment will result. Therefore, Beatrice will have a claim against Florence.

[8] While this would seem to deal conclusively with the matter, still discuss the requirements under s.24A in order to demonstrate your knowledge and add to the level of evaluation in your answer.

✓ Make your answer stand out

- Using authorities such as *Harnett* v *Bond* [1925] A.C. 669 and *Warner* v *Riddiford* (1858) 4 C.N.B.S. 180, discuss also the possibility of a claim of false imprisonment against the police for preventing people from leaving Parliament Square.

- From your general academic reading, include some material so as to explain in a bit more depth some of the theoretical basis which underpins trespass and why it has strict liability and is actionable *per se*. You can also draw further on the views of Lord Goff in cases such as *Collins* and *F* for this purpose.

! Don't be tempted to ...

- Define assault again when you come to discuss Sylvia's claim against P.C. Hugo.

- Go into aspects of false imprisonment which are not relevant, such as whether the claimant knew they were restrained.

- View the question as quite straightforward and just race through an application of the law to the facts. Make sure you still try to evaluate the law, such as with regard the need for hostility in battery, and use this to develop your argument. Otherwise, you will miss out on marks for the depth of you analysis and evaluation.

❓ Question 2

Francesco and Edoardo were walking home from university one day, taking the path which runs alongside the Montgomery River, a very wide, deep and fast-flowing river. As they were walking they saw Bubba and Dustin approaching on the other side of the river on their way to the local golf course. The four had recently had an argument after Edoardo had reported Bubba and Dustin for cheating in an exam which saw Bubba get expelled while Dustin was found innocent.

When Bubba saw Edoardo he yelled: 'You are dead for reporting me; I am going to put you in hospital for that!' Edoardo, feeling scared, decided to run so he could get home quickly. Feeling aggrieved by being reported when he was innocent, Dustin decided to chip a golf ball across the river at Edoardo as he ran off. However, he misjudged the shot and instead struck Francesco in the back of the head who had decided to carry on walking home.

When Edoardo got home he decided to get his own back by ringing Bubba's house and playing a prank on Bubba's elderly grandfather, Zach, whom Bubba lived with, by informing him that Bubba had been run over and killed on his way to the golf course and that the police would probably be with Zach shortly. Upon hearing this, Zach went into shock.

Advise Bubba, Dustin and Edoardo as to any liability they may face.

Answer plan

→ Define assault and consider whether there is sufficient reasonableness and immediacy to Bubba's threat.

→ Outline the requirements for battery and consider the issue of transferred intent in relation to Dustin's act.

→ Advise Edoardo as to the rule in *Wilkinson* v *Downton* and apply it to his call to Zach.

Diagram plan

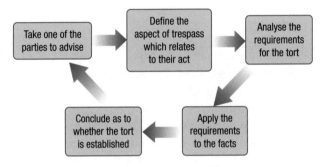

A printable version of this diagram is available from www.pearsoned.co.uk/lawexpressqa

Answer

[1]By briefly demonstrating your understanding of the tort, you can get to the main premise of the question quickly so that you have enough time to fully evaluate the issues arising from the facts. You can then refer back to the tort's nature as required.

[2]Keep this brief as it is only the introduction. Set out in depth what the tort is about when you come to discuss Edoardo's liability. Simply show that you have appreciated that the rule is distinct and requires discussion.

In advising Bubba and Dustin as to their potential liability, both will need to be advised as to assault and battery respectively which form the tort or trespass to the person. These protect a person's bodily integrity and are actionable without proof of actual harm. This reflects the importance that tort places on this interest.[1] Edoardo's advice differs slightly in that he faces liability under the rule in **Wilkinson *v* Downton** [1897] 2 Q.B. 57 which, while related to trespass owing to it having an element of intention, is a separate tort.[2] Each will be advised in turn.

The tort which Bubba may be liable for is assault. This is intentionally causing a person to reasonably apprehend the immediate infliction of a battery. The fact that Edoardo ran off scared after hearing Bubba's threat would suggest that he felt he was going to attack

[3]The reason for only including the name of the case in here is that you are seeking to draw a parallel with the facts of the case in order to use this as the authority for the argument which you will go on to advance. There will be no need to then state the facts, as the marker will know from how you have structured the sentence that the two aspects of the definition which you are discussing were at issue in *Thomas*.

[4]This is why, although 'reasonable' comes first in the definition, you should address it second in your answer.

[5]You will not need to write the full article title and citation, but provide the marker enough indication as to what work you are referring to.

him. However, Bubba should be advised that this is not sufficient to establish liability, and, as in **Thomas v N.U.M.** [1986] Ch. 20, there are two aspects of the definition which should mean that Bubba will escape liability.[3] The first is that the carrying out of the threat, the infliction of the battery, must be immediate. We are told that both were on differing sides of the river and from the description given it would appear that the Montgomery River is impassable. This would mean that it was not possible for Bubba to actually perform the unlawful touching necessary for battery immediately. Even though some delay is permissible (**R v Ireland** [1998] A.C. 147), Edoardo would still need to reasonably believe that the battery is imminent, which on the facts seems unlikely. This leads into the second aspect of the definition which is an issue here,[4] namely the reasonableness of the apprehension. It is not sufficient that Edoardo subjectively felt that he was about to be hit: it must objectively on the facts be reasonable for him to apprehend this event. As it seems there was no possibility of Bubba crossing the river, and therefore no immediate danger, any apprehension he felt was not reasonable as Bubba was not going to be able to carry out the threat.

Dustin faces liability under the tort of battery. This is defined as an intentional, immediate and direct act which causes unjustifiable physical contact with the claimant. From the facts, there is clearly no issue around the requirement for an immediate act. Additionally, although it is a golf ball which makes contact rather than Dustin physically touching Francesco, this will also not matter; it is clear from case law that direct does not mean instantaneous and an intervening object can be used (e.g. in **Hopper v Reeve** 129 E.R. 278 where throwing water over someone was a battery). Dustin should be advised that even though his intention was to hit Edoardo rather than Francesco, this will not enable him to avoid liability. What must be intended is the act and not the result (**Bici v Ministry of Defence** [2004] E.W.H.C. 786): Dustin's intention to hit Edoardo will simply be transferred to hitting Franceso. The application of the concept of transferred malice was first acknowledged in English law in **Bici** and one of the reasons for its application is by analogy with the criminal law. However, its application has been firmly rejected by Beever (2009)[5] who argues that, unlike in criminal law, in tort the identity of the claimant has significant importance and is essential to the cause of action and therefore, the analogy does not work and the

[6]This is why it is worth commentating on the academic discussion around this issue, as it could form the basis of Dustin avoiding liability, which is what your task essentially is. More importantly, this also allows you to add to the analytical depth of your answer.

[7]Although the question is not on negligence, show your wider knowledge of tort by highlighting that you have seen further potential liability from Dustin's actions.

[8]By highlighting why Edoardo could not be sued in trespass, you not only show more depth to your understanding of that tort but also create a platform from which to introduce the rule in *Wilkinson* v *Downton*.

[9]Your aim is to pass comment on the rule, not to argue whether there is negligence. As the rule has been subjected to significant criticism, you should reproduce this and assess whether it is a suitable basis of liability for Edoardo.

doctrine should not apply. If this were the case, then Dustin by not intending to strike Francesco would not be liable to him for battery.[6] Therefore, as **Bici** is only a High Court judgment, it is open for Dustin to defend any claim by Francesco on the basis that the doctrine should not apply in tort, but he should be advised that as the law currently stands he will be liable for battery. However, Dustin should be advised that, even if successful on this point, it may instead lead to him being liable in negligence.[7]

In relation to Edoardo, the harm which his actions have led to did not flow directly from what he did: it was more indirect harm. As such, he could not face any claim under trespass.[8] However, where someone intentionally conducts themselves in a way which causes indirect harm, the rule in **Wilkinson** v **Downton** may be used to impose liability. In **Wilkinson** a prank call caused the recipient to suffer psychiatric injury, which was not recoverable at the time in negligence. The judge found the defendant liable on the basis that he had wilfully done an unjustified act calculated to cause harm, therefore, the intention to cause the harm which occurred was imputed by the judge. This appears very similar to what has happened with Edoardo. The rule was subjected, though, to extensive analysis in **Wainwright** v **Home Office** [2004] 2 A.C. 406, where it was held that imputed intention should not be used and that there must be an actual intention to cause harm, or the defendant would need to have acted without caring whether he caused harm. We are not told that Edoardo had an intention to cause harm, but it would seem that he was at the very least the latter. The question is what sort of harm Edoardo's phone call has caused. We are told that Zach went into shock but no more. If this is a fully recognised psychiatric injury, then Edoardo is very likely to face liability either under the rule or in negligence. In **Wainwright**, Lord Hoffmann felt negligence was the better cause of action but subsequently the rule was used for this type of injury in **C** v **D** [2006] E.W.H.C. 166.[9] However, if the 'shock' was in fact merely a case of distress, then it would appear that Edoardo will not face any liability. Lord Hoffmann stated that the rule does not provide a remedy in such instances and while he was cautious about creating a tort of intentionally causing distress to deal with such a scenario Lord Scott was strongly opposed to the idea, a view adopted in **Mbasogo** v **Logo Ltd** [2007] Q.B. 846.

In conclusion, Bubba is unlikely to face any liability for assault, but Dustin is likely to be liable for battery; even if Dustin can avoid this, he may instead be liable in negligence. Determining the position of Edoardo requires more evidence as to the nature of Zach's injury. If it was simply distress that was suffered, he will not be liable, but if he suffered a medically recognised psychiatric injury, he will face liability under the rule in **Wilkinson v Downton** or alternatively negligence.

✓ Make your answer stand out

- Read the article by Allan Beever (2009) 'Tranferred malice in tort law?', in Legal Studies 29 (3): 400–20 in full; be able to add further points to your argument regarding Dustin and whether he should be liable for battery.
- Consider in more depth the future role of the rule in *Wilkinson* v *Downton* and whether there should be a tort covering the intentional infliction of distress.

! Don't be tempted to …

- Get too sidetracked regarding the merits of applying transferred malice in tort; make sure you stay focused structurally on applying the law to the issue.
- Discuss negligence. If you do refer to negligence, avoid going through and applying all of the requirements. This could lead to your marker thinking that you have misidentified the main essence of the question, which is trespass, and you will also risk running out of time. By highlighting it, you will have shown an appreciation of that tort by way of the fact that you have seen its potential application.

? Question 3

Malcolm and Glen are two homeless people who were sitting on a street corner drinking cider one day when Julius, who owned a nearby shop, approached them. As he did, Julius said: 'If you two filth-bags do not clear off away from my shop I'm going to force you away.' Julius then spat at Malcolm as he turned around to go back to his shop.

Glen fearing that Julius was going to get something to attack them with decided to get in first and swung the glass cider bottle at Julius, hitting him in the head and causing a severe cut. As Julius fell, he hit his head and lost consciousness.

At the hospital Dr. Mannion diagnosed Julius as needing emergency surgery and a blood transfusion. Such a procedure is against Julius's religious views and so he would have refused this had he been conscious. Julius also confirmed when he gained consciousness that he was simply going back to the shop to work and was hoping Malcolm and Glen would have gone on their own accord.

Advise the parties as to their liability under the tort of trespass to the person.

Answer plan

→ Explain what assault is and discuss the relevance of the condition which Julius had attached to his words.

→ Indicate how Julius will also be liable for battery for spitting at Malcolm.

→ Outline the requirements for battery in full in relation to Glen hitting Julius.

→ Consider whether Glen can claim self-defence in light of Julius's assault and battery.

→ Advise Dr. Mannion as to battery, explaining whether his actions were justifiable owing to necessity.

Diagram plan

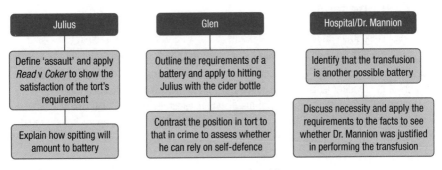

Julius	Glen	Hospital/Dr. Mannion
Define 'assault' and apply *Read* v *Coker* to show the satisfaction of the tort's requirement	Outline the requirements of a battery and apply to hitting Julius with the cider bottle	Identify that the transfusion is another possible battery
Explain how spitting will amount to battery	Contrast the position in tort to that in crime to assess whether he can rely on self-defence	Discuss necessity and apply the requirements to the facts to see whether Dr. Mannion was justified in performing the transfusion

A printable version of this diagram is available from www.pearsoned.co.uk/lawexpressqa

Answer

[1]By highlighting these factors here, you show that you have identified all the topics in the question and where the complications may lie.

The potential liabilities of the parties all relate to trespass to the person and the torts of assault and battery. While these torts are actionable with proof of damage, clearly some damage has occurred here. However, the issue, particularly for the latter two acts, is whether the actions were justifiable in the circumstances owing to self-defence and necessity.[1]

[2]Obviously, you have not defined battery yet, so provide a brief explanation here. This will enable you to apply the requirements of assault to this situation more easily.

[3]Do not forget to apply this aspect. Generally, you would need to substantiate this statement but here, on the facts, there really is no issue of this not being a direct act. Therefore, this would suffice.

[4]As this is a distinct point on the requirements for an assault, give it its own paragraph to clearly distinguish it and spread the detail of your answer out. This will make your argument easier to follow.

[5]Because of this authority and the exact similarity of the case to Julius', simply state this and deal with the definition of battery at the start of your advice to Glen, which naturally is going to be more in depth on the subject.

[6]Again, this is self-evident, so you should simply state this fact after explaining what battery is and move on to main discussion point of whether the touching was justified as an act of self-defence.

[7]Although a tort answer, you are still making an assertion of legal principle to set out your argument, so you should cite the criminal law authority for it. Your aim is to compare the two approaches and show that you have a real grasp of the basis of tort law and the principles underpinning it.

The first issue is whether Julius is liable for assaulting Malcolm and Glen. Assault is causing another to reasonably apprehend the immediate infliction of a battery, the unlawful touching of that person[2] and requires an intentional and direct act. Arguably, Julius has a clear intention as he wants them to go away from his shop and the threat was designed to make them leave; and the act is obviously direct.[3] Julius should be advised that this is likely to be a reasonable apprehension by Malcolm and Glen even though he gave them a way of avoiding any battery. His words simply amount to a conditional threat and do not negate any apprehended threat (**Tuberville v Savage** 86 E.R. 684). Provided that his words would objectively cause the apprehension of the battery, Julius will be liable for the assault: **Read v Coker** 138 E.R. 1437.

The fact that Julius turns away and goes to return to the shop may suggest that any battery was not going to be immediately inflicted;[4] however, an apprehension of an imminent battery is sufficient under (**R v Ireland**). Julius had a reasonable means of inflicting a battery at the time, but even if it was reasonable to think that Julius was returning to his shop for a weapon, owing to its close proximity, this would still be imminent.

In any event, clearly under **R v Cotesworth** 87 E.R. 928, Julius spitting at Malcolm will be a battery.[5] Therefore, the fact a battery occurred supports an assertion that the apprehension of one was reasonable, even though Julius had turned away and was not going to physically strike them.

Glen also faces liability for battery. The unlawful touching must be an intentional, direct and immediate act of Glen's. It is clear that by swinging the cider bottle Glen has satisfied all of the elements of the tort.[6] The only way that Glen can avoid liability is proving that his touching of Julius was in self-defence and thus not unlawful, as this makes the touching of another, and the violation of their personal integrity, justified. Glen's issue is that while he felt Julius was going to attack him imminently, he was mistaken. In terms of criminal law, acting under an honest but mistaken belief would be sufficient for self-defence, regardless of how reasonable the mistaken belief was (**R v Williams (Gladstone)** [1987] 3 All E.R. 411).[7] However, self-defence in tort is different. **Ashley v Chief Constable of Sussex** [2008] U.K.H.L. 25 determined that it must

[8]All of the judges stated an opinion on this, so remember to be specific as to whom you are referring, as this shows that you have a greater level of knowledge of the case.

be reasonable to hold the mistaken belief. Lord Scott[8] felt that the purposes of tort and crime differed, and that if tort adopted the same approach the wrong balance would be struck between a person's right not to be subjected to physical harm and another's right to prevent an imminent attack with reasonable force. While not imposing criminal sanction on a person in such a situation is justifiable as their liberty is at stake, an unreasonably held belief is an unjustifiable basis for setting aside one's right to physical integrity. Therefore, Glen's liability rests on the reasonableness of his belief that he was going to be imminently attacked. Arguably, it is reasonable to believe that as Julius was outnumbered he may want a weapon. However, it is more likely that this was not a reasonable belief. Julius's words do not necessarily indicate an imminent physical attack, and when viewed with the fact that Julius was turning away from Glen it would seem less reasonable to believe such an attack was about to occur.

[9]In terms of advising Dr. Mannion of his liability, this would be an important piece of information for him and impacts ultimately on whether he would be held liable or not. Although no specific mention is made of advising the hospital, or of vicarious liability, by mentioning this you will gain marks for having recognised that the doctrine will operate here.

Even if Glen can satisfy the requirement from **Ashley**, his act must also be proportionate to the threat posed by Julius (**Lane v Holloway** [1968] 1 Q.B. 379). Here Julius was, at the time in question, unarmed and turning away from Glen yet Glen struck him around the head with a glass cider bottle. Therefore, even if Glen was acting under a reasonable belief, his act was disproportionate to Julius' conduct and so Glen would be liable for the battery.

The final issue is whether Dr. Mannion can be liable in battery for operating on Julius without his consent. By performing the transfusion, the elements of a battery are clearly present. Dr. Mannion should be advised that, if liability is found, any claim would likely arise against the hospital as they would be vicariously liable for his performance of the operation[9] (**Cassidy v Ministry of Health** [1951] 2 K.B. 343). The issue is whether this was a justifiable intrusion of Julius's physical integrity because the situation was an emergency.

[10]The point of writing your answer in this way rather than talking about the 'defence' of necessity is that it indicates you have a deeper understanding of the tort in recognising that, if the touching is not unlawful, there is no tort from the start – not that there was a tort but a defence applies to negate liability.

Ultimately, the liability for the operation will rest on whether the situation was one of necessity, as if this was the case it will justify the intrusion and mean that the fundamental essence of the tort, unlawfulness, is missing.[10] This is governed by **F v West Berkshire H.A.** [1990] 2 A.C. 1. For this to be an instance of necessity, it first needs to be shown that the touching was necessary in the circumstances and that it was not practicable to communicate with the claimant. Julius was unconscious from the fall and so it was not possible to ask whether he would object to the transfusion. An assessment is needed as to whether the transfusion could have waited until Julius regained consciousness. If the action was required to save Julius's life or prevent permanent damage, then it will be reasonable to not wait as clearly the situation was one of necessity. We are told that the situation was an emergency because of the loss of blood from the cut, and so this suggests that it was necessary not to delay.

It must then be shown, though, that the action taken was reasonable in the circumstances in which they occurred, with a reasonable body of medical opinion supporting such action. We are not told whether this was the case; if it was then there would be no liability under **F**.

Therefore, in conclusion, Julius is likely to be found liable for assault and battery; Glen is also likely to be liable for battery, unless he act was deemed reasonable, but even then it was potentially dispro-portionate. The hospital will, however, not be liable owing to the necessity of the situation.

✓ Make your answer stand out

- Explain in more depth whether it is right that tort takes a different approach to criminal law when it comes to self-defence. For example, are the differing underlying principles of each area of law sufficient to warrant a separate approach or could they be reconciled?

- Consider what the merits are of tort adopting the third solution discussed by Lord Scott in *Ashley*. This would require you to think of the consequences of such a change and its merits. To aid this, you may want to look at the Court of Appeal judgment from the case and particularly paragraphs 63 to 78 where Lord Clarke MR discusses this.

- Do ensure that you explain why the hospital is vicariously liable for Dr. Mannion. It is something which should be considered but which can easily be forgotten in the exam room, especially when the question is not specifically on vicarious liability.

> **!** **Don't be tempted to ...**
>
> ■ Avoid the debate over self-defence or deal with it too briefly, as this is arguably the key point in the question where you can gain extra marks for the level of evaluation within your answer.
>
> ■ Turn your answer into an essay on the nature of self-defence. It may seem tricky but you have to strike an appropriate balance between demonstrating a deeper level of knowledge and understanding and adding analytical depth with the fundamental need to employ a good structure and answer the question that has been set.
>
> ■ Discuss other defences which have no application on the facts just to show that you know them. This will just show that you have not understood the question properly and is indicative of a descriptive, narrative type answer.

🖎 Question 4

'At the level of enforcement, rights do not permit trade-offs between the interests of the right-holder and of the right-infringer. Such trade-offs take place at the earlier stage of right-definition. This is mirrored in the distinction between defences and justifications: justifications are part of the definition of the right whereas defences are trade-offs at the level of enforcement.'

P. Cane (1999) 'Fault and strict liability, for harm in tort law', in W. Swaddling and G. Jones *The Search for Principle: Essays in Honour of Lord Goff of Chieveley*, OUP

Evaluate the function and requirements of trespass to the person in light of this statement.

Answer plan

→ Discuss the purpose of the overall tort explaining its rationale.

→ Evaluate battery, illustrating its aim and showing how its requirements aid the overall purpose.

→ Repeat this process for assault.

→ Consider false imprisonment in the same way.

Diagram plan

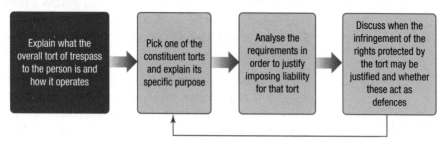

A printable version of this diagram is available from www.pearsoned.co.uk/lawexpressqa

Answer

[1]Structurally, it makes more sense if you deal with the generic theoretical aspects of the tort first before going into depth on each component tort. This passage should be written as an extended introduction and then it can act as your foundation for the answer from which the rest of your arguments build from.

[2]This may just read like a restatement of the quote, but it is important that you include a passage such as this in your answer, in your own words. This shows firstly that you understand what the quote means and allows you to tie it in to the overall theory and purpose of the tort.

Trespass is one of the oldest torts protecting the individual from unjustified intentional harm inflicted. Consisting of battery, assault and false imprisonment, it seeks to provide meaning to one's right to physical integrity and liberty by imposing liability without the need to prove any damage was suffered because of the intentional infringement of the right.[1] As Cane suggests, strong protection is provided by not preventing vindication of the right through the pleading of a defence. However, this raises problems in terms of criminal justice and freedom of action. Therefore, certain actions are permitted in order to balance the competing rights of others. Where the defendant's actions are justified, there is no tort in the first instance as the key characteristic of unjustness is missing; however, a defence to an action implies that a tort has been made out initially.[2]

Battery is the direct and intentional unlawful touching of another, although subjective recklessness will suffice (**Bici v MoD** [2004] E.W.H.C. 786). It aims to protect physical integrity by prohibiting any form of unjustified molestation, not just touching which causes injury (**F v West Berkshire H.A.** [1990] 2 A.C. 1). This reflects the sacrosanct nature of physical integrity, which means that the smallest infringement, even an unwanted kiss, is prohibited.

Such a strong approach is warranted owing to the defendant's intent. If actual harm is necessary, the protection afforded is greatly reduced; the system for vindicating one's rights is made far simpler by merely requiring that there should be no touching rather than

219

assessing the degree of touching. Liability also arises even if an object is used to make contact with the claimant (**Pursell v Horn** 112 E.R. 966), or if the intentional act was directed at a third party (**Bici**). In this latter scenario the intention is transferred to the person who was actually touched.

Clearly, this could greatly restrict one's right to freedom of action; greater harm to the claimant could even be caused if all touching required consent to be justified. For example, doctors could not perform emergency operations on unconscious patients. Therefore, the law has sought to reasonably restrict the tort's application by creating categories of lawful touching. It is for this reason that Cane highlights the distinction between defences and justifications in trespass.[3] These situations go to the heart of what battery is and thus negate its existence. The key categories are necessity (**F**), self-defence (**Ashley v Chief Constable of Sussex** [2008] U.K.H.L. 25) and all touching within the bounds of what is acceptable as part of everyday life (**F**).

The first of these is clearly a justified intrusion so as to prevent a greater harm such as death or serious injury and covers the medical scenario above. The second is also needed as it allows one to prevent their physical integrity from being infringed themselves. The third category covers 'the exigencies of everyday life' such as jostling in the street (*per* Lord Goff in **F**). However, reflecting tort's overall approach to balancing conflicting rights and interests, none of these automatically make the touching lawful; there are set requirements outlined in the cases which must be satisfied in order to justify the touching.[4]

Physical integrity can also be infringed without actual touching, hence the need for assault. Assault requires that the defendant must have done an intentional, direct act which causes the claimant to reasonably apprehend the immediate infliction of a battery.[5] The fact that a battery is unlawful means it is equally right to impose liability when someone intentionally causes another to apprehend that one is forthcoming. Power and control can be exerted simply by threat of violence and one's quality of life should not be hindered by the constant apprehension of a battery. One's right to physical integrity would be hollowed as liability is avoided simply by not carrying out the threat, yet the consequence may be the same.[6] Causing such a

[3]Remember that the question asks you to evaluate the tort in light of the statement, so refer back to it in support of your points. Including a line such as this at the stage of introducing justifications for touching someone also shows that you have understood what Cane is suggesting in the quote.

[4]The question does not expressly ask for details of these, but at this stage of your answer check how you are doing for time and perhaps add some detail here. The important point is to at least get across that the categories of justifications are needed to provide the balance which tort strives to achieve.

[5]As battery is in the definition of assault, it is best to discuss battery first as then you will have already defined this term, allowing you to now get straight into assault.

[6]Offer some reasoning as to why the operation of assault is justified; this stops your answer from becoming a descriptive piece on each tort. Instead you are showing analytical skills which will help you get more marks.

state of mind cannot be justified on any public policy basis. It should also be noted that as with battery a subjectively reckless act will suffice (**Bici**). Perhaps the most significant word in the definition of assault is 'reasonable'. It is too great an infringement into another's freedom of action if the claimant could succeed by simply perceiving a threat in non-existent circumstances, particularly when great emphasis is now placed on freedom of expression. Requiring reasonableness ensures that any encroachment of freedom of expression is justified. A good illustration is in **Thomas v N.U.M.**, where the striking miners had no way of actually reaching the non-strikers[7] and so any apprehension was unreasonable. This also reinforces how the full context must be considered. An assault can be carried out by simple gestures, words are not needed (**R v Ireland**); however, if words are present alongside an action, they must be considered in order to assess whether they reinforce the reasonableness of the apprehension or in fact negate it (**Tuberville v Savage** 86 E.R. 684).

Finally, false imprisonment is the total restraint of someone without lawful authority for however short a time (**Bird v Jones** (1845) 7 Q.B. 742). The tort, therefore, protects one's liberty, a fundamental right under the ECHR. Reflecting the importance of personal liberty under the law, liability arises from a restraint lasting the smallest amount of time and the claimant may not even need to realise they were being restrained (**Murray v MoD** [1988] U.K.H.L. 13). However, there is some doubt as to the validity of this view. **Murray** approved **Meering v Graham-White Aviation** (1919) 122 L.T. 44 on this point but the issue was only *obiter*. In the later case of **R v Bournewood Mental Health Trust** (ex parte L [1999] 1 A.C. 458), the patient did not know that if he left his actual ward he would be detained. However, because he could physically leave the ward, there was held to be no total restraint present as he could in theory leave that area. This would mean that knowledge of the restraint is required by the claimant. Significantly, the minority was favoured in **HL v UK** [2004] E.C.H.R. 471 regarding a claim under Article 5; thus, arguably, if the situation arises again, the **Murray** position will be adopted.[8] This would better reflect the purpose of the tort: otherwise a person drugged, then taken but released before gaining consciousness, would have no claim.

[7] All you need here is to state enough of the basic facts to illustrate the point which you are making. So do not feel the need to go into more factual depth here than is stated.

[8] Although this is not an English law authority, it is worth mentioning as it involved the same claimant – thus showing that you know this and understand the implications of the case.

Clearly, there must be justifications for certain restraints, otherwise the criminal justice system would be inoperable. Therefore, PACE 1984 provides the power to make arrests. However, in order to allow the police to perform their function, while also ensuring that the function is not abused and due process is observed, certain procedures must be followed. This is crucial in any democracy to prevent the devaluing of the tort's protection.

[9]The key to your conclusion is to offer a personal view as to whether a good balance has been struck between the rights that the tort protects and the conflicting interests of society. This should be a restatement of what you have been advancing throughout your answer.

Therefore, the three torts play a vital role in protecting one's key right to personal integrity. The fact that they have existed for so long without any fundamental restructuring of principle suggests that they are doing this job effectively while not causing problems for day-to-day society by justifying actions which would otherwise infringe one's physical integrity.[9]

✓ Make your answer stand out

- Try and read the chapter on trespass in Fifoot's (1995) *History and Sources of the Common Law: Tort and Contract* (Stevens & Sons Ltd) as well as the essay from which the quote is taken. The first will provide you with material as to the historical purpose of the tort which you can use in your answer. Reading the essay from the question will also help you to understand the distinction which Cane is making between defences and justifications, which will allow you to discuss this more confidently in your answer.

- Expand the discussion of the distinction when it comes to defences or justifications in trespass. The idea is that justified actions remove the key element of the definition of each tort and so prevent it from ever coming into being. This is contrasted to defences which acknowledge the presence of the tort but prevent liability.

- Provide some more details as to specific requirements for the conduct in question to be justifiable and thus negate the existence of each tort.

! Don't be tempted to ...

- Talk independently about the justifications too much as the question does tell you to focus on the requirements of the tort. You will, therefore, limit your scope to explore these in depth and show your analysis and evaluation of the torts.

- Give excessive factual detail of cases in order to explain your points. The question is more concerned with the theory of the tort and the underlying principles, and so you just need to discuss the facts to the extent that they help to illustrate these. Simply give enough to help substantiate the point and act as the basis for the issue which you are dealing with at that time.

Defamation

How this topic may come up in exams

The topic's scope and its prominence in the media make this a popular exam area. You should check your module and see whether, and to what extent, it covers the misuse of private information and the development of a tort of privacy as these are related to defamation. The structure of the tort and the various defences which have their own criteria and tests to apply means it lends itself well to problem questions. However, essays are also common, focusing on the balance between protecting an individual's reputation, and nowadays their privacy, and another's freedom of expression. Therefore, it is important to know the influence of human rights on the topic.

■ Attack the question

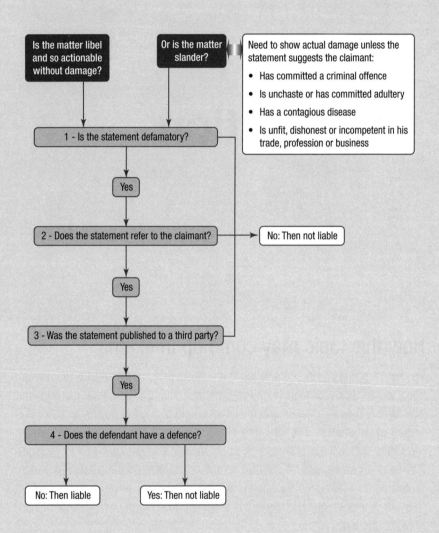

Is the matter libel and so actionable without damage?

Or is the matter slander?

Need to show actual damage unless the statement suggests the claimant:

- Has committed a criminal offence
- Is unchaste or has committed adultery
- Has a contagious disease
- Is unfit, dishonest or incompetent in his trade, profession or business

1 - Is the statement defamatory?

Yes

2 - Does the statement refer to the claimant?

No: Then not liable

Yes

3 - Was the statement published to a third party?

Yes

4 - Does the defendant have a defence?

No: Then liable

Yes: Then not liable

A printable version of this diagram is available from www.pearsoned.co.uk/lawexpressqa

🅿 Question 1

Michael Paxman is an investigative reporter for the *Westminster Echo,* a weekly political magazine. He has been looking into a local MP, Peter Seldon. Peter Seldon is also currently the housing minister with responsibility for planning applications, and before entering Parliament was a director of a national house-building company. Michael's investigations have uncovered that Peter's previous company has received preferential treatment in planning decisions. Additionally, he has established that Seldon had retained shares in the company which he has just sold for a sizeable profit after the company had obtained planning permission for a new town development. Michael has now published his investigation in the latest edition of the *Westminster Echo*; an extract on the front page reads:

> Today we reveal how housing minister, Peter Seldon, joins the list of corrupt MPs who shame Parliament. Evidence indicates he is favouring former business associates in deciding planning applications. Not content with doing favours for those associates, he has also pocketed thousands of pounds from a share holding in the company.

Inside the magazine, however, the story states that Peter had registered the shares in the register of members' interests, and stresses that there is no evidence of him receiving financial payments from the company for the decision.

During a televised debate in the House of Commons on housing policy, Peter responds: 'Michael Paxman, a two-bob journalist with a history of fabricating and plagiarising stories: it is he who brings shame on his profession.'

Advise both parties as to whether they have a claim for the respective comments in defamation.

Answer plan

→ Define what defamation is and establish that we are concerned with libel.

→ Apply the three requirements of defamation, in turn, to the newspaper story and ensure that you identify the key allegation against Peter.

→ Consider the possible defences which could apply to the paper, namely justification and qualified privilege. If not applicable, advise of the remedy available.

→ Repeat the application of the requirements of defamation to the comments by Peter.

→ Discuss the defence of absolute privilege for Peter.

Diagram plan

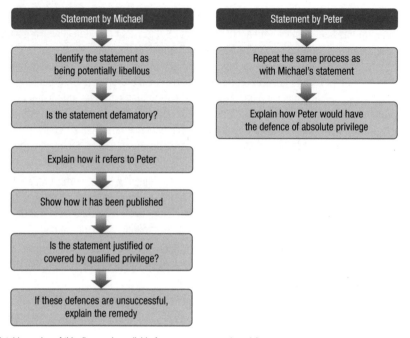

```
┌─────────────────────────────┐      ┌─────────────────────────────┐
│    Statement by Michael     │      │     Statement by Peter      │
└─────────────────────────────┘      └─────────────────────────────┘
              ↓                                     ↓
┌─────────────────────────────┐      ┌─────────────────────────────┐
│   Identify the statement as │      │   Repeat the same process as│
│   being potentially libellous│     │   with Michael's statement  │
└─────────────────────────────┘      └─────────────────────────────┘
              ↓                                     ↓
┌─────────────────────────────┐      ┌─────────────────────────────┐
│  Is the statement defamatory?│     │   Explain how Peter would have│
└─────────────────────────────┘      │  the defence of absolute privilege│
              ↓                       └─────────────────────────────┘
┌─────────────────────────────┐
│   Explain how it refers to Peter│
└─────────────────────────────┘
              ↓
┌─────────────────────────────┐
│  Show how it has been published│
└─────────────────────────────┘
              ↓
┌─────────────────────────────┐
│   Is the statement justified or│
│   covered by qualified privilege?│
└─────────────────────────────┘
              ↓
┌─────────────────────────────┐
│  If these defences are unsuccessful,│
│   explain the remedy        │
└─────────────────────────────┘
```

A printable version of this diagram is available from www.pearsoned.co.uk/lawexpressqa

Answer

The issue to consider is the validity of claims by both parties for defamation. Such claims bring into focus the tension between protecting one's reputation while recognising free speech and the need for a free press. This is significant here as the matter involves investigative journalism into parliamentary corruption. It will be argued that while both statements appear defamatory, the defence of privilege will protect Peter, and in its qualified form it may defeat his own claim.

Advising Peter first, it should be noted that while the comment was by Michael any action should be brought against *The Echo*[1] as ultimately being responsible for the story. He should also be advised that defamation can take two forms: libel or slander. The former is where the comment is made in a permanent format and thus is

[1] In a defamation action it is important to note who the claim is against as it is an expensive process. A media organisation is well equipped to fight such claims, as opposed to an individual journalist, and this may have a bearing on whether Peter will want to bring a claim, especially if you advise him that the claim may not succeed.

actionable *per se*. As the comment has been printed, it would be libel and significantly means Peter will not need to show damage from the statement. Defamation is the publication of a statement about a person which lower's their reputation in the eyes of society. As such, three elements need satisfying.

The first is whether the statement is defamatory. This requires Peter to be lowered in the estimation of right-thinking members of society (**Sim v Stretch** [1936] 2 All E.R. 1237). This is determined with reference to the fair-minded and not unduly suspicious reasonable man (**Lewis v Daily Telegraph** [1964] A.C. 234). There appears to be no issue here: looking at the front page extract, the allegation is that Peter is corrupt making ministerial decisions for profit. However, under **Charleston v News Group Newspapers** [1995] 2 All E.R. 313, a passage cannot be taken in isolation where other parts negate the effect of the libel. From the overall story, it is clear that no financial wrongdoing is alleged. Therefore, Peter could not base a claim on such suggestions, but the story does not negate the allegation of corruption by favouring associates,[2] which would lower the reputation of a politician in the public's eyes.

The second and third elements that the statement refers to the claimant and is then published to a third party, respectively, are clearly satisfied, as the article is about the housing minister, Peter Seldon, and has been printed in a national magazine.[3]

While Peter may have a claim for defamation, reflecting the need to create a balance with freedom of expression, tort recognises several defences which may assist *The Echo*. The first would be if the story is true. The key statement is that Peter is corrupt for favouring former associates in determining planning decisions. *The Echo* would only need to prove this to be substantially true to defeat the claim (**Alexander v North Eastern Railway Co.** (1861) 6 B. & S. 340). As we are told that Michael has evidence that Peter's former company has received preferential treatment, this may be the case.

The Echo may prefer to use the defence of qualified privilege as they do not need to show truth. The defence applies where the defendant has a duty to make the statement and the person to whom it is made has an interest in receiving it. Here it can be said that there is a duty on the media to report parliamentary corruption as there is certainly a public interest in knowing that it is occurring. The press

[2]Not only is it important that you clarify for the purposes of this element which statement may be actionable, but it is also important when you discuss defences, so make sure you spell out what exactly it is that was said which was defamatory.

[3]As there are no contentious issues in the facts on these points, keep them brief to save you time to discuss the more relevant aspects.

do not have their own head of privilege for reporting political matters, but because of the public interest the defence is to be applied in a more relaxed fashion to ensure important stories are published (**Reynolds v Times Newspapers Ltd** 2 A.C. 127). Peter should be advised that to succeed with the defence, a two-question test must now be satisfied (**Jameel v Wall Street Journal Europe Sprl (No. 3)** [2006] U.K.H.L. 44). Firstly *The Echo* would have to show that the subject matter of the article, taken as a whole, was in the public interest. This would undoubtedly be the case here, owing to the overall nature of the story. The public would want to know all aspects of the story as it involves how the government is operating and making important decisions notwithstanding any suggestions of corruption. However, while the overall story may be in the public interest, the inclusion of the defamatory statement needs to be justifiable. Peter must be advised that allowance must be given for editorial judgement here and it is arguable that the statement in issue – preferential treatment – is sufficiently integral to the overall story to warrant inclusion: indeed it is the story itself. The second question to then ask is whether the publication met the objective standard of responsible journalism. As such, the story cannot be motivated out of malice. Peter should be advised that we lack information on this point.[4] There is nothing to suggest malice or any underhand reporting practices in obtaining the information from which the story is based; other relevant factors would be the extent to which the evidenced was verified. As this is a weekly publication which has published the story following an investigation,[5] it suggests that this was not a spur-of-the-moment decision to publish. Therefore, it would have been irresponsible not to have checked the validity of the claims, especially in view of their potentially defamatory nature. It could be argued that writing the front page extract in the manner that they did was irresponsible as it created a false impression which the main story did not support. However, in view of **Charleston**, this may not matter. If irresponsibility is shown,[6] Peter should seek a claim for damages to his reputation; and if there were any further allegations from the investigation, an injunction.

Advising Michael, the matter would again be libel as, although it involved spoken words, the debate was televised (Broadcasting Act 1996, s.166). The words spoken are therefore published and by naming Michael directly it would be considered as referring to him.

[4]Highlighting this shows that you appreciate the requirements for the defence and have read the question properly. However, you then need to ensure that what you then write does not come across as a definitive position: you are simply evaluating the potential situation.

[5]Rather than discussing this point in the abstract, use the facts of the question to give strength to the argument.

[6]As you cannot state for certain whether it will you need to take care leading into a discussion of remedies and so should use an introductory phrase like this.

Even on the basis that it is a common name, the context clearly means it refers to Michael (**Jameel**). There is also no apparent issue with the statement being defamatory as it clearly suggests that Michael makes up his stories and copies the work of others.[7] However, Peter will have the defence of absolute privilege. MPs, under Article 9 of the Bill of Rights 1689, cannot be questioned in court on statements from parliamentary proceedings. As the statement was made during a parliamentary debate, the defence will apply, and unless Peter waives his right to the defence under the Defamation Act 1996, s.13, Michael will have no action.

[7] As before, you just need to simply apply the elements to the statement and show how they are made out.

In conclusion, it appears that *The Echo* may well have a defence to any claim by Peter, although more information would be needed to firmly establish this; however, Michael would be unsuccessful in any claim against Peter.[8]

[8] Although you have effectively concluded each party's claim and this may seem like repetition, you should round off the answer with a summary of the position.

✓ Make your answer stand out

- Consider the position for the parties for any republications which may occur.
- Discuss whether the statement that Peter is corrupt could amount to honest comment, as an opinion based on the facts of the investigation.
- Highlight the human rights implications regarding freedom of expression underlying the tort.

! Don't be tempted to …

- Discuss aspects of the tort, such as whether the statement was published, which are not issues in dispute.
- Make definitive statements as to the liability of the parties, as the facts do not support such findings.
- Give detail as to slander, as it is not the form of defamation within the question.

? Question 2

Warwick is a celebrity TV chef who has just opened an upmarket new restaurant in Mayfair. Following the opening, a review appeared on the online website of *The Afternoon Yardstick* newspaper, which then had a comments section for bloggers to discuss the restaurant and review. Taking advantage of the ability to post under a pseudonym, a blogger called Restaurant Nemesis posted the following comment:

> This guy cannot cook for toffee; I was there last night so I should know. The food pulled off the great achievement of being burnt and cold! Don't even get me started on the decor of the place; if this is an upmarket restaurant suitable for Mayfair, I'm the Queen of Sheeba. I've been in posher greasy spoon cafes.

To leave a comment, however, a blogger must register their personal details with the newspaper. To gauge the response to the opening, Warwick went online to read the review and the comments customers had posted. Upon seeing this comment, Warwick complained to *The Afternoon Yardstick* about the comment, fearing it may turn people away from the restaurant. However, several days later the comment was still there and he has been informed that the blogger's identity cannot be revealed.

Advise Warwick as to his options in bringing a claim against the blogger for defamation.

Answer plan

→ Define defamation and identify what form we are dealing with.

→ Apply the criteria for the tort in turn to the blogger's comments.

→ Explain the steps that Warwick will need to undertake in order to obtain the registration details of the blogger from *The Afternoon Yardstick*.

→ Touch on any defences the blogger may have if he is identified.

Diagram plan

A printable version of this diagram is available from www.pearsoned.co.uk/lawexpressqa

Answer

Warwick requires advice as to the tort of defamation and its application to comments made online. This is an important issue as it involves the competing interests of protecting one's reputation, on one hand, and freedom of expression and the press on the other. The issue is further complicated by the Internet itself which emboldens people through perceived anonymity to express their views with even less inhibition.[1] It will be argued that while Warwick potentially has a claim against the blogger this is likely to be successfully defended; however, he may have a better action against the newspaper.

Warwick should be advised that there are two forms of defamation: libel and slander. Although blogging can be seen to be analogous to slander in that it is similar to an oral conversation, it has been held to be libel (**Nigel Smith v ADFN plc** [2008] E.W.H.C. 1797). This is important as it means that no proof is needed of actual damage.[2] Defamation is 'the publication of a statement which reflects on a person's reputation and tends to lower him in the estimation of right-thinking members of society generally, or tends to make them shun or avoid him' (Rogers 2010). Therefore, there are three elements to the tort which need to be established for a successful claim.[3]

The first is that the statement is defamatory. This requires the statement to lower the regard with which the claimant is held by right-thinking members of society (**Sim v Stretch** [1936] 2 All E.R. 1237). Applying this to the comment, the natural meaning of the post which Warwick will seek to apply is that he cannot cook and the restaurant is downmarket and not suitable for its location. It is unlikely that people will shun Warwick personally but they may now avoid his restaurant. Similarly, as he is a professional chef, it could cause people to lower the regard that they have for his cooking. However, Warwick should be advised that the comment could instead be viewed as simple abuse. Abuse can amount to defamation in libel (**Berkoff v Burchill** [1996] 4 All E.R. 1008), but following the **Nigel Smith** case it would need to be shown that the comment was intended to be taken seriously by casual readers; this was noted as not often being the case. Arguably, this is a comment on a review of the restaurant by a diner who had apparently visited the restaurant: a

Margin notes

[1] This provides some context to your answer which you can draw on later. It also demonstrates that you are aware of the human rights issues which influence the area and the difficulties faced by the law.

[2] By stating this you are illustrating that you are aware of the difference between libel and slander without using up time fully explaining what slander is.

[3] Follow up the quote with an explanatory statement to show that you understand and to link into the next part of your answer.

[4]Where you have two contrasting positions, make sure that you take a view on which is best, and use the facts to show why. Otherwise, your answer will not make total sense as to why you are proceeding with your advice.

[5]Do not just assume that this element is satisfied as the comment does not use his name. Therefore, you have to discuss the following point.

[6]Refer to this so that you show that you are aware of the practicalities of bringing a claim and issues such as the limitation period.

[7]It would be important to phrase this along these lines as you would have indicated some doubt as to their defamatory nature previously.

[8]While this is relevant to the answer, it also shows that you are aware of the context in which decisions are taken.

casual reader may well take this to be a reflection of Warwick and the restaurant, particularly if the overall review is somewhat negative.[4]

The next element is that the statement refers to Warwick. Although the comment does not directly refer to Warwick, this element should still be satisfied.[5] It will be clear that ordinary sensible people will believe it to refer to Warwick as the comment states 'The guy cannot cook for toffee' in response to an article reviewing Warwick's new restaurant. It is therefore reasonable, in light of the facts, that people would believe Warwick is being referred to (**Morgan v Odhams Press Ltd** [1971] 2 All E.R. 1156).

Finally, the statement must be published to a third party. This is relatively straightforward and is satisfied once the comment was posted on the website (**Godfrey v Demon Internet Ltd** [2001] Q.B. 201). Warwick should be advised that every download of the page will be another publication although only one action will result.[6] The amount of any damages will be reflected by the overall scale of publication (**John v MGN Ltd** [1997] Q.B. 586).

However, even if all the elements are satisfied, Warwick still has the issue of identifying who the tortfeasor is as only a pseudonym is provided. Warwick should be advised to apply for a Norwich Pharmacal Order which, if successful, means the newspaper has to reveal the blogger's identity, which it will have as users need to register their details. The requirements for obtaining such an order were outlined in **Mitsui Ltd v Nexen Petroleum UK Ltd** [2005] E.W.H.C. 625. Firstly, Warwick will need to show that he has suffered a wrong. On the basis that the elements of defamation are met,[7] this will be satisfied. Next, it must be shown that the Order is needed in order to bring an action against the wrongdoer, which is also satisfied, as Warwick only knows the tortfeasor as 'Restaurant Nemesis'. Lastly, Warwick will have to show that the newspaper has been involved in the wrongdoing so as to have facilitated the wrong and also be able to provide the information needed to bring an action. The latter part of this requirement is satisfied as all users register their personal details with the newspaper. The first part will also be satisfied following **Sheffield Wednesday F.C. v Hargreaves** [2007] E.W.H.C. 2375, which is a similar case. However, acknowledging the privacy concerns of such users of websites,[8] it was stated that courts have discretion to grant the order where the statement,

[9]Make sure that you do
not repeat your previous
argument, but relate the issue
back to add to your structure
and ensure that you are
not just stating a series of
isolated points.

while strictly defamatory, is more trivial in nature. This is an issue for Warwick because, as noted previously, the post could be said to simply be abusive and understood as a joke. Again, this may turn on the overall tenor of the newspaper's review which, if favourable, may detract from the seriousness of the post.[9]

However, if the court grants the order, the next issue for Warwick to overcome is any possible defences to the claim. As the post is a reply to a blog reviewing the restaurant, which naturally invites comments, the blogger may claim honest comment. This is significant as the blogger need not show the truth of his statement, merely that they were exercising their freedom of speech when making the comment. The main requirement is that the opinion was honestly held even if the view is exaggerated and in forthright terms (**Nigel Smith**). The defence will be defeated, though, where the maker of the statement is motivated by malice. The viability of this defence cannot be assessed until the identity of the blogger is known; but Warwick should be advised that in the absence of malice, it is likely to be successful for the reasons stated in **Nigel Smith**, where Eady J stated that it is 'fanciful' in such situations as this to suppose that the blogger does not believe the comment.

[10]Although the question says to advise Warwick regarding a claim against the blogger, the facts allude to a possible claim against the newspaper, so do not dismiss it, especially as the claim against the blogger may fail.

In conclusion, Warwick may satisfy the requirements for a defamation claim and thus have the identity of the blogger revealed. However, owing to the nature of the comment and where it was published, it is likely that the blogger will succeed with a honest comment defence, unless malice can be proven. In such an event, Warwick could instead successfully claim against the newspaper[10] as a publisher who then, when notified of the content of the post, took no action (**Godfrey**).

✓ Make your answer stand out

- Discuss how if there was evidence of only limited publication any claim could be viewed as an abuse of process (*Jameel* v *Dow Jones & Co. Inc* [2005] E.W.C.A. Civ. 75).
- Explore the merits of the analogy of blog posts to slander and consider the consequences for Warwick as this could prove crucial to his claim.
- Expand on the possibility of bringing a claim against the newspaper.
- Use recent cases which are to do with blogging and the Internet rather than applying old, albeit more well-known, cases to a new situation. This will show that you are up to date with developments and the new context with which the law is operating in.

! Don't be tempted to ...

- Go into too much detail as to the general nature of slander, as Warwick's situation will be libel.

- Show your knowledge regarding innuendo, as the sentiment within the comment is clearly expressed.

- Simply conclude that the comment will not be defamatory and not consider the consequences of it being found to be defamatory.

- Dwell on the elements for establishing defamation which are not really in issue, as you will not get on to the other issues.

 # Question 3

'While it is right that a person should not suffer injury to their reputation, the defences provided by the law against a claim of defamation are of fundamental importance in ensuring that individuals can exercise their right to free speech.'

Evaluate the defences to defamation and assess whether the law has achieved a fair balance between these competing principles.

Answer plan

→ Overview the two types of defamation and the difference between them, discussing why the tort is needed.

→ Explain the elements of defamation.

→ Balance the need for the tort with an evaluation of the defences, assessing whether they tip the balance too far back in favour of the defendant or do not go far enough.

→ Consider the need for reform if the balance is not right.

Diagram plan

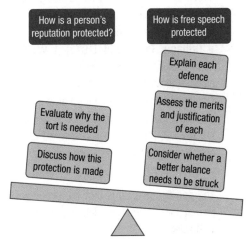

A printable version of this diagram is available from www.pearsoned.co.uk/lawexpressqa

Answer

Defamation seeks to balance the seemingly irreconcilable issues of protecting one's reputation with the right of others to say what they want. A satisfactory balance is vital so that unfounded claims do not ruin lives while allowing a free investigative press to flourish. It is argued that, while the requirements and defences balance, it is the cost of litigation which causes the problems.

Defamation is where a person is lowered in the estimation of society and takes two forms depending on the permanency of the statement. Slander is transient statements and generally requires proof of financial loss, or loss which is capable of financial assessment. However, libel, which is permanent, is actionable *per se*, thus putting one's reputation on a par with their personal integrity under trespass. It may seem questionable to put reputation on such a level, particularly at the expense of another's free speech; however, reputations are important assets and the justification is that the permanence means more people may see the statement and cause greater damage.[1]

To receive the tort's protection, certain requirements must be met which ensure that a sufficient nexus exists between the statement and the claimant to warrant restricting the maker's free speech.[2]

[1]After defining defamation, you ought to consider whether such protection is justifiable and judge the merits of the defences against that.

[2]Rather than just explain the elements of the tort, explain the purpose of the elements. You should consider whether insisting on these counters the harshness of not needing to show damage.

Firstly the statement must refer to the claimant. Where reference is direct, there will generally be no issue; however, it is sufficient if the reasonable person, having knowledge of the circumstances, would understand the statement as referring to the claimant (**Morgan v Odhams Press Ltd** [1971] 1 W.L.R. 1239). The statement must then be published, which requires communication to a third party; otherwise, there is no damage to their reputation. Finally, the statement must be defamatory. Fair-minded people within society, as a whole, must think less of the claimant (**Lewis v Daily Telegraph** [1964] A.C. 234). Protection extends also to situations where the ordinary words themselves are not defamatory but they contain an innuendo which is damaging.

[3]The point here is to provide a judicial reason for permitting an otherwise highly protected interest.

[4]The fact that the law presumes that you are lying requires you, in light of the statement in the question, to explain the justification for such a position, as it would seem to tilt the balance away from the claimant.

The primary defence is that the statement was true, as damages cannot be awarded for injuring a false reputation (**M'Pherson v Daniels** (1829) 10 B. & C. 263).[3] However, statements are presumed to be untrue and the defendant must prove otherwise. This is compliant with Article 10 (**Jameel v Wall Street Journal Europe** [2006] U.K.H.L. 44) and justified as one should have to substantiate their claims.[4] However, allegations can be difficult to prove, particularly when they are specific. Minor inaccuracies are permissible. Under the Defamation Act 1952, s.5 in a case of multiple statements the defence will not fail because every statement is not true; the lack of concrete evidence combined with the cost of defending an action – which owing to the reversal of evidential burden may be more forthcoming – may deter people from making statements which are in fact true.[5]

[5]After stating why the law adopts the position it does, it is important to evaluate the consequences of that position and where it leaves the balance between the parties.

[6]As with truth, as these are exceptions to when you can injure a reputation, you ought to start with the reason for the defence and then assess its merits against the importance of protecting reputations, as seen in the discussion on *Branson*.

The next substantial defence is honest comment, which embodies the whole idea of free speech as it protects one's right to criticise another;[6] crucially the comment does not have to true.[7] However, so that reputations are protected certain requirements must be met. Firstly, the statement must be fair. Malice will defeat the defence, although a court will not find malice where the defendant can show that the opinion was honestly held (**Branson v Bower (No. 2)** [2002] Q.B. 737). To insist on anything more was said (in **Branson**) to negate the whole point of the defence which is to allow strong comment to be conveyed on issues.

[7]By stating this aspect of the defence at the start, you strengthen the flow from the previous defence which is based on truth and allows you to argue that this defence affords more protection for free speech.

The next requirement is that the statement is indeed comment. While the comment itself need not be true, it must be drawn from a set of true facts, although s.6 of the Defamation Act 1952 provides that inability to prove the truth of every fact is not fatal so long as the comment is fair, having regard to those which can be proven which aids the defendant's case. However, the statement must be comment and not fact. This means that the comment must refer to the facts on which it is based or be based on facts which are common knowledge (**Kemsley v Foot** [1952] A.C. 345); otherwise, the statement is one of fact and the defence of truth would need to be pleaded. However, reflecting the Internet's use, the facts in question need only be indicated in the comment in general terms (**Spiller v Joseph** [2010] U.K.S.C. 53).

Finally, the comment must be on a matter which the public has a legitimate interest in, or is something which has been submitted for public review such as a film (**London Artists v Littler** [1969] 2 Q.B. 375). The rationale for this is, that if one's reputation is to be justifiably injured by someone passing comment on it, the public must be concerned with hearing that comment.

The next substantial defence is privilege. The defence may be absolute, which applies regardless of motive and acknowledges the situation is one where free speech is too important to restrict. The defence is commonly relied on by MPs making parliamentary state-ments which are not actionable regardless of how defamatory they are, but it also applies to instances such as witness statements in court.[8]

[8]Demonstrate that you know that the defence is more widespread than the more well-known application to parliamentary matters.

The other form of the defence is qualified privilege, where motive is important as malice will defeat the defence. It applies where there is a duty on the maker to make the statement and a corresponding interest in the recipient to hear the statement (**Adam v Ward** [1919] A.C. 309). Reflecting the importance to democratic society of an investigative press, **Reynolds v Times Newspapers Ltd** [2001] 2 A.C. 127 adopted a more flexible approach for the media, with Lord Nichols providing 10 non-exhaustive factors to consider, with various weight given to each depending on the facts. Owing to the continued restrictive application of **Reynolds**, the principle was restated in **Jameel** with the questions to be asked being that, taken as a whole and in context, the article was in the public interest, and the publication met the standard of responsible journalism. Lord Hoffman felt judges should not make editorial decisions with

[9]As it is a relatively recent adaptation, you should offer an opinion as to its merits and what the outcome, in terms of the need for balance, is likely to be.

the benefit of hindsight. Subsequently, the test has been held to apply to anyone writing responsibly in the public interest (**Seaga v Harper [2008] U.K.P.C. 9**) and is easier to satisfy than the old requirement in **Adam**. This provides stronger protection when highlighting potential wrongdoing. Employing responsible methods, such as verification and including a riposte in the story, it avoids publication of unsubstantiated claims and protects reputations by pre-empting litigation.[9]

[10]Relate this back to your initial discussion on the elements; if they are meant to act as a hurdle for claims but then are too easy to overcome, does this mean the balance is in the claimant's favour?

However, while the defences afford suitable theoretical protection of free speech, particularly the adaptation of qualified privilege, the relative ease in satisfying the requirements for defamation means the threat of litigation restricts speech.[10] Indeed, the cost means that the prospect of financial ruin is detrimental to both parties; damaged reputations may go unchallenged and damning information of public importance left unpublished. Therefore, the litigation process, rather than the tort itself, requires urgent reform.

 ## Make your answer stand out

- Refer back to the quote in your answer when assessing the importance and justification for each defence.
- Draw on some of the wider causes of concern regarding the tort, such as cost and libel tourism.
- Look out for recent high-profile cases from the news which you can use to show that you are aware of recent developments.

! Don't be tempted to ...

- Dwell too long on the requirements for a claim. The question is focused on the role of the defences, so you will not leave yourself enough time to address these, otherwise.
- Discuss every defence as you will not have the time to do so in the required depth and provide any worthwhile evaluation. Stick to the substantive defences which provide a full defence to an action.

Question 4

'The power wielded by the major multi-national corporations is enormous and growing. The freedom to criticise them may be at least as important in a democratic society as the freedom to criticise the government.' *Per* Baroness Hale (dissenting) *Jameel* v *Wall Street Journal Europe Sprl (No. 3)* [2006] U.K.H.L. 44.

Critically evaluate whether proof of actual damage should be proven in order for a trading corporation to claim libel.

Answer plan

→ Set out what defamation is and what it seeks to protect.

→ Distinguish between libel and slander.

→ Discuss the justifications for not requiring proof of damage in libel and why this is not contested for individuals.

→ Comment briefly on the challenge to the rule in relation to governmental bodies.

→ Evaluate which reasoning best suits the modern trading corporation.

Diagram plan

The minority

• Companies can be just as powerful as government institutions

• Reflects the importance of freedom of expression

• The rule helps to protect the soul of an individual which companies do not have

• Injury to commercial assets in other torts requires proof of damage

The majority

• Company reputations are of monetary value

• Their profits flow from the amount of custom, which in turn is dependent on the public's perception

• Impacts on the quality of staff they can attract

• Creates different rules for different corporations or hits non-trading corporations

A printable version of this diagram is available from www.pearsoned.co.uk/lawexpressqa

Answer

The issue here is whether corporations should be treated differently from individuals when it comes to libel and have to prove damage. This is important as corporations place great value on their trading reputation, but the current rule could protect them from legitimate criticism as they can easily bring actions over less powerful individuals. It is submitted that the rule should be changed for corporations in order to protect the public interest.

Defamation's purpose is to protect one's reputation from harm where a statement is published which refers to them and would tend to lower their reputation in the minds of right-thinking people. Defamation takes two forms: slander which is a transitory statement, or libel, which is a statement in permanent form. Reflecting the fact that this permanence means the statement is more easily disseminated and any reputational damage is more durable over time, there is no requirement in libel to prove the damage did occur. This is further justified on the basis of the difficulties of an individual establishing that the loss was due to the statement.[1]

This rule applies to all claimants (**South Hetton Coal Co. Ltd v North-Eastern News Association** [1894] 1 Q.B. 133) regardless of their nature. However, the first successful challenge was in **Derbyshire C. C. v Times Newspapers Ltd** [1993] A.C. 534. It was held that any government institution could not bring a defamation action. To have held otherwise would have been fundamentally at odds with the public interest, as defamation claims could be used to censor criticism and restrain free speech. In a democracy, governmental bodies should be subject to criticism: otherwise, party political systems could not function[2] as they are based on trying to undermine confidence in your opponent's competence. The 'chilling effect' of libel claims may prevent matters of public importance coming to light.

That a company should be able to bring an action has always been acknowledged; what is in issue is whether they should benefit from the same rules as individuals.[3] In **Jameel** the majority felt they should, favouring the principle in **South Hetton** that the rule should be the same for all claimants.

[1] This is the most important part of this paragraph as it explains why we have the rule. Therefore, focus more on this than what defamation is, as this will provide the foundation upon which the actual arguments take place.

[2] While this may seem slightly off tangent, you should briefly cover this case and the principle which it determined as you can use this later in support of Baroness Hale's view when you look at the minority view in *Jameel*.

[3] Using this wording here gives you the scope to seamlessly proceed to discussing the majority or the minority, depending on your viewpoint. Remember to lay out the view that you ultimately favour second, as this will mean your answer will end on a stronger note and flow into your conclusion.

Lord Scott opined that a corporation's reputation is an asset of monetary value; this is why so many advertise on TV shows and sponsor events. Companies try to enhance their reputation by association for commercial advantage. However, if their reputation suffers, these opportunities are reduced, leading to lost custom and ultimately profits. Weir (1972) suggests that as this is financial injury it can be proved evidentially, unlike with individuals, and thus should be proved.[4] At first glance this seems a strong point; Lord Scott, though, felt that it was not so simple for companies to prove this loss and attribute it to the statement. Trade variations happen for a variety of reasons and so it is difficult to show that loss resulted from the published statement. Lord Bingham's opinion dovetailed with these sentiments, highlighting that a corporation's reputation also impacts on those who want to work for it. Therefore, reputations should be protected by a favourable judicial verdict as this carries more weight than a denial by press release; the verdict makes people take note. Significantly, Lord Scott also noted that such a change would exclude corporations from obtaining interlocutory injunctions.

Lord Hope's opinion was that arguments for revising the rule solely for companies could not be soundly based in principle as it singles out trading corporations for differential treatment from non-trading corporations. While this could be resolved by altering the position for all corporations, this was not argued in **Jameel** and Lord Hope felt that bodies such as charities would find it even harder to put a value on the loss and to actually prove it. Therefore, a change for all would be detrimental, while a change for the one group would seem unfair in light of the equal asset value of a reputation to trading corporations.

Notwithstanding the **Derbyshire C.C.** case holding that there were distinctions between public authorities and corporations, Baroness Hale felt that, today, the boundary is blurred with multinational corporations wielding enormous power.[5] As such, she felt it may well be of democratic interest to similarly open such corporations to 'uninhibited criticism'. It is important to reiterate that Baroness Hale was not suggesting removing standing from trading corporations; indeed, she did not even advocate that loss must be caused: simply that they must prove that the statement was likely to cause them financial loss. This position, a slight modification of the position

[4]By including this here, you make the arguments in favour of the rule stronger as you are fully testing them at the same time. You will also have a greater degree of cohesion to your answer than if you include this later on with the specific arguments of the minority.

[5]This links your answer to the discussion of *Derbyshire C.C.* and why you discussed the issue of public authorities.

[6]By highlighting these you show some wider knowledge, and strengthen the assertion that this would be a modest development of the law with wider support.

[7]Include some practical examples to how the majority's arguments can be rebutted, as these will carry more force than a purely jurisprudential argument.

[8]Obviously, as the House was split, it is worth showing your knowledge of each judge and explaining what side they were coming from.

[9]As you have just ended the previous paragraph with why there is no practical reason for the rule, it is beneficial to highlight that you are now addressing the remaining arguments advanced by the majority. As the answer is about arguing against the majority, it is important to include Lord Hoffmann's brief views on the issues as this allows you to counter the theoretical reasons of the majority.

[10]This allows you to end on a strong note with high-level judicial endorsement for your concluding argument.

advanced in **Derbyshire C.C.**, also reflected the view of the Faulks Committee on Defamation.[6]

This obviously raises the contention of the majority that proving such loss may be difficult. However, this is not necessarily the case. Companies, particularly large corporations, will have year-on-year sales figures and so can contrast the period following the publication to previous years'.[7] As companies do now, an assessment of external factors could be made in order to determine whether any loss was caused by those factors such as bad weather or the holding of national events. Furthermore, under Baroness Hale's proposal concrete evidential proof is not required: thus causative uncertainties would not be detrimental. It would just be necessary to show that the loss was 'likely' to have been caused by the statement. This is easy to do by looking at the size of the loss and the nature of the statement in light of the external factors. Therefore, on a practical basis there is no need to maintain the rule.

Lord Hoffmann, supporting Baroness Hale,[8] somewhat countered Lord Hope's theoretical issues regarding creating distinctions[9] by noting that as the company's reputation is just a commercial asset, not requiring proof of damage would mean that defamation is at odds with other torts such as malicious falsehood. It could be argued that this is justified because defamation serves a different purpose, but His Lordship felt that the justification for not requiring proof by individuals is that their reputation is part of their 'immortal' self – it is their soul. Therefore, it warrants greater protection. However, a company has no soul and, therefore, there was no reason to treat it more favourably in defamation than in other torts which deal with harm to commercial assets.

Therefore, while there are strong practical and theoretical difficulties for aligning a trading corporation with an individual, these can be overcome. Further reflecting the new landscape identified by Lord Steyn in **Reynolds v Times Newspapers Ltd** that the starting point should be free speech, they *should* be overcome.[10] To favour the protection of a company's reputation without proof of damage is, in Weir's view, a 'grim perversion of values'.

✓ Make your answer stand out

- Read *Jameel* in full so that you can draw on all of the judicial opinions in support of your arguments, as each judge says something different. You can then show deep and wide-ranging knowledge of the issue.

- Also read the Report of the Faulks Committee on Defamation (1975), Cmnd 5909 to which their Lordships referred and which made a recommendation on this point. It would also be beneficial to look more closely at the views of Weir (1972) in his case commentary of *Bognor Regis Urban District Council* v *Campion* in 'Local authority v critical ratepayer: a suit in defamation' [1972A] C.L.J. 238.

! Don't be tempted to …

- Spend too long on what defamation is; you can take it almost as a given in the question that it is known. The question is assessing your understanding of what its purpose is and thus why the damage rule is needed or not.

- Avoid stating which position from the case you prefer, as this is ultimately what you have been asked to argue.

15

Privacy and the misuse of private information

How this topic may come up in exams

The debate around the right of privacy is arguably the most topical issue in tort at the moment, along with defamation, because of a range of high-profile cases. The wide-ranging arguments as to whether there should be a general tort protecting privacy, and the influence of human rights in developing a tort of misuse of private information, means that it is lends itself extremely well to essay questions in an exam. However, do not discount a problem scenario requiring you to apply how the developing tort offers some protection for a person's privacy.

Attack the question

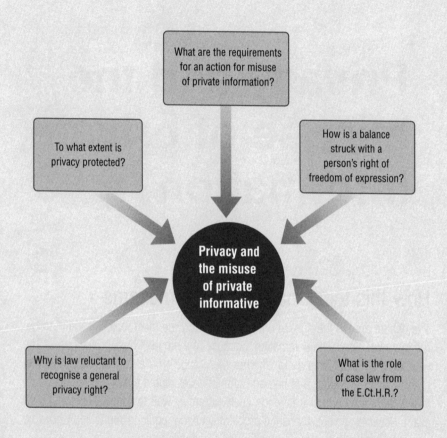

Question 1

'*Wainwright* v *Home Office* saw an emphatic repudiation of any notion that English law now recognised a general right to privacy.' M. Arden (2010) 'Human rights and civil wrongs: tort law under the spotlight', Public Law, Jan: 140–59

Critically evaluate the extent that the tort of misuse of private information has negated the need for a general tort protecting against the invasion of privacy.

Answer plan

→ Outline the position stated in *Wainwright* v *Home Office* [2003] U.K.H.L. 53.

→ Evaluate the reasoning for this position.

→ Consider how privacy is protected through the existing tort.

→ Determine the effectiveness of the protection.

→ Discuss whether its continued development means that we effectively have a general privacy tort by the back door.

Diagram plan.

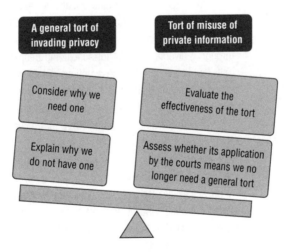

A printable version of this diagram is available from www.pearsoned.co.uk/lawexpressqa

Answer

The issue to determine is the extent to which the courts have responded to the need to protect privacy by developing the tort of misuse of private information, and whether the presence of this tort means that the lack of a general privacy tort should be a concern. As privacy is a fundamental human right, this is extremely important.[1] However, it is argued that by developing this tort in line with the E.C.H.R. an effective privacy regime exists, negating the need for a general tort.

The importance of a citizen's right to a private life has long been recognised, even prior to Article 8 of the E.C.H.R. 1950. The rationale is to prevent the state from unjustly intervening in the day-to-day activities of its citizens.[2] The right is the embodiment of Mill's 'harm to others' principle, i.e. people should be free to do what they like in private so long as they are not hurting anybody else. As such, it is a fundamental aspect of democracy.

While the UK signed the Convention and has incorporated it into law through the Human Rights Act 1998, this only means that a citizen has protection from state intrusion. It does not correlate to equivalent common law rights actionable against private citizens; the Act has no direct horizontal effect.[3] The common law, though, has always provided a patchwork quilt of horizontal protection through a diverse range of torts including trespass, defamation and malicious falsehood. Yet these options did not always fully deal with the situation complained of and as such there was a gap when it came to privacy (as illustrated in **Kaye v Robertson** [1991] F.S.R. 62).[4] Nevertheless, it was felt in **Kaye** that moves to a general right should come from Parliament. Arguably, the most effective action was the equitable doctrine of breach of confidence, from which the new tort derives. However, that no general tort protecting invasions of privacy exists was emphatically stated in **Wainwright** where Lord Hoffmann stated that it was not a principle of law which could be directly applied to individual claims. His Lordship even noted doubt as to what the concept of 'invasion of privacy' means, while also highlighting the lack of need for a high-level principle for compliance with Article 8. Indeed, he noted that in the USA, where a general right exists, it is broken down into several loosely defined torts. Lord Hoffmann felt that privacy was simply an underlying value which

---

[1] While this may not seem like it is adding much, you want to get across that you appreciate what privacy is and, therefore, know the context in which you are writing.

[2] Naturally, you start by introducing the right. However, remembering the sentence in the introduction, you need to go further and explain why it is a right; explain why it is important.

[3] This is something which often gets misunderstood, so it is vital that you show you do know how it operates. Remember that it is because of this fact that there is a need to develop a form of horizontal protection.

[4] You would not need to get into *Kaye* here; your aim is to reinforce what you stated above regarding the need to develop an effective action that would protect a person's privacy against interference by another citizen.

points the way for developing existing law, which has proved to be the case.

Baroness Hale has argued (**Campbell v MGN Ltd** [2004] U.K.H.L. 22) that, although the E.C.H.R.'s incorporation does not mean that new rights can be created in a dispute to give effect to Convention rights, existing rights must be interpreted and developed in a manner which is compatible with Convention rights, as the court is a public authority under s.6 and thus expressly obliged to act compatibly[5] (a view previously adopted in **Venables v News Group Newspapers Ltd** [2001] Fam 430).[6] While the other Lords in **Campbell** did not opine on the matter, all accepted that the confidence action was the best vehicle to develop, and as such the requirement of a prior confidential relationship was removed. Reflecting this development, Lord Nicholls rechristened the action as the tort of misuse of private information. This terminology was adopted by the Court of Appeal in **McKennit v Ash** [2008] Q.B. 73 which, in reviewing the opinions in **Campbell**, set out the requirements for the new action.

The first requirement is that the information in question is indeed private, thus protected by Article 8. For this, the courts assess whether the claimant had, in relation to the information, a reasonable expectation of privacy. In **Campbell**, Lord Hope suggested that an expectation exists where the information is obviously private or easily identifiable as such. However, where there was doubt as to whether an expectation should exist, he suggested recourse be had to the 'highly offensive test' from **Australian Broadcasting Corporation v Lenah Game Meats Pty Ltd** (2001) 1 A.L.R. 185. This involves asking what a reasonable person of ordinary sensibilities would feel if found in the claimant's position. While there were doubts about using this test among other judges – such as Lord Nicholls who felt it blurred the differing questions of what is private and what interference is proportionate – their views are compatible in that it is what the claimant objectively thinks which matters – a view shared in **Murray v Big Pictures (UK) Ltd** [2008] E.M.L.R. 12.[7] This is therefore more effective in giving claimants protection than the approach of the Court of Appeal in **Campbell** which looked at what the reader felt.

Even if the information is private, the second question to determine is whether this right to keep the information private should, on balance, outweigh the competing right of the defendant to publish

---

[5] Following your previous discussion and how the Act works, it is important to get across that you are aware of this development: otherwise, your answer may seem contradictory.

[6] By briefly including reference to this case you add some judicial support to Baroness Hale's argument which you are now advancing. This is beneficial because, as you may go on to explain, the other Lords did not discuss this, so questions could be raised as to how authoritative the view is.

[7] Naturally, you have to evaluate the differing views in *Campbell*, but this then gives the impression of a law in a state of confusion. By referring to what later cases have said on this point, you can argue that the new tort is coherent and understood. If it wasn't, there would be questions as to how effective it is, which would impact on the quality of the proposition which you are advancing.

the information. Clearly, this balancing act needs to be undertaken to give effect to the freedom of expression, which is essential in a democracy as part of a free press. However, the merits of a free press must be balanced with ensuring responsible behaviour and respecting the rights of people to a private life. This requirement is not surprising as both Articles 8 and 10 state that each right may be restricted where necessary in a democratic society so as to give effect to the other; neither takes precedence.

In **Campbell**, Baroness Hale stated three factors to consider when performing the balancing exercise to ensure that any interference is proportionate and necessary. Firstly, there must be a pressing social need, essentially a similar issue as the first requirement of whether disclosure is in the public interest. This has allowed the tort to be used in relation to photographs (**Murray**).[8] Secondly, any interference must be proportionate to the legitimate aim of meeting that social need. As such, the extent of the interference must be enough to protect the opposing right and no more. Finally, the reasons advanced for the interference must be logical and sufficient to justify it. The party which satisfies these most effectively will succeed in the aim of preventing or obtaining publication. This will be warranted as they have demonstrated that their interference with the other's right is necessary to give effect to the social need while not being too overbearing.[9]

The new tort offers protection, going further than simply revealing private information, as seen in claims regarding photographs. The sensible development of the tort in line with E.C.H.R. jurisprudence means that a general right exists by default, yet this has not been detrimental to free expression nor restricted the press. The balance at the tort's heart provides the flexibility to ensure that the latter is only curtailed where justified.

[8] You need to discuss how the tort, once established, has been applied as this goes to the heart of how wide-ranging the protection is and, therefore, whether a general tort is needed.

[9] Outline how the balancing exercise works, then give an opinion as to what this means and how the results flowing from the exercise arise. Someone's right will have been interfered with and so you need to decide whether this has been done fairly, as this goes to the heart of whether the tort is good or not.

✓ Make your answer stand out

- As well as the Arden article in the question, read in full A. McLean and C. Mackey, (2007) 'Is there a law of privacy in the UK? A consideration of recent legal developments', E.I.P.R. 29 (9): 389–95, which makes the argument which lies at the heart of the question.

- Make sure you leave plenty of time for discussion as to how the tort works and whether its application means a general tort is not needed, as this is the principal premise of the question, not why we don't have a general tort.

! **Don't be tempted to …**

■ Feel the need to discuss *all* of the different cases which have taken place recently. Stick to those which have added something new to the development of the tort and assess the merits of that development.

■ Get too tied down by a discussion of the other actions which may be brought, as the question is directing you to focus on the misuse of private information.

[?] Question 2

Kyle Springer is a famous Christian TV presenter who during his shows regularly advocates a life of purity for his viewers. The gambling industry is often a target for his tirades against immoral living and he calls those involved in organising gambling events 'parasites on the poor and vulnerable'. His strong moral convictions have led to his TV show attracting millions of viewers and resulted in his receiving a vast income through endorsing various products.

However, investigative reporter, Morgan Douglas, found out that Kyle hosted a weekly poker night at his mansion. To protect his reputation, the poker nights are strictly private and by invitation only; as such the guests only ever include Kyle's closest circle of friends. On the night of the March event, using long-range photography, Morgan managed to secretly take a photo of Kyle standing in his doorway with a pack of cards and some poker chips in his hand.

A fortnight later, Morgan's newspaper, the *Daily Reflection*, ran a story with the headline: 'Springer's gambling shame! "Moral" star in regular gambling sessions'. The photos were also published alongside the story. Prior to the publication, Kyle had checked himself into rehab, acknowledging that he had a gambling addiction which he cited as the reason for his anti-gambling tirades. This fact was also published within the body of the story.

Traumatised by the publication of the poker nights and details of his rehabilitation, Kyle now seeks your advice over the matter.

Answer plan

→ Outline what the cause of action would be.

→ Explain why there is no general tort regarding the invasion of privacy.

→ Set out the requirements for the tort of misuse of private information.

→ Balance Kyle's right to privacy against the *Daily Reflection's* right to freedom of expression.

→ Consider whether the details of the story and the inclusion of the photos were a necessary and proportionate response to any public interest in publishing.

→ Assess what remedy Kyle could expect, if successful.

Diagram plan

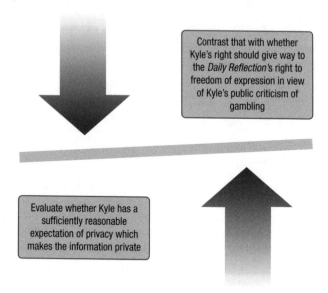

Contrast that with whether Kyle's right should give way to the *Daily Reflection*'s right to freedom of expression in view of Kyle's public criticism of gambling

Evaluate whether Kyle has a sufficiently reasonable expectation of privacy which makes the information private

A printable version of this diagram is available from www.pearsoned.co.uk/lawexpressqa

Answer

[1] Indicate your awareness of the extent of privacy protection in tort and what Kyle's action could be.

The issue to determine here is the extent to which Kyle may have redress in tort for the publication of his hosting of poker nights and his subsequent rehabilitation. This will involve assessing the extent to which the law recognises rights to privacy and protects them under the tort of misuse of private information.[1] It will be argued that Kyle may be entitled to damages because of the parallels with **Campbell v MGN Ltd** [2004] U.K.H.L. 22,[2] depending on the level of detail published in relation to his treatment.

[2] By mentioning *Campbell*, you show the parallels between Kyle's situation and *Campbell*, and how that authority will form the basis of your answer.

[3] Use this wording to show your awareness of the context around the debate on privacy protection and the workings of the Act. This allows you to develop this point later to show how Kyle's action may come about.

Notwithstanding that privacy is a fundamental human right under Article 8 of the ECHR, which has been incorporated into English law by the Human Rights Act 1998, the absence of any horizontal effect between private citizens[3] means there is no general tort protecting invasions of privacy as has happened here. This was clearly stated in **Wainwright v Home Office** [2003] U.K.H.L. 53 which saw no need for its creation, particularly by the judiciary. However, Kyle should be advised that this does not mean he automatically has no redress. As Hunt (1998) has argued, while the courts do not have the power to create new rights to achieve compatibility with the ECHR, as public bodies they must develop and interpret existing laws in a manner which is compatible with Convention rights. Therefore, Kyle may have an action under the tort of misuse of private information which has developed out of the equitable doctrine of breach of confidence. In developing this in light of the HRA, the requirement for a prior confidential relationship has gone[4] (**Campbell**).

To bring an action, Kyle will have to demonstrate that the information published was private and thus protected by Article 8, and then demonstrate that his interest in this information remaining private outweighs the paper's right of freedom of expression under Article 10 (**McKennit v Ash** [2008] Q.B. 73).

In proving the first requirement, the courts, following **Campbell**, employ a 'reasonable expectation of privacy' test. In **Campbell**, Lord Hope[5] explained that where the information published is obviously identifiable as being private, a reasonable expectation of privacy would result. The fact that the poker games occurred in Kyle's own home, and by strictly private invitation only, suggests that this information can objectively be identified as private. Objectively looking at the situation, as **Campbell** said we should, it would appear that people should have an expectation of privacy in relation to what they legally[6] do with their friends at home, particularly as it has been held to attach to routine daily acts (**Murray v Express Newspapers Plc** [2008] E.M.L.R. 12)[7]. The information of his gambling addiction and rehabilitation is clearly private and thus would warrant protection under Article 8. Therefore, it seems that Kyle had a reasonable expectation of privacy in relation to the matter.

However, Kyle should be aware that, just because he has an expectation to privacy, it does not mean he has an automatic right to keep the information private. Under the breach of confidence action a public interest defence always existed which has now been developed to balance Articles 8 and 10, which both Articles themselves make clear should happen where it is necessary for a democratic society. Therefore, Kyle will have to show that his interest in keeping the information private outweighs any public interest in the story. Kyle may have problems here as the thrust of

[4]Demonstrate your knowledge of the background to the action and how it arose to make existing laws compatible with the Convention.

[5]While there appears to be some agreement on this point by the majority, they all gave separate opinions and the minority only dissented on the application of the balance to be struck in the instant case. Therefore, you should be specific as to whom you are referring when referencing aspects of *Campbell*.

[6]Including this avoids questions as to your logic; if this were an illegal drug-taking party, it might be harder to say that it should carry an expectation of privacy. You prevent the marker having issues with the proposition.

[7]Mentioning this reinforces that acts within the home are capable of having a reasonable expectation of privacy.

the information is that he is a habitual gambler when he has made a career out of denouncing such activities. This obviously leaves him open to charges of hypocrisy and as he is a public figure creates a public interest in highlighting this. The same issue was the basis for the claim in **Campbell** except that concerned drug-taking. In **Campbell** it was accepted by all, including the claimant, that a public interest in publicising her drug-taking existed in light of her previous denials. That marks an important distinction between these situations, as **Campbell** involved not only hypocrisy but also illegal activity, whereas Kyle's gambling is legal. However, it must be considered that Kyle has made substantial sums of money from criticising those who organise gambling activities. Therefore, while legal, his actions do carry a sufficient public interest and thus there is sufficient reason for the paper to interfere with his privacy right.

Notwithstanding this potential public interest, Kyle should be advised that the information published must be proportionate to the legitimate aim that is being pursued by the paper through the exercise of their freedom of expression: otherwise, a claim will succeed. This was explained in **Campbell**, as again involving a balancing exercise between the two conflicting rights. In **Campbell** the publication of the information of the claimant's condition and the fact that treatment was being sought was deemed to be a proportionate response. However, the reason why **Campbell** succeeded in her claim was because the newspaper published details as to the nature of her treatment as well as photos of her leaving the treatment centre. This information was held to be disproportionate to the legitimate aim of highlighting her illegal drug-taking. To advise Kyle further we would need to know whether the paper merely stated that he was attending rehabilitation or went further.[8] If it was just the former, then under the authority of **Campbell** any action would not succeed, but if further information as to his treatment was published, he could have a successful claim under the tort. While we do know that they have published photos of Kyle, these are distinguishable from **Campbell**[9] in that they were simply of him at his house with the cards and poker chips. Although taken covertly, of him and of his house, these could be said to simply provide credibility to the claims in the story which the public has an interest in knowing, as a form of factual evidence unlike the **Campbell** photos.

[8]Remember we are not told this definitively and so you should not frame any statement more assertively than this.

[9]Owing to the factual similarity to *Campbell*, a lot of your answer will require demonstration of your factual knowledge of *Campbell* and understanding of the law in order to compare and contrast it to Kyle's situation and what Kyle may do.

[10]This highlights your awareness that, unlike with libel, any action is not likely to bring much compensation. Further, it is good to include as it is the sort of information a client may want to know before deciding whether to bring a claim.

[11]While we are not told if this is the case, it is often how newspapers work in order to prolong stories over time; therefore, by referencing it in this way you show your knowledge of the other remedies available but in a context relevant to the question.

In conclusion, Kyle should be advised that it is unlikely he would have a successful claim merely for the revelation that he is a gambling addict receiving treatment, with the publication of the photo unlikely to change this. However, a claim may succeed if the story featured specific details as to his treatment. If this is the case, Kyle would be entitled to damages, although these tend to be low.[10] He could also seek an order for delivery of any remaining photos and copies of the information which the paper still holds. He should also be advised that if the paper is seeking to publish a further story, he could then seek an injunction in order to prevent that additional publication.[11]

✓ Make your answer stand out

- Read the article by M. Hunt (1998) 'The "horizontal effect" of the Human Rights Act 1998', Public Law, Autumn: 423–43.
- Make sure you fully understand the case of *Campbell* and use your knowledge to substantiate your answer by drawing parallels and/or distinctions.
- Consider what options Kyle may have if the paper were to have further stories which they want to publish.

! Don't be tempted to ...

- Spend too long discussing why there is no general tort and whether this is justified. Remember there is a recognised action which he could use, and it is your knowledge and understanding of that action which the question is seeking to assess you on.
- Give a long factual account of *Campbell*; while you need to compare the two situations, this does not necessarily mean you have to provide a detailed factual account of *Campbell*. Concentrate on applying the legal principles to Kyle and using *Campbell* to simply support your reasoning.
- Include numerous references to other cases just to show you know them. If citing them adds substance to your argument, then do so, if not then leave them out.

16

Liability for animals

How this topic may come up in exams

Animals themselves may feature in a number of topics such as negligence, nuisance or trespass to land; however, here we are looking at the specific topic of liability under the Animals Act 1971. Although a small area, it can be quite complicated. You will need to know the wording of the statute and understand how the words have been interpreted by the courts. The Act's complexity means that you should not discount a question on the suitability and effectiveness of the legislation. In terms of problem questions, you should make sure that you have also learnt the more fringe provisions of the Act as well as the main duty provisions.

Attack the question

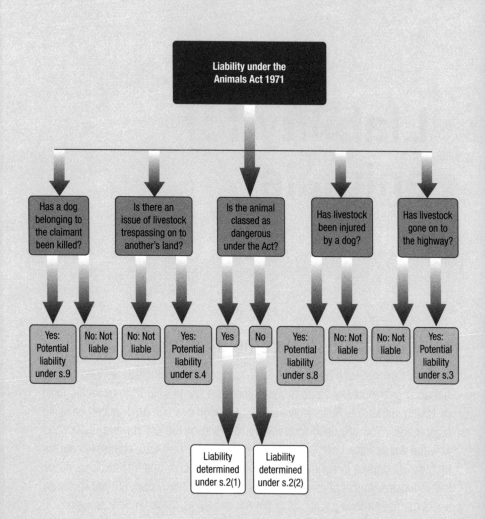

❓ Question 1

Miranda, and her 8-year-old son, Rupert, are visiting Langleybury Farm one summer afternoon. Rupert has brought his pet Labrador, Bonnie, with him, even though she has just given birth to puppies. Bonnie is normally a good-natured, playful young dog but, since the birth, has appeared agitated when away from her litter. Suddenly, the farm's peacock, Moses, appears from around the corner and startles Bonnie, who starts to bark wildly. This, in turn, frightens Moses, who turns and flees. Bonnie makes a dash towards Moses, and Rupert is not strong enough to keep hold of the leash.

Alerted by the commotion, Jonty, one of the farm workers, manages to grab Bonnie, who in turn bites him hard on the arm forcing him to release her. The gash in Jonty's arm requires 10 stitches and he has to stay off work for several weeks. Bonnie catches up with Moses and corners him in the sheep pen. At this point another farm worker, Hyacinth, fearing for Moses' safety, shoots Bonnie dead.

Meanwhile, a sheep from the farm, Basil, is startled by the sound of the shotgun and runs off through an open gate out of the farm and on to a neighbouring field owned by Hector, trampling all of his prize vegetables.

Advise all of the parties as to their potential liability in light of the Animals Act 1971.

Answer plan

→ Establish who potentially has a claim and against whom.

→ Take the issue of Jonty's injury first and establish the type of animal you are dealing with.

→ Work your way through s.2(2), outlining and applying the requirements for liability.

→ Then deal with the issue of the killing of Bonnie.

→ Finally, establish whether there is a claim for the damaged vegetables.

Diagram plan

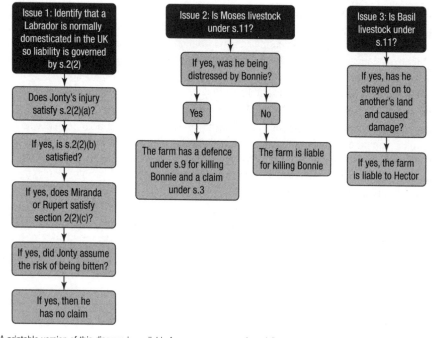

A printable version of this diagram is available from www.pearsoned.co.uk/lawexpressqa

Answer

[1] Save yourself time in the exam by shortening the Act's name so you do not have to repeat the name of the legislation.

[2] As each issue relates to a different provision of the Act, separate them out and deal with each in the order that they occur.

The incident raises several issues regarding the provisions of the Animals Act 1971 (the Act),[1] which may result in the various parties having claims. It will be argued that Miranda will be liable to Jonty as the ultimate keeper of Bonnie; the farm will not be liable for killing Bonnie and may in fact have a claim if Moses suffered any injury, but they are likely to be liable for the damage caused by Basil.

The first issue[2] is the liability for the bite suffered by Jonty. Miranda should be advised that although Bonnie is Rupert's pet, he cannot be liable as under the Act only the 'keeper' is liable. The keeper, under s.6, is normally the person who owns, or has possession of, the animal, and where this person is under 16 the keeper will be the head of the minor's household. We are not told whether Miranda

[3]Use the wording of the Act
where you can to demonstrate
why you are discussing the
issue and your knowledge
of it.

[4]As matters within the Act are
dealt within whole sections of
the Act, your answer will look
better if you can be specific
as to which part of the section
is relevant for the point that
you are making.

[5]As the first limb has not been
satisfied, there is no need
for you to explore the second
limb.

is 'the head of the household';[3] however, as Rupert's mother she is likely to satisfy the Act's wording for the purposes of liability.

In determining whether Miranda will face liability, the next issue is the nature of the animal in question as different criteria applies depending on whether the animal is classified as dangerous or not. Miranda should be advised that s.6(2)[4] provides a two-limb definition, providing firstly that a dangerous animal is a species not commonly domesticated in the British Isles. A dog is commonly domesticated in Britain and so liability for Bonnie will be determined by s.2(2) which deals with non-dangerous animals.[5] The subsection provides a three-limb test for liability. Firstly, the damage must be of a kind which Bonnie was likely to cause unless restrained, or which, if caused, was likely to be severe. This is satisfied as a dog can be said to be likely to cause a bite injury unless restrained. Even if Miranda were to argue that a Labrador is less likely to bite in comparison to other subspecies of dog, it has been held in **Curtis v Betts** [1990] 1 W.L.R 459 that dogs are dealt with as a general category and not by subspecies. The next requirement is that the likelihood of the damage was either down to permanent, abnormal characteristics for that species, or due to normal characteristics which arise in the species at particular times or in particular circumstances. Since **Mirvahedy v Henley** [2003] U.K.H.L. 16, it is settled that these are alternative reasons for liability. As we are told that Bonnie has become agitated whenever she is away from her litter, the bite could be said to fall under the latter basis. This is supported by the fact that the bite occurred when Bonnie was being restrained. Therefore, the bite was a result of the particular circumstances of the case. Finally, for liability to be imposed under the subsection, the keeper needs to have actual knowledge of the characteristics. From the facts, it would appear that Miranda would have known of these characteristics, particularly as we are concerned with dogs biting at particular times – facts which are widely known.

Miranda may argue that Jonty assumed the risk of being bitten by trying to restrain Bonnie. While this may have some merit, Jonty's position is perhaps more akin to that of a rescuer and so the defence will fail. However, depending on how he tried to restrain Bonnie, it is possible that a partial defence of contributory negligence is present: more facts will be needed to determine this.

The next issue to advise Miranda on is the killing of Bonnie. Normally, this gives rise to an action under the tort of trespass to goods. Miranda should be advised that any potential claim could be brought against the farm rather than Hyacinth under the doctrine of vicarious liability. This is because we are told that Hyacinth is an employee of the farm and it would seem clear that she was acting in the course of her employment, as she was seeking to prevent Bonnie attacking Moses. In the event that this is not the case, a claim could still lie against Hyacinth individually. However, s. 9 provides a defence where the defendant can show that a dog was killed while protecting their livestock. The first point to note is that a peacock falls within the definition of livestock within s. 11.[6] Section 9(3) stipulates when a person will be deemed to be protecting livestock. Importantly for the present incident, paragraph (a)[7] states that this will be where a dog is worrying livestock, and there is no other means of ending the worry. It is clear that Bonnie was still worrying Moses at the relevant time as she had already chased him and then had him cornered. Miranda should be advised that, while she may argue that the worrying could have been ended by some other means, this is unlikely to be successful as Jonty had already tried to restrain Bonnie and was bitten. This suggests that, when combined with the time factor that Bonnie had Moses cornered, Hyacinth could legitimately claim that there was no other means of protecting Moses.[8] This is particularly likely to be the case under s. 9(4) as this requirement is satisfied if Hyacinth reasonably believed this to be the case. However, if Hyacinth was not acting in the course of her employment and, therefore, was the sole defendant, the defence would not apply as Moses was not her livestock but the farm's. However, Miranda should be advised that the farm's defence will be lost under s. 9(1)(b) if the farm did not notify the police within 48 hours of the shooting. If this was not done, then she would have a successful claim against the farm. Miranda should also be advised that if Moses has suffered any injury as a result of being chased by Bonnie, then the farm would have an action for this injury under s. 3 of the Act.[9]

The final issue is the farm's potential liability for the damage caused by Basil to Hector's vegetables. The farm should be advised that Basil also falls within the definition of livestock; as he has caused damaged by straying on to land owned by Hector, they will be liable for the extent of that damage. The farm should be advised that even

[6] You need to mention this first as the defence is only for the protection of livestock. Therefore, if Moses is not livestock, the matter is closed and the farm would be liable for Bonnie's death.

[7] While you should be precise as to the subsection in question, remember not to waste your time by outlining provisions which are not directly relevant to the present discussion, such as paragraph (b) here.

[8] By analysing the facts of the incident within the actual question, you will strengthen your answer by giving firmer justification to your reasoning.

[9] Although we are not told of this, you should raise it to show your knowledge as it is potentially an issue, indicating what the position is either way.

if Basil was only able to enter Hector's land because it was unfenced, it would not be considered Hector's fault and thus negate the farm's liability. This would only be different if Hector had a duty to fence the area in question. On the basis that Hector did not have such a duty, the farm would be strictly liable under s. 4.

To conclude, it appears that Miranda would have no redress for Bonnie's death and, in fact, may well be liable for claims under the Act by Jonty and the farm for the harm caused by Bonnie. The farm is meanwhile likely to be liable to Hector for his damaged vegetables.

✓ Make your answer stand out

- Illustrate your understanding of the doctrine of vicarious liability by going into more depth if you feel that you will have the time.
- Be precise with the provisions that you refer to by indicating the subsections of the Act. This will show that you have a much stronger level of knowledge of the Act.
- Illustrate your understanding of the wider law by discussing the possibility that if the farm did not inform the police, there is a similar common law defence from the case of *Cresswell* v *Sirl* [1948] 2 K.B. 311.

! Don't be tempted to ...

- Spend too much time on the vicarious liability aspect of the question or, alternatively, ignore it altogether in order to save time.
- State as definite certain facts, or presume their non-existence, just because the question is silent on the matter: for example, whether the farm has a claim under s. 3 of the Act.

Question 2

'My Lords, [m]any difficulties have arisen in interpreting and applying the provisions of section 2(2) of the Animals Act 1971.' *Per* Lord Walker in *Mirvahedy* v *Henley* [2003] U.K.H.L. 16 at [133]

Analyse s.2(2) of the Animals Act 1971 and evaluate whether *Mirvahedy* v *Henley* has resolved the many difficulties.

Answer plan

- Outline the overall purpose of the Act and the specific aim of s.2(2) and the general difficulties that have been faced.
- Outline the provisions of the subsection, stating the three requirements.
- Contrast the judgments and differing approaches of the Court of Appeal prior to *Mirvahedy*.
- Explain the decision in *Mirvahedy* and evaluate the consequences.
- Consider the need for any reform.

Diagram plan

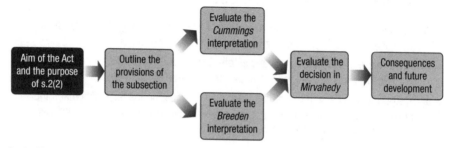

A printable version of this diagram is available from www.pearsoned.co.uk/lawexpressqa

Answer

The issue to discuss is the extent to which the House of Lords in **Mirvahedy v Henley** has resolved the previous difficulties surrounding liability for non-dangerous animals under the Animals Act 1971. The case was significant as previous authorities had reached different interpretations of s.2 which created uncertainty. It is argued that the case has resolved the difficulties by clarifying the law, and despite the initial concerns regarding the decision, the law is now in a settled and satisfactory state.

[1] By quoting passages from specific judges in the case, you will show a deeper level of knowledge of the case.

Prior to the Act, liability for animals under the common law was described by Lord Nicholls[1] in **Mirvahedy** as 'notoriously intricate and complicated'. The Act sought to simplify the law, but the language employed in s.2(2) resulted in uncertainty. Section 2(2)

[2] Although the question is concerned with s.2(2), you still need to discuss what is said by s.6 as this dictates what animals are governed by s.2(2)

deals with liability for injury by all non-dangerous animals. This phrase, owing to s.6[2], captures all animals which are commonly domesticated in Britain regardless of whether certain subspecies may be more dangerous than others: for example, Rottweilers compared to Labradors. The fact that the subsection is to be applied in such a vast range of scenarios heightens the need for clear wording and a solution to the previous lack of clarity which caused the difficulties.

The subsection has three requirements which must be satisfied in order for liability to be imposed. Two requirements, paragraphs (a) and (c), have been successful in simplifying matters. Paragraph (a) provides that the damage must be of a kind which the animal is likely to cause unless restrained, or which if caused, is likely to be severe. Paragraph (c) requires that the characteristics of the animal which cause the injury be known to the keeper, their servant, or a member of their household who is under 16. The key requirement is paragraph (b).[3] This links to paragraph (a) by providing that the likelihood of damage or the likelihood of it being severe must be due to characteristics of the animal. The difficulty regarded what the requirement meant, and the nature of the characteristics in question as the requirement, clearly has two limbs. The paragraph states that the cause must be a permanent characteristic of the animal which is abnormal for that species, 'or' the cause was a characteristic which 'is not normally so found except at particular times or in particular circumstances'.[4] The purpose of this paragraph,[5] according to Lord Nicholls in **Mirvahedy**, is to limit the circumstances when liability will be imposed by providing a precondition of liability in addition to (a) and (c). However, it has been said of the wording that it is 'inept', *per* Nourse LJ in **Curtis v Betts** [1990] 1 W.L.R. 459) and has an 'elusive' meaning (*per* Lloyd LJ in **Breeden v Lampard** (unreported) 21 March 1985).[6] It is the second limb which has caused difficulty, with contrasting judicial opinions over whether it was an alternative head for imposing liability, or merely a clarification of the first limb. Clarity was hindered by the fact that the cases forming both sides of the debate were not before the court in the opposing cases.

The first interpretation comes from **Cummings v Grainger** [1977] Q.B. 397 which concerned a guard dog biting a trespasser. It was held that while dogs are not normally prone to bite, when they are guarding their territory they may do. Therefore, even though this

[3] As this is the paragraph of the subsection at the root of the problems, this should form the main part of your answer, so you should just briefly outline what paragraphs (a) and (c) state.

[4] As you will highlight in your answer, this phrase is not clear and could be worded better. However, by using the actual statutory wording, you illustrate why there have been difficulties and set up your later discussion.

[5] To fully assess the correct interpretation of the paragraph, you ought to explain what the purpose of it is. Then you can use this purpose as a basis for assessing each interpretation.

[6] As these two judgments form the opposing schools of thought as to how the section operates, by quoting their criticisms you will reinforce the idea that there were widespread difficulties with the section.

[7]As you are assessing and contrasting two opposing interpretations, offer a view as to the merits or otherwise of each interpretation. If you do not, your answer will be lacking in terms of analysis of the section, which is what you have been asked to do.

[8]This is a general example which the cases use to simply illustrate the issue to be determined.

could be considered normal behaviour in the circumstances, were it not for a valid defence, liability would have arisen. The merits of such view are that it falls within a literal interpretation of the statute.[7] The use of the word 'or' would indicate that this is an alternative to the first limb. The difficulty with this interpretation is the generality of the meaning it gives. It results in liability always arising, as one would always be able to point to a set of circumstances and say that they are particular to that species. Liability would be imposed even though the behaviour was normal, such as a bitch biting someone who approaches her pups.[8]

The second interpretation comes from **Breeden v Lampard**: here a characteristic was said to not warrant being classified as abnormal, and thus subject to strict liability, when it was normal for the animal in those particular circumstances. Therefore, the scenario of a bitch protecting her pups would not bring liability as that is a character-istic which is normal in that scenario. Imposing liability in the view of Lloyd LJ would not have any sense. He felt that the second limb of the paragraph was merely refining what is meant by abnormality. Oliver LJ also could not believe that Parliament intended to impose liability for actions which were normal in the animal in the circum-stances in question. There is force to these views in that otherwise a non-dangerous animal is being treated the same as a dangerous animal; as the Act makes the distinction, it would seem strange to then treat them alike. Therefore, in contrast to the **Cummings** interpretation, the **Breeden** interpretation would essentially never result in liability.

The issue to be determined in **Mirvahedy** was whether a keeper is liable for damage caused in circumstances when the animal's behaviour was normal for the animal in question in the particular circumstances of the case. Lord Nicholls felt that neither inter-pretation 'provides a compelling clear solution'. However, he felt there was nothing in the section's wording to support the **Breeden** interpretation. Adopting it would depart from the scheme origi-nally advanced by the Law Commission without any evidence to suggest that Parliament intended such a departure. Lord Walker acknowledged that the distinction made as to the dangerousness of the animal implied that strict liability can never arise for a non-dangerous animal which is behaving entirely normally, as their behaviour would have to be abnormal. However, he also noted that this implication was not clearly spelt out and as such the language of the Act suited the **Cummings** interpretation 'more naturally' as a matter of language.

In conclusion, **Mirvahedy** appears to have settled the matter, and looking at the literal wording of the Act it is hard to disagree with the adoption of the **Cummings** interpretation. The use of 'or' is critical to defeating the reasoning in **Breeden** that the second limb is a refinement of the first. Without anything to support a counter purpose to the section, the adoption of the literal rule for statutory interpretation had to be undertaken. Fears that liability would now always result caused a vast increase in animal insurance premiums, leading many riding schools to close. However, these fears have proved unfounded, with subsequent cases not finding liability.[9]

[9]If you highlight this, it helps to illustrate whether the case was right or wrong. Depending on your view, put these in the order that you think helps the point you are making.

✓ Make your answer stand out

- Draw on more of the background to the Act, such as the Law Commission report, to more fully support what the purpose of the section was.
- Draw on the dissenting opinions of Lord Slynn and Lord Scott as to why *Mirvahedy* should have been decided differently.
- Explore the cases following *Mirvahedy* in more depth to discuss whether the fears over the decision were misplaced.

! Don't be tempted to ...

- Get into the rules in specifics of statutory interpretation.
- Demonstrate your knowledge of the wider provisions of the Act.

Bibliography

Arden, M. (2010) 'Human rights and civil wrongs: tort law under the spotlight', Public Law, Jan.: 140–59

Beever, Allan (2009) 'Transferred malice in tort law?', Legal Studies 29 (3): 400–20
Buckland, W.W. (1935) 'The duty to take care', 51 L.Q.R. 637
Buckley, R.A. (1984) 'Liability in tort for breach of statutory duty', 100 L.Q.R. 204

Cane, P. (1999) 'Fault and strict liability for harm in tort law', in W. Swaddling and G. Jones (eds) The Search for Principle: Essays in Honour of Lord Goff of Chieveley, OUP

Davies, M. (1982) 'The road from Morocco: Polemis through Donohue to no-fault', Modern Law Review 45 (5): 535–55

Fifoot, C.H.S. (1995) History and Sources of the Common Law: Tort and Contract, Stevens & Sons Ltd

Giliker, P. (2006) 'The ongoing march of vicarious liability', 489 C.L.J. 492
Giliker, P. (2010) 'Lister revisited: vicarious liability, distributive justice and the course of employment', L.Q.R. 126 (Oct): 521–4

Hedley, S. (1995) 'Negligence: pure economic loss: goodbye privity, hello contorts', C.L.J. 54 (1): 27–30
Heuston, R. V. F. and Buckley, R.A. (1996) Salmond and Heuston on the Law of Torts, 21st edition. London: Sweet and Maxwell
Hodges, C. (2001) 'Compensating patients: case comment on A v National Blood Authority [2001] 2 All E.R. 289', 117 L.Q.R. 528
Hoffman, L. (2005) 'Causation', L.Q.R. 121 (Oct): 592–603
Howarth, D. (2006) 'Many duties of care: or a duty of care? Notes from the underground', 26 O.J.L.S. 449
Howells, G. and Mildred, M. (2002) 'Infected blood: defect and discoverability: a first exposition of the EC Product Liability Directive', 65 M.L.R. 95
Hunt, M. (1998) 'The "horizontal effect" of the Human Rights Act 1998', Public Law, Autumn: 423–43

Law Commission (1969) Report No. 21 'The interpretation of statutes'

Markesinis, B.S. (1989) Negligence, nuisance and affirmative duties of action', 105 LQR 104
McDonald, B. (2005) 'Blameless?', P.I.L.J. 34 (May): 15–17
McLean, A. and Mackey, C. (2007) 'Is there a law of privacy in the UK? A consideration of recent legal developments', E.I.P.R. 29 (9): 389–95
Murphy, J. (1996) 'Expectation, losses, negligent ommisions and the tortious duty of care', C.L.J. 55 (1): 43–55
Murphy, J. (2004) 'The merits of *Rylands* v Fletcher', 24 O.J.L.S. 643
Murphy, J. (2007a) *Street on Torts*, 12th edition. Oxford: OUP
Murphy, J. (2007b) 'The juridical foundations of common law non-delegable duties', in Neyers, J. *et al.* (eds) *Emerging Issues in Tort Law*, Hart

Nolan, D. (2005) 'The distinctiveness of *Rylands* v *Fletcher*', L.Q.R. 121 (Jul): 421–51

Ogus, A.I. (1969) 'Vagaries in liability for the escape of fire', Cambridge Law Journal 27: 104
O'Sullivan, J. (2007) 'Suing in tort where no contract claim will lie: a bird's eye view', Professional Negligence 23 (3): 165–92

Reece, Helen (1996) 'Losses of chances in the law', Modern Law Review, 59: 188
Rogers, W.V.H. (ed.) (2010) *Winfield and Jolowicz on Tort*, 18th edition. London: Sweet and Maxwell

Stapleton, J. (1994a) 'In restraint of tort', in P. Birks (ed.) *The Frontiers of Liability*, vol. 2. Oxford: OUP
Stapleton, J. (1994b) 'Product liability', *Law in Context*, Butterworths

Teff, H. (1998) 'Liability for negligently inflicted psychiatric harm: justifications and boundaries', 57 Cambridge Law Journal: 91–122
Todd, S. (1999) 'Case comment: Psychiatric injury and rescuers',115 L.Q.R. 345: 349

Weir, T. (1972) 'Local authority *v* critical ratepayer: a suit in defamation', [1972A] C.L.J. 238
Weir, T. (1992) *A Casebook on Tort*, 7th edition. London: Sweet & Maxwell
Weir, T. (2006) *An Introduction to Tort Law*, Clarendon Law Series, p. 129
Williams, G. (1960) 'The effect of penal legislation in the law of tort', 23 M.L.R. 233
Winfield, P.H. (1934) 'Duty in tortious negligence', Columbia Law Review, 34 (1): 41–66

Index

INDEX

INDEX